CULTIVATING
**GARDEN
STYLE**

CULTIVATING GARDEN STYLE

Inspired ideas and practical advice to unleash your garden personality

For Rob, Meredith & Isaac. Because you are
my most favorite people in the whole wide world.

Rochelle Greayer

TIMBER PRESS
PORTLAND × LONDON

Introduction

Making a garden should never be less than a deeply fulfilling experience. There is no need to feel overwhelmed by landscaping plans and plant choices; the task can be approached as you might undertake a kitchen update. This book will share ways to create outdoor areas that, like our interior rooms, charm our design sensibilities, are comfortable and appealing to our personal tastes, and reflect our individuality. While I hope you find endless inspiration in these pages, I will also help you understand basic design concepts, garden construction, and plants—what makes them grow and look beautiful together, and why they are important to the nature that surrounds us.

A great garden welcomes you in the same way that a wonderful hotel sweeps you away to another place. The best gardens are adventures, filled with discovery and exploration, and each chapter in this book will take you on a journey through a particular garden style. The image collages share my inspiration and illustrate the process I use to gather ideas for a garden. I suggest you let them form the starting place for layering in the story of your own landscape. The follow-on pages will help you define the special features of your own garden and will guide you through ideas for the plants and beautiful objects that will reside there.

To create a garden that is a perfect reflection of you and whoever else lives in it, you must insert yourself into the experiment. Henry David Thoreau wrote that "it's not what you look at, it is what you see," and you must perceive the garden as an opportunity to transcend the ordinary. Don't be afraid to express yourself and do whatever crazy thing you might have always thought wonderful.

They say that smell is the most powerful sense for drawing us back to a particular place and time, but I think gardens and plants have remarkable time-machine powers. Certain landscapes can take me back to when I was a kid building grasshopper graveyards with little stones in the dirt, counting the shades of green on my grandmother's Montana ranch, or sniffing nettle (thinking it was mint), only to learn of its painful effects on my nose. These adventures that start with plants are so valuable for us as adults, and even more important to build into our children's lives so that they mature into people who not only cherish and protect the environment, but are also happy people.

We go outside to grow things, breathe fresh air, regenerate, and relax. Trying to conquer the forces (such as storms and pests) that act against all our best garden intentions is counter to what we seek in nature. It is much wiser to recognize that you are just one part of the design and no matter what your initial vision, the final outcome will never be just as you intended. But if you learn to work as a team with the garden, you will enjoy some wonderful, unanticipated surprises.

I want a garden to live in, one that reflects my character and taste as much as the things I wear and with which I choose to fill my home. But a garden is a specific kind of challenge; it changes and has a life of its own, and that presents challenges in a way that no other design practice does. A garden has to weather, well, the weather. It has no roof or walls—though you can define them if you want—and the confines arguably don't even stop at the property lines. Stuff lives in a garden; things move and change all on their own, and they create intricate relationships with other things around them (whether you the garden maker likes it or not). When you think about a garden's ecosystem in this way, the practice of garden design starts to resemble some sort of Frankensteinian experiment in evolving beauty. Which is, of course, exactly what it is.

If I achieve one thing with this book, I hope it is to spur you to imagine something more for your garden—to discover the ways in which it can feed your desires and provide an extraordinarily satisfying place for you to live, play, and become rejuvenated.

GETTING INSPIRED

Who wants a cookie cutter house anymore? No one I know. It is much more fun to let your character and taste shine through. We express our personal style every day in the choices we make: clothes, home decor, food, and products we buy. As far as I am concerned, a garden is just another room of the house, another place to define and dress however *you* see fit. There are many ways to gather and organize motifs, moods, and samples in order to get in touch with your taste and personal style. Here are some of them.

Mood boards

I used to make mood boards by cutting images from magazines, but now I curate boards online much like the ones you'll see at the start of each

chapter in this book. There are several social media websites that allow this kind of image gathering, including Pinterest. I use an online picture-organizing tool both for my own projects and as a way to get on the same page as a client and quickly share ideas with them.

The best way to get started on your project is to go to whatever website you are using and do a few simple searches of words such as "garden," or a term associated with a style you like (for example, "bohemian"). When starting to gather, forget about organizing ideas or designing your garden —just "like" images. Liking is freeing; you can do it instantaneously and avoid overthinking the decision. You want to go with your gut—no questions asked, no further thought.

Next, go back and take a look at your likes. Do you see any common themes? A color, a mood, a mix of materials? A shape or a type of planting? A good designer can help you find yourself in these images, but you can do it on your own, too. Once you have a whole bunch of things you like, start organizing the ones that go together (most sites will offer online boards where you can place your likes), and you will begin to see a theme emerge. I put a few key words to these themes (as I have done here in the book) to help shape the design and guide me as I fill in the blanks, creating a unique and personal final project.

Garden tours

Garden tours are fantastic for assessing the possibilities in your area. Neighbors who open their gardens put their hearts on their sleeves when they share their personal spaces. Take them up on their openness and ask them where they buy their plants or why they grow certain things and not others. Talk to them about their trials and tribulations. Not only will you learn something, you will find that universally (at least in my experience), garden makers are among the nicest and most generous people around.

Botanic gardens

Local botanic gardens almost always have displays to help you learn about plants that are native to your area or that do well in your climate. They are planned by professionals and can be great catalysts for new ideas and for learning detailed information about issues specific to your region.

Nurseries

Each nursery has its own unique personality. Some carry more shrubs and trees, others primarily stock annuals; some promote chemical-intensive gardening, others help those seeking organic options. Natives, alpines, large specimens—whatever the specialty, it is worth taking the time to step away from the big box stores, visit a range of nurseries, and learn about the distinct selection each offers. You will undoubtedly find one that suits you and your garden goals.

Fashion

If you struggle to know what your garden style preferences are, you need only start with the clothes you choose (or wish you could choose). Fashion is a place we can look for color possibilities; it can also reveal a sense of the styles that appeal to us. Do you prefer crisp, clean cuts in straightforward colors, or more avant-garde shapes in offbeat hues? Being drawn to a feeling that fashion conveys offers direction for how we might capture the same in our garden design.

Art

Much like fashion, art gives us a bird's-eye view of someone else's inner expression. If we are drawn to an expression and we find personal meaning and significance in it, that will help to guide and shape our own expression. When you love an image or a piece of art, try to sort out what is drawing you in. Is it the material, the texture, the shape, the emotion, or something else? This will help you understand your own preferences and spark your creativity.

Interiors

The most obvious place to look for garden inspiration is actually inside—to extend what we love about our interiors to the outdoors. As a designer, I cringe to meet new clients who have just moved into their house and haven't had a chance to personalize the space, because there is no better way to understand what someone is all about than to see something they've created. If you have remodeled or decorated your home in a way that you love, there is no reason to think you can't extend that same style right through the back door.

USING THIS BOOK

Once you have begun to establish a style that suits your taste and lifestyle, you can identify the main elements that will define the character of your garden. And, you can start putting concepts into action.

To help you as you move through this process, each chapter of the book represents a specific garden style. These style chapters are grouped into four overarching themes, or sections. Within each chapter are five recurring elements that are integral to helping your garden take shape.

The Big Ideas

The Big Ideas section of each chapter describes the key motifs of that chapter's style. It is equally important, however, that the ideas fit your location in practical terms. Professional landscape designers assess every site for a variety of factors, starting with understanding the history of the space and what led to its present state. Conditions such as weather and soil quality are also important considerations. When analyzing your garden, you should spend some time thinking about these factors, too, so you can feel confident that your plan will be successful.

Make It Your Own

There is nothing like a nice new party dress to necessitate a night out on the town. Just the same, finding a perfect garden chair or an accessory that fits the mood and spirit of your garden will encourage you to keep building and expanding the scope of your private utopia. When a new set of mating birds takes up residence in the charming birdhouse you found, I guarantee you will want nothing more than to find more ways to make them feel like welcome guests. This section suggests product ideas to help you understand how to bring together items to achieve the look you want.

Putting Down Roots

Plants are the heart and soul of a garden. Their beauty is usually the most impressive thing in a landscape. It takes time to learn their personalities and how to get along with them (just like any new relationship) and there is nothing wrong with starting with the most agreeable varieties before getting better acquainted with those on the fringes of popularity. The plants in these pages will help you discover new options and make choices to capture the style you seek. You'll also learn a bit about how to place and take care of your garden inhabitants. But don't stop there; the plant world is vast and this is just an introduction to what you'll turn up on your own journey.

A Garden Story

I have tremendous appreciation for the gardeners who have shared their work in these pages. Some of the outdoor retreats have been built by homeowners alone and others have involved designers, but all embrace their own aesthetic. They are spaces that ooze personality and style. The ingenuity and cleverness exhibited demonstrates the resource that we can all be to each other. None of the gardens are static; in fact, some changed just moments after being photographed. But that is the nature of such places; they are never done and will always be spaces where something new can be discovered.

Learning, Doing, Growing

At the conclusion of each chapter are practical design and horticultural projects, tips, and information covering a diverse range of topics, from lighting choices to mulches to container planting. This will help you get going and growing, as well as offering guidance that I hope will be useful once you have gotten your hands dirty.

ARTIFACT

12
RETRO ROCKERY

24
CULTIVATED COLLECTOR

"Mix at will!
It all can be
changed.
Think an
arrangement
is too 'granny'?
Add
something
modern
and watch it
become oddly
cool."
— Reuben Munoz

36
ENCHANTED BOHEMIAN

Gardens inspired by special objects are always surprising and unique. Meaning and memories flow freely from these cherished possessions, enveloping us in their stories. Each of these chapters celebrates artifacts in a wholly distinct way, yet all offer delicious proof that our lives and gardens are made richer by well-loved treasures.

"I sought to construct this garden as a particular space of sheltering intimacy bounded by a courtyard of walls."
—Topher Delaney

Retro Rockery

funky

saved

sassy

The key to taking cues from any period is to avoid looking like you live in a time capsule. I don't know about you, but I'm a little unsettled by people who seem stuck in another era; they kind of spook me. What is charming, however, is an appreciative nod to another time, an embracing of happy memories and the objects we associate with them, and celebrating the classics of design with a dash of whimsy—all while keeping at least one foot firmly in the present. I enjoy the stories that come with vintage objects, even if it's only the story of how it was rediscovered.

To me, rockeries are the perfect old-school gardens because they are about details. You could argue that rock gardens celebrate the plants within them more than most other styles; often each plant in a rockery is separated from its friends by gravel or a boulder or other similar formations that give each its own frame. Alpine plants and the rugged shrubs that populate these gardens have characterful details that invite you to study them up close. When rockeries and retro sensibilities are combined, a wonderland of quirky, fun possibilities is created.

vintage

comfortable

Iconic elements

Nothing is more satisfying than the end of a successful hunt for a vintage treasure—except perhaps discovering the find you weren't even looking for, or the moment you place the newly found object in the spot where you can most enjoy it and the story it tells.

Simple lines, clean finishes

Simplicity allows natural beauty to shine through. Uncomplicated layouts also don't compete with fun accessories and interesting plants. Too much to see will just look a mess, so embrace basics. Let the patio be plain gray concrete, or gravel. The excitement will come from the adornments.

Rocks

You can't have a rockery without rocks. If your garden is filled with stones to begin with, this style is a perfect way to put all those natural gifts to work. If you don't have rocks on site, you will have to harvest them elsewhere. Look around at local sources—construction sites are always a good resource. Notice each rock's size and color and enjoy examining it from all sides. Place your stones in a way that will highlight their very best qualities.

Vintage colors, period patterns

Whether you are aiming for the '50s, '80s, or somewhere in between, colors from these eras were often derived from nature (think mustard, avocado, tangerine, sun gold) and put together in combinations to be striking and provocative. Whatever period you're channeling, there are many easily researched color palettes that can help infuse your rockery with vintage charm. Patterns also help set a tone, and can be added to architectural elements as well as to fabrics.

Boldly Brady

Incorporate the colors and retronaut shapes of the late '60s and early '70s. Vintage light fixtures can be refitted with solar-powered bulbs or exterior lighting. Modern gnomes, bullet planters, and psychedelic fabric complete the ensemble.

Psychedelic
floral fabric

Yellow
clam chair

Come & knock on our door

Casual, bright, sunny, and mod captures the spirit of the '70s. Incorporating the ubiquitous aluminum folding garden chair might seem uninspired, but by reimagining it with updated and upmarket details such as wood handles and contrast stitching, old becomes fresh and new. Perhaps seek furniture that recalls woven styles of macramé and wicker. Use black and white and brown to offset the bright colors of this generation.

Vintage
circles fabric

Upscale folding
lawn chair

Madison Ave.

With a martini in hand, dress your garden in the seductive, steamy blues of the early '60s. This glamorous mid-century modern lounge bench is even heated—because who wants a chill when sitting in the garden? Paired with patterns of the era and a sexy fireplace, the mood is set. Vintage-feeling but modern butter-colored planters give a perfect color contrast.

Jungalow fabric

Heated
lounge bench

Ward, June, Wally & the Beav

The sweet innocence of the '50s favored pale pastels, simple planes, and geometric shapes; chintz and other patterns featured everyday items. It was spartan compared to revival styles of earlier decades. A simple wedding cake planter paired with vintage furniture sets the basic style. Accessorize by looking for period pieces such as chair swings.

Chintz fabric

Vintage
chair swing

Vintage patio
pendant lights

Green
bullet planter

Ceramic gnomes

Malm fireplace

Steel and
wood vessels

Color block
wall planter

Astro fire pit

Pod planters

Metal plant rack

Pink wedding
cake planter

BREEZE BLOCK WALLS

Easy to construct and strikingly appealing, decorative concrete block walls or architectural screen blocks are indicative of mid-mod architecture. They can be difficult to source in places where this style isn't common, but are worth seeking out for adding exterior interest to nearly any house and garden built from the '40s to the '70s—and they also work well with modern architecture. Common uses include screens, fences, built-in benches, and embellishment on solid walls.

Dianthus alpinus

Acantholimon ulicinum

Phlox stolonifera

Helichrysum splendidum

Aethionema saxatile

Saxifraga paniculata

Sempervivum

Mini shrubs

Though they remain small, dwarf shrubs often live longer (some have been documented at over a thousand years old) than most other garden plants. Dwarf by definition means the plant will never grow larger than 10 feet (3 meters) in any direction. The sometimes rough and rugged nature of these plants will impart agelessness and give the garden a framework. Make sure to have a good mix of evergreen and deciduous types so the garden will look good through all seasons.

Deutzia gracilis 'Nikko'

Gentista lydia

Creepers, cushions & rosettes

Many rock garden plants originate in high mountain climates or similarly harsh locales. (The Mediterranean might seem like a nice vacation spot, but to a plant it can be hard work!) Adapting to their environment, plants from these places often grow in distinctive ways. Hugging the ground, they can creep and spread over rocks and stony meadows while conserving water. Cushion-like formations of dense foliage that sometimes formalize into rosettes enable them to withstand extreme conditions. Creepers, cushions, and rosettes give the rock garden its stereotypical style and help to blend the rocks together. In the nursery, look for plants referred to as "alpine" or "Mediterranean."

Chlorophytum

ROCK GARDEN BASICS

Look for the word "prostrate" (or versions of that word—such as "prostrata") in the name when shopping for shrubs. This means that the plant will grow low and spread over the terrain.

- Don't be tempted to over-improve your soil. Many rock garden plants prefer a rocky, sandy soil, so make sure that in addition to adding a water-retaining substance (peat or other), you maintain or create soil that is rocky and ready for these plants.

- Don't over-plant. Being able to see plants without others tumbling over the top will help you appreciate each species' special qualities.

- Use gravel for mulch; it will blend the garden together better than other mulches. Also, mulches move around more without bed edging—something that doesn't come with rock gardens. So ease your stress and choose gravel; it can easily be put back in place without worrying about materials mixing.

Old-school plants

Give the garden some personality with plants that can't help but be associated with another era. Ponytail palms, fiddle leaf figs, umbrella trees, spider and jade plants, philodendrons, asparagus fern, hardy geraniums, and mother-in-law's tongue (*Sansevieria*) are all inextricably linked to the height of chic '70s style. Most are indoor plants of tropical origin and will love a little summer vacation in the garden, rewarding you not only with a few extra pots to play with in the summer, but also with extra growth and vigor as they come back inside in the fall.

Crassula

Ficus elastica

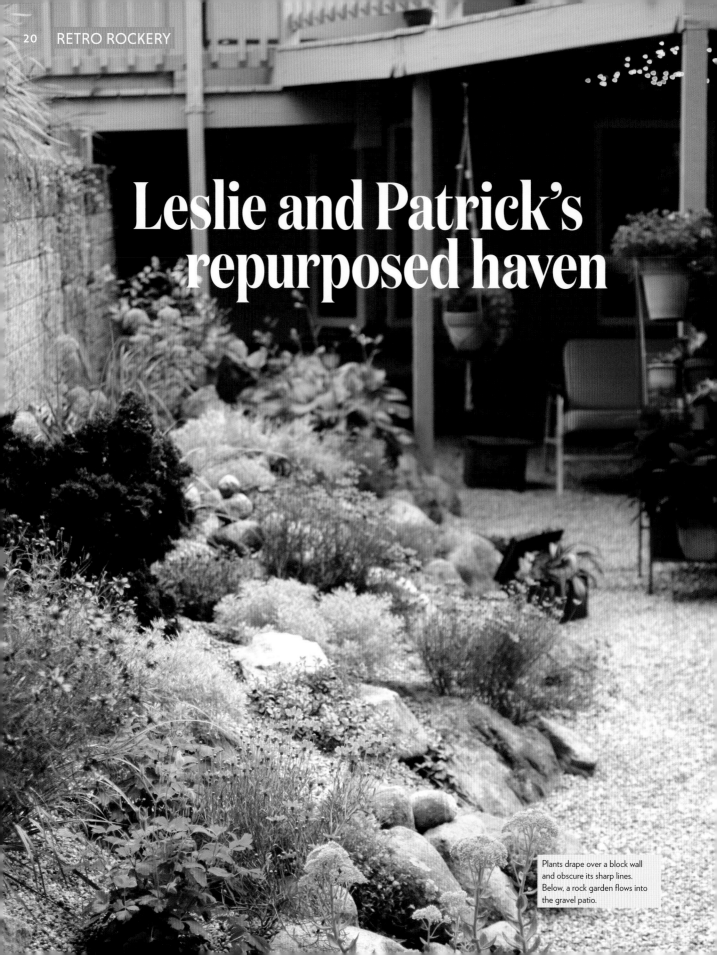

Leslie and Patrick's repurposed haven

Plants drape over a block wall and obscure its sharp lines. Below, a rock garden flows into the gravel patio.

"Many of the elements we found in a scrap metal pile. Now we forget our troubles by the fire, crank Hank Williams, and chill." — Patrick Bunnell

Rustic and reclaimed elements such as an old tool box make for interesting plant homes.

A vintage cola sign adds character and ties together the upper deck and lower gravel patio.

An uneven dirt patch that was beneath and overlooked by Leslie and Patrick's wooden deck was an obvious place to establish an extended outdoor family room. Building on their passion for and burgeoning collection of antiques and vintage ephemera (as well as their ability to throw a really good party), the area was transformed into a rock garden lounge. One side was carved into a rockery by adding boulders and large rocks rolled in from other parts of the property, and the rest of the area was leveled and covered with a thick layer of gravel. A fire pit anchors a comfortable seating area, and there is plenty of room between the upper and lower decks for large gatherings of family and friends.

BUYING PLANTS

Buying plants can seem overwhelming, particularly if you don't know how to navigate a garden center. Here are some tips for managing the nursery or flower market.

Have a list. While I wholeheartedly recommend walking through a garden center for the sheer joy of it, don't buy unless you have researched your choice and know where it will succeed in your garden. If you were going to make a nice dinner, you would have the recipe in mind and know its ingredients; the garden is the same. Know what you need before you go.

Don't buy onesies and twosies. Unless your garden is truly tiny or you are shopping for large trees and shrubs, even the smallest plot will benefit from repetition and the coherence it brings. If you must make an impulse buy (we are talking annuals and perennials here), don't regret it by buying only one. You will get it home, put it in the ground, it will be perfect, and I can almost guarantee that when you return for a few more, they will be gone. You will be forced to wait until you can split the plant or take cuttings to enjoy the rhythm of a garden with good repetition.

Be careful with substituting. Have confidence in your first design decision and either seek out the original choice somewhere else or wait until you can research the suggested sub thoroughly. Often a substitute won't meet your exact requirements. A great garden center with highly knowledgeable employees can help, but you should feel that they are sending you home with the right thing—not just *some* thing.

Ask questions. There are no dumb questions when it comes to buying plants (or anything, really).

Give the plants a good physical. Check them out from top to bottom. Do they have lots of leafy stems? They should. Make sure you don't see any suspicious pests or signs of disease (yellowing leaves, for example). Large weeds growing in the pot with your plant is a sign of neglect. Take a look underneath. Are there large amounts of roots coming through the drainage holes? Just a few are okay; they imply the plant has a healthy root system. But massive amounts suggest the plant is root-bound and probably not a good choice.

Carefully consider plant size. Often in larger nurseries there are multiple sizes of the same plant. The bigger the pot, the more you pay. When making this choice, consider your budget first. Buy the largest you can afford, but I think it better to get more of a smaller variety than just a few sizable versions. They will all grow together nicely in time, and often smaller plants (particularly trees and shrubs) will establish more quickly than their larger counterparts. I like to strategically pick a couple things to go big on (for instant gratification), but save on everything else. It is also important to examine plants side by side. Sometimes a plant in a small container might actually be the same size as the variety in a bigger, more expensive pot, due to different planting times. Make sure you get your money's worth.

Don't choose a plant that is in full bloom. Look for its friend that is a little less showy. So long as you can confirm the color, it is better to buy a plant that has fewer flowers than more. You might even want to nip off blooms when planting, so the plant puts its energy into establishing itself.

ONLINE PLANT SHOPPING

I love Internet shopping for plants because the varieties available are vastly greater than most local nurseries tend to offer. Specialty nurseries in particular thrive online and if you hanker for that just-right variety, you can often get it via mail order. But buying plants sight unseen can be a little scary, so here are a few tips to get you comfortable.

Know your planting zone and what will work in your garden. Your local nursery serves just your area, so its selections have been edited to include only things that will work for you. Online, you have to narrow your choices and ensure you aren't buying something that won't survive in your garden. Many sites offer zone searches, which I head for straightaway. I like to narrow things down first so I am not even tempted to think I can keep things alive that aren't for my region.

Make sure you know what you are buying. Look at multiple images of the plant to get a range of expectations for color (photos do lie). You might want to do a Google image search to find things on other sites as a cross-reference. Also make sure you are clear on size—mail-ordered plants tend to be smaller than you would buy nearby and they often come bare root and need to be planted sooner.

Pay attention to shipping costs. They can be high due to the special requirements of plants. I don't buy anything online that I can easily get nearby.

Make sure that damaged goods will be replaced easily. Before buying, make sure you understand the company policy for plants that arrive a little worse for the journey.

Read online reviews and buy from reputable companies. Otherwise, you risk not only wasting money but also infecting your other plants with disease or insects.

HOW TO GET A PLANT BARGAIN

- **Buy in the fall.** You may not be able to see the color or the leaf if it has already disappeared. But if you are in a trusted garden center and can stand a surprise or two, you can get a great deal late in the season.

- **Look for slightly damaged plants.** Trees or shrubs with a broken limb or other slight imperfections can often bring the price down. Just make sure it is cosmetic and not life threatening. Root-bound, weedy, or neglected plants can also be bargains, but make sure you are prepared to nurse them back to health.

- **Look for untagged plants.** Many nurseries discount these since the variety is often unclear.

Cultivated Collector

adventures

I come from a long line of collectors. People who get great joy from the hunting and gathering of highly specific items. My mom has little houses, one aunt has miniatures, another has Elvis ephemera, and my grandmother collected buttons, antiques, and dollhouse pieces that I am pretty sure were additions to a collection started and handed down from her mother. They all collected plants, too. I have until recently shunned this familial hobby because it not only takes time and resources, but the finding part is only half the story. The other half is displaying, and this, in my opinion, is a far greater and more seriously considered challenge.

This garden style can be the summation of many collections or simply one grand assemblage. It can be as small as a terrarium or acres and acres of trees and plants. These gardens are among my favorites to explore—particularly if the collector has a knack for arrangement. I love them because they are the gardens that most deeply reflect passion and enthusiasm, and they are more than just a beautiful landscape—they are the culmination of the joy the creator found, having fed and nurtured a desire. Collections can satisfy a sense of personal aesthetic or they can be made up of strange and eclectic items that express individualism. Most people collect to please their personal tastes, but it is ultimately about passionate possession.

specimen

arrangement

details

curiosities

Gather like with like

Unless it is something truly remarkable, one by itself is lonely and often nothing special. But many of something—anything— becomes a statement and gains interest with each addition. Take advantage of this and place the pieces in your collections together; the gathered items will lend each other credence.

Use architecture to organize

Most collectors collect more than just one item. If this is the case, you need to find ways to break things up and keep them separately organized. If you don't, you run the risk of looking like you live in a discombobulated junkyard. Break your garden up into distinct areas—garden rooms—through the use of walls, hedges, and other structures, so that you can dedicate areas to particular collections.

REORGANIZE, REWORK, REPEAT

For collectors, a new possession or addition means taking considerable time and energy to reorganize and make room for the latest element. Displaying the pieces in fresh and interesting ways is a design challenge that is often as much of an investment as the collection itself. Keys to success in maintaining a collector's garden include indulging (and forgiving) oneself and allowing for constant rearranging. It is the curating that turns what might be boring objects into a fanciful and exciting assemblage. Make vignettes and celebrate the details, giving the eye a million places to wander. There are infinite possible garden collections, but these are some I have enjoyed.

Antiques
Antlers
Birds
Birdcages
Birdhouses
Bird's nests
Bonsai
Bottles
Bugs
Butterflies
Chimes
Crystals
Daylilies

Decoys
Driftwood
Flotsam
Flowers
Grasses
Hammocks
Ladders
Leaves
License plates
Multiple items of
    the same color
Old church
    windows

Rare plants
Rocks
Sculptures
Seeds
Seed catalogs
Seed packets
Shells
Signs
Tools
Toys
Tractors
Trees
Tropical plants

Make art

Depending on what you collect, you can give your items cohesion by using them as the building blocks of a greater piece. Driftwood (for example) is a lovely thing to collect from vacations at the beach. Each piece carries with it a memory of a certain time and place. A pile of driftwood might look a mess, but organized and elevated into something intentional, the gathered wood can become a beautiful focal point.

TIPS ON CURATING

- **Tell a story.** Perhaps the narrative is about color or material, or maybe there is a more personal thread that runs through the pieces. Impart meaning.

- **Don't follow trends.** Collect only what you love, what gets you excited, or what you think is extraordinary.

- **Be picky.** Take pride in your collection; seek out the most-prized pieces or those that are closest to your ideal. Collections can get out of hand quickly and being picky will help keep them at a maintainable size.

- **Do your research and know your collection well.** Gather a depth of knowledge and become an expert—it will help you see treasure where others can't.

- **Display creatively.** Reimagine uses for items or display them in a way that is outside of the expected. This will help others appreciate how special your collection is.

Ginkgo tree

Porcelain
garden stool

Bamboo fencing

Teak
deck chair

Balinese
stone carving

Coleus

Blue ceramic
Buddha

Ipe chair

Fuchsia

Ammonite sculpture

Forsythia

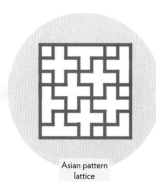

Asian pattern
lattice

Fresh from the Far East

Collections evolve as we journey through life, and can be gatherings of anything. Early garden collections arose from the exotic travels of plant collectors who made great voyages to uncharted lands. Asia was a particularly fruitful area for early specimens of plants we regularly use in our gardens. For a crisp spring look, combine the ancient ginkgo (which grows wild only in China), an easy-to-move Asian ceramic stool, the bright blooms of forsythia, and a trellis screen with a pattern indicative of *chinoiserie* (details and motifs that are not actually Chinese, but rather artistically derivative of Asian design).

Ruby grass

Hurricane lanterns

African adventure

Capture the spirit of another place, perhaps an ancestral homeland, by assembling a collection of culturally influenced furniture. Add to it some plants that originated from the region—in this case, a beautiful ruby grass could offset a bamboo fence. Hurricane lanterns like those found in grassland camps can be placed around the garden for simple and beautiful lighting that doesn't require an electrician.

Fragrant jasmine

River stone
container

Indonesian islands

Balinese carved stone in traditional motifs and blazing blue Buddhas are delightful details that capture the exotic nature of the East Indies. Combine elements that tickle the senses. Textural river pebble–covered pots and luscious, colorfully painted South Asian native coleus create a visual feast, but no Indonesian garden can be without jasmine, the national flower. Its blooms are sacred and symbolize purity and grace, while providing a heady scent that permeates a garden.

Alstroemeria lilies

Brazilian
chita fabric

South American sojourn

Ipe (or epay) furniture is made from trees of the genus *Handroanthus*. The wood is prized for its hardness and rot resistance. Ipe is also particularly lovely for other garden features such as decks. This deeply colored South American wood mixes nicely with the rich purples and exotic pinks of fuchsias and alstroemerias, which are native to the Caribbean and southern South America, respectively. Keep the mix thoughtful and playful with accessories like brightly colored chita fabrics and ammonites that recall the region.

A plant collector's greenhouse

Establish havens

Some collections require a special home. Lovers of carnivorous plants may have to consider a greenhouse; those desiring an orangerie will need an indoor room large enough to accommodate potted trees. To be at their best, plant collections—particularly those housed outside of their natural homes—must have their needs met. This may be as simple as amending soil to make it just right, or it may require more significant gestures.

Species collections

Collected hostas

I find that a plant collector's garden is often part laboratory, part orphanage, and part hospital. Collectors always seem to have a soft spot for the less than perfect, a willingness to bring whatever it is home and give it a little TLC. Because a collection is about the whole being greater than the parts, it is quite common that a newcomer on the scene will kick off a string of adjustments to the whole design (which, of course, is part of the fun).

If you are a plant collector, try to think in advance and admit that you are afflicted with the gleaner bug—and leave room for additions. Moving things around too much can get tiring for you and distress the plants. Also, before you commit a plant to a spot in the ground, move the potted specimen from place to place and try it out in lots of different arrangements in your garden.

Tie things together

Tropical pond at Butchart Gardens

If your collection is large or difficult to display (say, totem poles or farm implements), it can be helpful to bring it together with something else—like plants or a certain type of path. Imagine a collection of totems set in lush, ferny settings throughout a garden, or large-scale art or antique farm tools in a giant meadow with gorgeous mown paths linking them. Garden focal points can help tie a collection together, too. A water feature provides a perfect rallying point for a collection of tropical plants, giving the plants a logical place to hang out together.

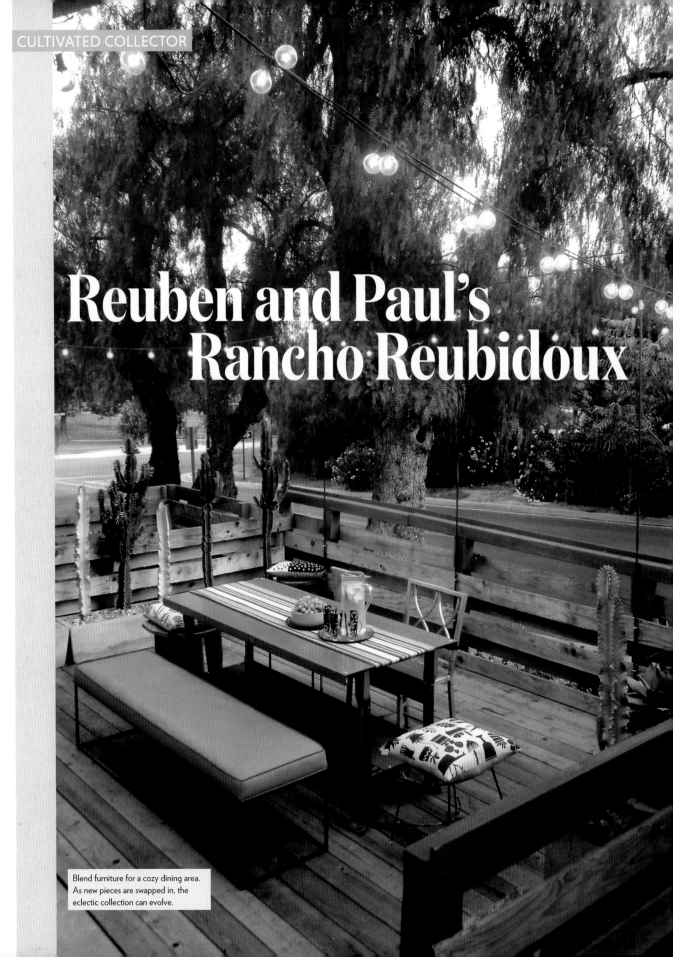

Reuben and Paul's Rancho Reubidoux

Blend furniture for a cozy dining area. As new pieces are swapped in, the eclectic collection can evolve.

"Mix at will!
It all can be
changed.
Think an
arrangement
is too 'granny'?
Add
Something
modern
and watch it
become oddly
cool".
— Reuben Munoz

Rearrange pieces and take photos—not only to document the creation but to help you see objects in a new way.

Reuben and Paul bought the worst house on the block in 2007 and eagerly set about "subtracting all the negatives." The back of the lot housed long-neglected shrubbery, fruit trees, a tangled lawn, and the homeless. In front, there was a threadbare lawn and hedges. All were removed to create a blank canvas for the garden they named Rancho Reubidoux. Terracing and endless caravans of gravel (with weed block beneath) formed the backdrop for the collecting to begin. Succulents and cacti, boulders, trees, vintage items, and industrial junk were the elements in Reuben's design palette, and he approached laying them out in the same way he approaches his work as a graphic designer. "I worked to create vignettes and groupings of objects to promote visual control within the scheme. My fave colors are rust, stone, and weathered wood; all work naturally and brilliantly alongside the colors of succulents. I truly believe the old adage 'anything goes'!"

Add interest by mixing materials. Variation is created with containers, wood, and widely spaced plants.

CREATIVE REPURPOSING: PLANTER SCONCE

Finding new ways to use old things takes a clever eye. There are a million online resources and ideas for reworking just about anything. The result almost always satisfies a basic need to reduce our carbon footprint, but often beautiful and special pieces can be made from inexpensive or free materials.

It may take only awareness to open your mind and notice the attractive shape or an alternative use for everyday objects. Reuben Munoz created a planter sconce from especially shapely palm tree debris he found in the road after a windy day. Here is how he made the transformation.

MATERIALS
- A palm scoop (found in the road)
- Metal mesh screening
- Coconut fiber hanging plant liner
- Array of small, colorful succulents
- Wire
- Wire-cutting pliers
- Hammer
- Rust-colored, large permanent marker
- Textured spray paint
- Staple gun
- Cactus mix soil
- Leather cord

1. Cut coconut fiber into a half-circle slightly larger than the size of the desired planting area.

2. Cut the metal mesh with wire-cutting pliers to an approximate size and roll it into a cone-like shape (use gloves for this step). Adjust the cone's size to fit snugly against the palm scoop. Anchor with small lengths of wire threaded through the mesh and twist to secure.

3. Mark the top of the planting cone with marker. Trim to fit with wire cutters. Spray paint the mesh to match the color of the scoop.

4. Place the cone on the scoop and use a staple gun to secure each side with several staples. If needed, use a hammer to drive staples in deep so that they hold tightly. Fit coconut fiber as a lining for the mesh cone. Make sure to leave excess at the top to push onto the raw edge of the metal mesh.

5. Cut an opening down the front vertically and roll it back so that plants appear to spill out the front.

6. Fill the bottom of the cone with cactus mix soil and add the first succulents, layering in dirt and succulents as you build toward the top (Reuben used plants with contrasting shapes and colorful foliage, including *Aeonium* cultivars with black rosettes). Once everything is planted, mark and drill a hole for a hanger.

7. Push a small length of leather cord through the hole from behind, then knot, providing a simple and effective hanger.

TEN DO-IN-A-DAY TASKS TO TRANSFORM A GARDEN

1. Paint the doors. Think of every door between the outside and inside of your home as an opportunity to make an entrance. Making these transitions special will heighten appreciation for garden rooms.

2. Flank doors with large containers or collections of plants. Keep it simple with an evergreen shrub or experiment with other groupings. A hit of green as you head outside will improve your mood instantly.

3. Refresh chipped paint and remove mold, dirt, and debris that are soiling the siding, decking, or any other surface. Your garden is like any other room in your home; you want it to be comfortable to live in. That won't happen if you have to walk across slimy floors, or if you stain your trousers every time you sit on dirty furniture.

4. Mow, weed, prune. It is no different from a quick swipe of the vacuum, a rapid pick-up of dirty laundry, or a quick tuck-away of paper piles. Everything will seem a whole lot nicer when this is done.

5. Plant something that is pretty and flowering. Sometimes you just need a refresher, akin to a new throw pillow, to give things a jolt.

6. Clean up the edges of everything. Who doesn't have a little OCD about furniture being straight and aligned with walls and rugs? Gardens are the same; most people feel better when they have drawn lines and colored within them. A half-moon edger is my favorite gardening tool—get one and use it like crazy; it is almost therapeutic.

7. Clear the debris from gutters, dark corners, and anywhere muck gathers. It is, however, okay to leave it in a big rotting pile. In the garden, we call that a compost heap.

8. Assess surrounding trees and large shrubs. Adjust branch height and coverage to flatter the house and to make sure you can enjoy your garden. Don't let forgotten arboreal tasks hide your home's best assets, keep you from soaking in a little sun, or interfere with your ability to view the evening stars.

9. Add light. Most of us are a little afraid of the dark, so take it easy on yourself. Install just enough light so you can move around safely and enjoy the shadows cast by plants and trees.

10. Incorporate at least one deeply personal, particularly characterful, or special thing. It can be anything, so long as when you see it you instantly love it and understand why it is special.

Enchanted Bohemian

Just thinking about creating a bohemian garden makes me start lusting after travel magazines, bookmarking exotic locales, and pining for a life where literary pursuits, art, music, and personal passions guide my every move. Bohemian style captures the spirit of a restless heart and fosters a look that seems effortless and unplanned. (One of my favorite books is Laren Stover's *Bohemian Manifesto*, which charmingly and humorously describes a variety of bohemian personalities. I find myself in the Gypsy category with a dash of Nouveau.) There are a few common threads to bohemian style, though. To pull off the look successfully you must have a collection of textiles, art, and oddities that you have collected in your wanderings. Then, you must display them as if you couldn't care less what anyone thinks of them. And this is much harder than it sounds.

keepsake

eccentric

gypsy

Bacchus

dreamy

Textural tension & methodical mismatching

When faced with making sense of a variety of pieces, it is important to find commonality. In a patio set, no two chairs have to match, but if they all have similar proportions, sameness of color, consistently strong silhouettes, or other matching qualities, they will come together. The design is energized by the contrast of elements. Planting should be similarly fanciful—let the plants mix and dance together in exciting combinations.

BOHO STYLE

- **Match nothing**, but make sure it all relates.

- **Relax** and eschew neatness.

- **Don't care** that the chandelier you've decided to hang from a tree doesn't work. That isn't the point.

- **Use tertiary colors on the color wheel**—such as sage, lime, charcoal, maroon, and aqua—to impart complexity.

- **Love everything you have collected.** Recognize that belonging to you is the shared connection. (If the grouping is truly muddled, you might want to subtract the few most disconnected things and replace them with mismatched wooden furniture and a few gilded items.)

- **Let ethnic flavors mingle.** If the pieces look a little Spanish or Moroccan or French or Persian, well, just put them all together and let them sing a little international symphony. Being bohemian is all about embracing an unconventional lifestyle and all the ideas, art, music, and people that go along with it.

Add depth & age

Use one-of-a-kind pieces to infuse a little whimsy. Let lived-in history shine through by resisting the urge to restore architecture and furniture. Try adding freestanding screens to make another textural layer in a space.

Exhibit wanderlust

The camper, the VW bus, the gypsy caravan: they can all become charming garden elements, perhaps even a crash pad for the after–garden party? Or maybe a sweet play spot. Bohemians are travelers, wanderers, adventurers, and vagabonds. Let your garden imply that you might just get up and go whenever you feel like it.

Nouveau bohemian

Traditional bohemianism takes a slightly different twist when mixed with contemporary design. Modern shapes and patterns are found in a woven string light fixture, a wavy indoor-outdoor rug, a cheery yellow bar cart. And they can all mix casually with a classic hanging chair that has irreverently been painted bright yellow.

Wave-patterned rug

Hanging chair

Gypsy bohemian

Gypsies are adept at establishing their own idea of nirvana wherever they happen to find themselves. The nomad bohemian gathers pieces that conjure a bit of mystery. Indigo batik prints for billowy curtains and upholstery layer well with a busy pattern on the outdoor carpet. Exotic lighting is moody and an unexpected fresh green peacock chair—with its hourglass shape and massive scale—makes anyone who sits in it feel like royalty.

Patterned outdoor rug

Peacock chair

Beat bohemian

Easy, breezy hippie style is simple to create. Beaded curtains set an undeniable mood; when you part their strings and walk through, you enter a space where anything can happen. Drifters with a penchant for art, beat bohemians have an easy come, easy go attitude. Crocheted rugs (from waterproof fibers), swirly sconce lighting, and pretty vintage rattan seating transfer hippie-chic fashion to the garden.

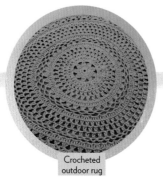

Crocheted outdoor rug

Rattan chair

Dandy bohemian

The dandy bohemian takes more care in making an impression than other bohemians, and is never without the ability to blur lines with a perfect cocktail (hence, the need for a striking bar cart). The elements almost veer into preppy—while still maintaining the telltale hallmarks of a magpie-like gatherer. Design the space with entertaining in mind: lots of comfy seating, an abundance of floor pillows, and lounging mats for lavishness.

Diamond-patterned outdoor rug

Venus rattan chair

Woven lantern

Lemon yellow
bar cart

Perforated lantern

Batik print fabric

OUTDOOR BAR CARTS

Interior furniture options continue to move outside and provide us with ever-greater garden living options. Bar carts with metal finishes and glass can easily go alfresco without modification. But new designs, made specifically for the great outdoors, feature liquor cabinets that attach to exterior walls, larger wheels for navigating bumpy terrain, and folding features for off-season storage.

Swirly
wall sconces

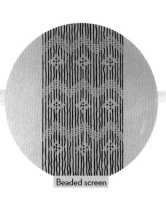

Beaded screen

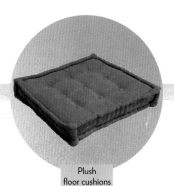

Plush
floor cushions

Green metal
bar cart

Airy & ethereal plants

Fine-textured plants lend fluidity to the garden. The floaty nature of these choices, which often hold tiny flowers high on dainty stems, means they can be used in large and mixed quantities, for a remarkable sense of lightness.

Gaura

Black mullein

Culver's root

Purple bell vine

Clematis

Tall verbena

Cow parsley

Grass

Mock orange

Nicotiana

Midnight gardens

Midnight gardens come alive in those dusky hours of early evening. The plants of these gardens all have special nighttime features. Some bloom only in darkness or seem to glow, others emit a special scent when the sun goes down. Combine a variety of these night owl additions to fashion a boho evening pleasure den.

Dusty miller

Evening primrose

Morning glory

BOHEMIAN SPIRIT

Muted colors, knee-high blooms, morning glories, and the musty scent of a garden will help set the enchanted mood. When planning the planting, let yourself be drawn to eclectic and sensual plants that come from all over the world. Layer plants not just for leaf texture but also for color and, most pleasingly, scent. Aim to satisfy no one but yourself and your cohorts. Bohemian poet Edna St. Vincent Millay planted the invasive and often reviled bittersweet vine in her garden to form an imposing screen around her pool, concealing a Prohibition-era bar and frequent no-swimsuits-allowed parties. I don't recommend adopting plants that you will live to regret, but don't be afraid to do as you please for your own reasons.

The summerhouse, used by artist and writer friends as a temporary studio, is new construction from salvaged materials. Aged details make it look generations old.

Clara's Isle of Wight bohemia

Summerhouse front

A favorite sunny spot, with views of the English Channel.

"we thought of painting the outside, but as it took shape it seemed to settle into the landscape, as if it had been there forever." — Clara Baillie

Water garden

Early-blooming tree peony takes center stage.

Mont Saint-Michel, tiny beach huts, peat fires, ocean views, and locally reclaimed materials were Clara's inspirations for her summerhouse and garden. When she had to have a tree removed (stump and all) she decided to make the most of the remaining hole and dug it into a pond. The summerhouse sits at the bottom of her garden, on the edge of the pond, and is a welcome refuge for Clara's family as well as many artist and writer friends who use it as a reading, writing, and quiet place. It is a place where "the world just disappears." Clara scoured the Isle of Wight's reclamation yards for materials, and the design of the summerhouse was ultimately driven by the pieces she found. The garden surrounding the summerhouse takes advantage of the warm microclimate of the local area; she is able to grow tree ferns, camellias, and crinodendron alongside viburnum, buddleja, clematis, roses, and wisteria. It all gives rise to an enchanting and extraordinary space.

SWINGING SEATS & DANGLING DAVENPORTS

When I think about some of the best and most important conversations I have had in my life, they all seem to take place around a swing. When I was a child, two chair swings on our back patio cocooned me while I consumed my first books. Before my sophomore year in college a dear friend and I worked out massive, life-altering decisions while idling over a tree swing. And these days, there is nothing more joyous than curling up with my little people in the hammock, to sway while we read stories. There is something magical about the cadence and I think that whenever possible all gardens, but especially those with bohemian intentions, should have some version of a place to perch and rock.

THE RIGHT WAY TO HANG A TREE SWING

BEAD SCREENS & CURTAINS

Garden passageways made of hanging beads have a variety of practical and less than purposeful uses. When planning your garden, consider using them for a variety of reasons.

PRACTICAL

- Establish separate garden rooms that can have different styles
- Create shade
- Provide structure for growing plants
- Soften hard architecture with fabric and strings

LESS THAN PURPOSEFUL

- Enjoy the clinking sound of beads as you pass through them
- Invoke the romance of softly billowing curtains
- Build mystery around what lies on the other side
- Take advantage of a fun and easily altered way to redecorate

Swings are best when they aren't just part of a playset. Look to hang them from trees, pergolas, porch overhangs, freestanding structures, or inside your outbuildings. Tree swing installation should take into account the safety of the tree and the riders. Here are a few pointers.

1. Find an appropriate tree with a good branch. Strong trees such as oak or ash are best, and the branch should be at least 6 inches (15 centimeters) in diameter.

2. Hang the swing as close to the trunk of the tree as possible without causing the swinger to come dangerously close to colliding with the trunk while swinging. Hanging the swing too far out will produce a lever action that can cause the branch to sag and break.

3. Use synthetic rope that is graded for at least double the weight you expect it to support. Rope feels nicer on your hands than a chain, and synthetic materials will not rot like natural fibers.

4. Use eyebolts screwed into the underside of the branch to secure your rope to the branch. If you drape the rope over the branch or wrap it in any way, the friction of swinging will, in time, wear away the protective layers of the tree branch and cause it to die.

5. If your swing or hanging chair needs more than one rope to suspend it, place the two attachment points slightly wider than the seat. This will help it to swing straight. Use a strong hitch knot attached to a carabiner (just like climbers use) to attach the rope to the eyebolts.

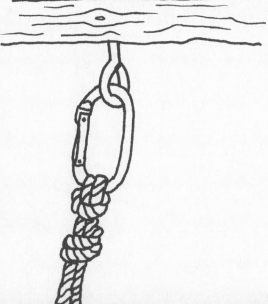

Abstract Vogue

daring

Artists have a certain way about them. I am endlessly fascinated with how, thanks to their trained eyes and ability to bring exquisite things to life, they help us see the world a little differently. When artists make gardens they tend to approach the whole project in a way most of us do not. They seem to either purposefully or unwittingly break every rule, setting about the project with a fearless confidence in their own self-expression, even if they don't know how to dig a hole. Their gardens are vogue; they have made their own rules.

Abstract art is about expression without being literal; rather than being overt, it uses shape and form to express ideas. An abstract garden is the same—it may not be filled with the things we expect all gardens to be filled with. A table and chairs might be gone and replaced with another composition. The garden may not be a place to be in, but rather a place to look over, or something else entirely. It might be filled with strange materials that challenge our definition of a garden. It will delight and instruct, take risks, be passionate and rich with ideas. In garden-land, to be abstract is to be avant-garde. Nothing is ordinary in the Abstract Vogue garden. The neighbors might not like it, but that is all part of the fun.

original

expressive

unconventional

esoteric

Fool the eye, follow the heart

Go for effect. Think about how you want your garden to feel— where you want to be transported to and the magic you want to sense. Nearly any mood can be created in any garden, and illusion can make a small garden feel bigger, hide an eyesore, or imply topography where there isn't any. As with other materials, water's reflective properties can also heighten drama and showcase the artistic quality of a design.

Punctuation

The garden, and the path you travel through it, can communicate a message. When you walk through any space, stop to think about how you feel at each stop. Perhaps it is anticipation and nervousness at the front door as you ring the bell, or discovery as you round the corner of a path whose end you couldn't see. Emotions rise and fall and you can design to highlight or diminish feelings. As you tell this story, it is always nice to let your audience know that you are done. Writers might do this with an exclamation point or a period; in the garden you can do the same with sculpture, plants, hedges, containers, fences, or a giant metal ball.

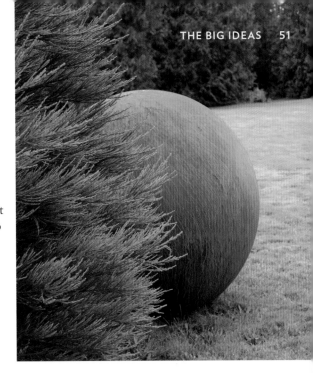

Experimentation

Throw out the rules and try something new. It may not work, but nothing innovative or exciting was ever discovered without a few flops. Test new materials, methods, shapes, and color combos, and embrace the failures as part of the artistic process. Soft-colored holiday ornaments strung together and wrapped around the trunk of a tree add texture and an interesting focal point.

Built-in pauses

Once you get the bug for confident self-expression, it can become addictive and you may be tempted to overdo it. Make sure that your best efforts are not lost in a sea of creative chaos—give equal thought to visual and emotional rest.

Color crazy

Let art captivate you. Use a favorite hue as a jolt of color
and joy in an otherwise green landscape, or devise a
planting palette from a favorite painting. There are plenty
of online tools to help you extract color schemes from
images; use them to make exciting new combinations in
the garden. If you want to keep it simple, plan a garden
around a single color and then inject a piece from the
opposite side of the color wheel. I imagine this fuchsia
lounger on a black-stained deck. Use contrast and
juxtaposition to let things get a little wild and fun.

Fuchsia stacking
lounger

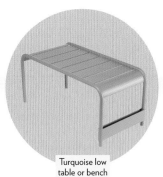

Turquoise low
table or bench

Sculpted shapes

Rectilinear bars of fire, perfectly round finials, and
triangular stands use elementary shapes to produce
dramatic sculpture. By combining shapes, more
complex and streamlined forms can be created, such as
a dodecahedron fire pit and a shapely rattan chair. Art
students learn how to simplify drawing complex figures like
the human body by combining basic shapes. Garden design
is no different; play with and combine shapes, smooth them
out, and experiment.

Sculpted
rattan chair

Bird café
with trellis

The universal palette

Art galleries tend to follow a few patterns. Walls are often
white or gray to let the works take center stage. The
molding might be particularly dramatic, or perhaps there
are one or two special pieces, such as a fabulous desk or
an amazing chandelier, but a classic and neutral palette
lets other attractions (paintings, sculpture, artifacts)
shine. This inflatable outdoor chesterfield (sofa) can go
anywhere (I imagine it happily providing a restful spot
in the middle of a gorgeous meadow), and shapely gray
planters look interesting, but let the plants within be the
primary focus. A red lamp adds a dash of whimsy for an
exciting outdoor gallery.

Inflatable sofa

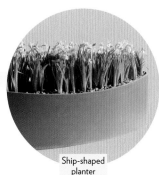

Ship-shaped
planter

Everything artful

A garden does not need dramatic lines or obscure sculpture
to be vogue. I would just aim to keep everything within as
artful as possible. Furniture can be chosen for interesting
shape, materials, construction, or design. Containers can
have an elegant twist on shape, and construction and
lighting can take on new form and purpose.

Nest chair

French spindle
planter

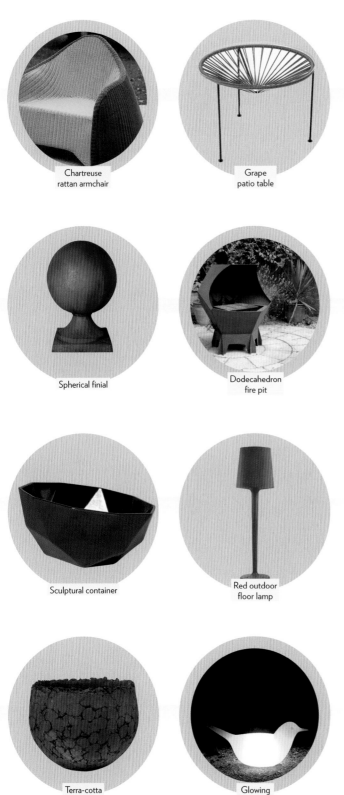

Chartreuse
rattan armchair

Grape
patio table

Blueberry
bistro set

Spherical finial

Dodecahedron
fire pit

Fire trough

Sculptural container

Red outdoor
floor lamp

Terra-cotta
lava pot

Glowing
bird light

CHOOSING OUTDOOR ART

Selecting art is always a deeply personal choice, but there are some practical considerations for art that you might place outdoors.

- **How will it temper with time?** Will it reveal itself in new ways as it weathers? What will grow on it, around it, and through it?

- **How does it relate to the area around it?** It should enliven a place and interact with its surroundings so that both the sculpture and the nature around it resonate in new ways.

- **What is its purpose?** Perhaps it is a focal point that wishes to draw the eye from elsewhere. Or maybe it provides the opportunity for contemplation.

- **How does the piece fit with the collection?** Does the collection have a voice and does that voice speak about the place? Curate so that there is meaning.

Lancewood

Catalina ironwood

Obscure plants

Those things that are rare and typically unseen can be vogue. Seek out obscure plants that have remarkable shapes and foreign features. Lancewood (*Pseudopanax crassifolius*) is a strange-looking tree with black, leather-like leaves and branches that native Maori used as spears because they were so straight (hence the common name lancewood). Catalina ironwood (*Lyonothamnus floribundus* subsp. *aspleniifolius*) is a special kind of fast-growing evergreen with luxurious, ferny leaves and beautiful, shaggy red bark. *Araucaria araucana*, the monkey puzzle tree, gets its common name from its sharp, twisted, blade-like foliage, which is impossible to touch without getting hurt.

Monkey puzzle tree

Plants as structure

Many plants can be used to form living garden structures. Weaving together willow branches can be a very cost-effective way to fashion a lattice fence, arches, tunnels, or other beautiful forms. If your locale permits, cactus-like ocotillo can be grown into fencing as well. Trees and shrubs such as hazel, hornbeam, beech, ash, and oak can be coppiced (that is, cut at the base to promote suckering) into hedge fences.

Big sugar beets
(Jette Mellgren, artist)

Cactus fence

Multicolored canvas

Form first

Topiary is often thought of as a staple of traditional or cottage gardens—quite the opposite of the Abstract Vogue garden—but shaped plants can be very avant-garde. You may also want to try sculpting earth mounds and cloaking them with turf or other ground covers. Tiny hills, cones, serpent-like shapes, or even growing chairs and sofas are all options.

Cloud-pruned tree

Paint with plants

There is magic in drawing up a planting plan (though I must admit I often forgo it). With pen and paper, I find I can organize plants in a way that I don't on the ground. A giant bed marked out with woven-together shapes that must be filled with something is like a paint-by-numbers project that I did as a kid—except I get to choose the colors. Thinking of a garden this way will help you imagine swathes of plants as strokes of a paintbrush. Perhaps you want a watercolor effect, where the colors wash together. Or maybe something more dramatic is on your mind, like the speckled mix of a Jackson Pollock painting. It could be something minimal, with only a few colors. Whatever it is, choose your paints and your application method.

Topher's striking fire garden

There is more than meets the eye in this uniquely romantic garden. Absent are carefree flowers and soft touches that we might consider typically sentimental. Instead there is a mirrored wall sculpture that spells out (in bar code) the name of an extraordinarily beautiful place (in Big Sur, California) that is personally important to the couple who commissioned this garden. Designer and artist Topher Delaney used the magnolia tree as the central building block to this design. Once the garden was stripped bare of other greenery, its powerful shape and form became more defined. The slate gray ground surfaces provide a perfect backdrop for shifting shadows, and a long sitting wall running the length of the garden offers a place from which to observe the constantly changing scene.

> "I sought to to construct this garden as a particular space of sheltering intimacy bounded by a courtyard of walls."
>
> —Topher Delaney

An encoded message is embedded in the mirrored strips, but at night, fire and blue light obscure the memory of language.

The magnificent magnolia is a reference to Marcel Duchamp's painting *The Bride Stripped Bare by Her Bachelors, Even (The Large Glass)*. No typical garden, the plan is more like a composed photo.

VERTICAL OPTIONS

Wall garden

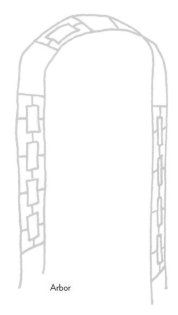

Vertical gardening isn't quite the latest, greatest trend it might seem. While the technology to grow plants on walls, hold them in place, and make sure they will thrive is relatively new and evolving, there are—and have been for awhile—many ways to make sure your garden goes beyond the horizontal plane. Gardens are three-dimensional, voluptuous beings and there are many ways to avoid being flat and boring.

Arbors and trellises. These help plants grow up. Support systems not only give vertical height but can become transitions from one area to another, screen eyesores, frame views, define paths, or provide a garden ceiling that makes an area feel cozier.

Wall gardens. When you have a very narrow space, there are a variety of options. You can choose plants that have a narrow profile and will climb a fence or wall feature, but you can also mount containers of all sorts that will hold dirt for growing plants. Trailing or vining plants will drape over the sides and help establish a green wall effect. There is also the option to utilize modern planting systems that allow plants to essentially grow sideways, by creating a layer of growing medium that is attached to and covers the wall.

Arbor

Hanging gardens. Use containers and baskets to hang gardens from balconies, overhangs, or any other place where you can gain a fingerhold. Hanging containers not only provide a lush look but free up floor space for other planters. Make sure to water regularly as these tend to dry out quickly.

Trees. Whether you leave them to grow naturally or interlace the branches, train them into shapes and hedges or espalier them, trees are the easiest and most obvious way to add vertical interest to a garden.

Trees

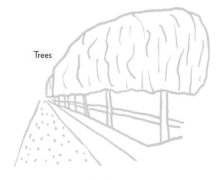

Rooftop gardens (green roofs). These gardens increase the green cover of a larger landscape and help to mitigate the heat island effect in urban areas. In a home garden, a green roof can be installed on a shed, a playhouse, or an outbuilding as an interesting focal point.

Rooftop garden

Living walls and crevice gardens. The most natural way to construct a wall garden is to encourage plants that might grow on walls naturally. Stone walls often have cracks and crevices where an opportunistic plant can take hold. Mosses, ferns, and lichens will often colonize a wall on their own (with time), but they can be encouraged by using moss mixes, or by carving out areas where tiny plants can be nurtured with a little dirt and TLC.

Hanging garden

Crevice garden

THE ART OF ILLUSION

If you are lamenting the size, shape, or view (or lack thereof) in your garden, you can employ a few artistic tricks to make improvements. These are some of the most common issues.

Make a small space seem bigger.
- Plant small trees far away and large trees up close. This creates a greater sense of perspective that will make distances seem farther.
- In a small garden, paving can be set at an angle to the house (30 degrees or 45 degrees work well) so that the grid lines of the paving can be as long as possible. This will give the illusion of a larger area.
- It might be counterintuitive, but a full space often seems bigger because there is so much to look at. Fill it up.
- If you can, forgo fences and borrow the view beyond. By not creating a visual boundary there is no sense of where your property ends.
- If you can't get rid of fences, try obscuring them with plants. Even in a very small garden, densely planted boundaries tend to imply endless depth.
- Add a mirror. The reflected space will double the perception of your actual space.

Disguise a flat square as something more interesting.
- Use plants to create rolling hills. Put low plants in front, build up to taller in the back, then taper back down again. The effect will be small hills. Alternatively, use different heights of ground cover to create smaller undulations.
- Cut and fill. This is less an illusion than a practical matter of changing topography through digging holes and creating mounds. But it is important to remember that in outdoor design, the floor doesn't have to be flat and the ceiling can be whatever height you want.
- Introduce curved paths and planting features. This will distract from the squareness and lead the eye gently around the garden.
- Create complexity, interest, and intrigue.
- Plant hedges and use screens to prevent the ability to see everything at once. What you can't see is exciting and mysterious.
- Cut holes in your screen or hedges, providing a window to what lies beyond. Little peepshows increase anticipation.
- If you have separated your garden into distinct areas, you can make the transition from one to another more exciting by adding arbors, tunnels, or other interesting entryways.

Distract and disguise.
- If you aren't happy with the way something looks and you can't change it, create a distraction. Strategically place a focal point that draws attention elsewhere, away from the eyesore.
- Vines and large plants are a great ways to hide walls, wells, and anything else that is less than pretty. Place the plant in front or let it grow over the mess.
- Use color in the same way. Dull colors will not grab attention but bright ones will. Use reds, yellows, and oranges to make something stand out, and use fewer outstanding colors to encourage things to hide.

CREATE TOPOGRAPHY IN THE GARDEN

Remember that if you dig, the depth of the hole is essentially equal to the height of the pile of dirt that you remove. The only risk in changing something flat into something undulating is that you must pay attention to where you are causing water to flow (hopefully not into your house or toward a neighbor's property). Also consider non-standard options such as ladders, string gardens, or repurposed materials like large feed sacks or construction bags that have been filled with dirt to form planting mounds.

Hollywood Froufrou

To the design layperson, it would be easy to assume that based on lingual similarities, Regency and Hollywood Regency are just regional versions of the same thing. But actually, about a hundred years of design evolution separate the two. Regency style emerged in England in the early nineteenth century and on the landscape front it evolved from the works of Capability Brown and Humphry Repton. Hollywood Regency was born in Southern California in the early twentieth century through designers such as Dorothy Draper and Billy Haines, who catered to stars of the Golden Age of film. So, quite different—but not unrelated.

Hollywood Regency is glitz and glamour covered in lacquer, chrome, and mirrored finishes. Every detail is meant to convey luxury and there is always the feeling that people should look good in the design—particularly if they are wearing satin bathrobes and sipping a cocktail. The opulence does take a cue from the original Regency period, though. There is a lovely, classical architecture in outbuildings, and the Doric temple of a place like Bowood House in England could easily be the broad-stroke blueprint for a poolside cabana.

Neither style can be taken too seriously—after all, between them there is a love of follies such as grottoes and hermit caves, colorful animal sculpture, and a full-on embrace of prissy details.

The best part of Hollywood Regency style, though, is the over-the-top, anything-goes attitude toward personal expression. Hollywood Regency loves bold blocks of color (in particular pink, turquoise, yellow, black, and white), juxtaposition (think about mixing English and French Regency with Greek Revival, Asian, and mid-century modern influences), and lots of memorable details. It's a smorgasbord of styles that miraculously come together to look elegant. In short, you have to have swagger to pull off a Hollywood Froufrou garden.

girly

dramatic

glamorous

staged

whimsical

Black & white

If you have trouble figuring out color, you almost can't go wrong by starting with black and white. The sharp contrast plus another color is an easy formula for achieving Hollywood Froufrou success. Play with nearly any color you like, but the more saturated and energetic the hue, the better.

Cabanas & bungalows

Lazing about and looking luscious (at least in pictures) is a key part of the Hollywood lifestyle. Hollywood Froufrou takes that into consideration. Gardens frequently have overtly decorated cabanas and bungalows where tea can be served, parties can spontaneously arise, and glamorous respite can be had.

Graphic patterns

Wide stripes, geometric patterns, neo-classical motifs, and Art Deco designs can be used not just in fabrics but also in the layout of the garden. Black and white checkerboard floors, Greek keys, rickrack edges, square scallops, and trellises are all patterns that are fun to mix and match. Throw in the odd animal print or furry pillow to finish it off.

Glamorous details

Metal furniture can be finished in extra-shiny colors or metallic tones to capture the love of lacquer. When choosing outdoor fabrics, not only should you use bold colors and patterns but also allow for lavish draping. Take extra care to add special touches such as contrasting piping and fabric edging. Ceramic whippets, greyhounds, poodles, foo dogs, camels, elephants, and monkeys are commonly found in playful pairs. Distinctive gems and minerals add panache. It is all about escapism and outrageous accents (which aren't mass-produced but express individuality) that help to dodge reality. Make sure that the whole thing isn't taken over by clutter, though; this isn't a minimal look but it is all held together by common threads of color and finish.

Gatsby glamour

It always starts with a cocktail party and conversation. Arrange the garden so that guests have plenty of seating and opportunities for tête-à-têtes. Crisp black and white recalls dapper formality. Keep furniture scaled to human proportions (as opposed to commonly manufactured oversized pieces) and low-slung, so that you look your best when perched atop.

Golden Age

Art Deco and Asian-infused details combine with warm, brassy, metal tones to produce a sexy Golden Age garden. This stylized vignette could just as easily be set around an amoeba-shaped pool behind a mid-mod house as between the classical columns of a generous porch. The mix of styles can extend beyond the accessories to include the architecture of the home.

Fifth Ave. flirt

Hollywood Froufrou is theatrical and unabashedly flirty. The bamboo chair relates to the bamboo-like pattern in the planters. Sticking with the white and baby blue scheme, the added animal elements of tiny birds and tassel-collared whippets add the right amount of outrageous detail.

China white

Popular since the seventeenth century, chinoiserie motifs such as lotus flowers and pagoda-like umbrellas give a fashionable sense of worldliness to the otherwise pristine white setting.

Cane-patterned ceramic stool

Portofino umbrella

Yellow flower garden stool

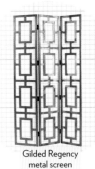

Gilded Regency metal screen

White Chippendale planters

Topiary planter

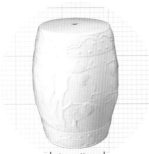

Lotus-patterned garden stool

Pagoda umbrella

Striped armchair

Petite
metal bench

Formal urns

Walter Lamb
lounge chair

Bronze ceramic
planter

Lacquered bamboo
garden armchair

Ceramic Italian
whippet

Swirly metal
armchair

Terra-cotta
flower planter

OUTDOOR THEATERS

Watching classic movies or even TV reruns is all the more charming when enjoyed under the stars. If you are serious about video quality and can't stand anything but perfect surround sound, you might want to stay indoors where the environment can be controlled. But if you appreciate the magic in hauling blankets and cushions out onto the lawn for an evening of entertainment under the stars—well, making that magic is easier than ever, thanks to modern technology. Here are a few main ingredients:

- **A backdrop.** A light and smooth wall of a house could work. I use a sheet strung over my laundry line, but all manner of homemade screens can be rigged.

- **A receiver.** If you have Wi-Fi, a laptop or tablet will likely pick it up even outside, enabling you to watch streaming online video.

- **A projector.** As with all technology, the next new thing will be here sooner than we can imagine. Inexpensive digital projectors are easily hooked up to a laptop or a handheld device.

Hydrangea

Pretty in pink

Pink is girly, romantic, naïve, and sweet—and it casts a flattering light. Planting in this style tends to be neat and tidy, but with splashes of color. If you choose just one color to incorporate into a planting scheme (and you probably shouldn't choose too many), start with pink. Soft pink will convey femininity and coyness and will recall design trends of the Golden Age. Pink hydrangea hedges for privacy are a good choice, as are arbors and pergolas covered with pink roses or dainty pink clematis.

Peony

Red-flowering currant

Camellia

Blowsy blooms

Flowers with big, beautiful blossoms give off an air of being so full of themselves that they might just fall apart and have to lie down on a fainting sofa. Roses, peonies, and dinner-plate dahlias are obvious choices but also consider ranunculus, camellias, and even some special varieties of big-bodied chrysanthemums.

Clipped boxwood
stair edging

Pruned greens

Carefully pruned hedging can be a
dramatic feature, and this style calls for
theatrics. Beyond just forming walls,
create twisted swirls of plants that give
an extra flourish to a staircase. There
are lots of options for hedges, but
boxwood, myrtle, holly, and privet are
great evergreen options. If you want to
be particularly glamorous, bamboo
is more exotic and unexpected.

Topiary twist

Michael's glamorous party pad

"Like a magpie, I love shiny, sparkly things."
— Michael Tavano

The metal cabana was powder coated using the same gold paint found on Ferrari automobiles. Pillows in outdoor velvet provide an exotic touch.

In the heart of New York City, a 242-square-foot outdoor space (11 feet by 22 feet, or 3.3 meters by 6.6 meters) is quite a luxury, but creating a functional and otherworldly garden within it can be quite a challenge. Designer Michael Tavano set out to construct a perfect outdoor entertaining space. He was inspired by the golden *paillettes* (spangles) that fashion designer Paco Rabanne used on his iconic 1970s dresses. Facing mirrors on either side of the dining table reflect light and dimension back at each other and a metal gazebo breaks up the space and gives it purpose. The layers of green planting all around effectively disguise the fact that this garden has city walls on all sides.

Inexpensive propane tank covers are turned upside down and topped with blue Lucite to create tables.

Touches of blue complement the dining set's gold accents.

TRELLIS BASICS

Trellises and lattice are some of the handiest but most underutilized design tools of the garden. They can take many forms, from purely architectural to functional plant support. They come in all shapes and sizes, so there is absolutely no reason to settle for the standard crosshatch variety if it's not what you want. Your usage will help you determine the best trellis solution for your project. Consider things such as pattern, privacy, strength, shadows, and placement.

Other uses for trellis include making freestanding modern art or arches to train plants over paths, decorating containers and furniture, and creating freestanding pyramids and shapes that can be used in the garden for decoration and support.

Flat lattice. Quite common and often the cheapest versions are those found in sheets at the hardware store, where thin strips of wood are held together in a crosshatch pattern with staples. More sturdy options use better joinery, but flat lattice does not have much structural strength. It can be fashioned in a basic diamond lathe pattern or a square crosshatch. The product is only the thickness of two thin strips of wood; because of this it plays better with light and shadow. The pattern will change with the angle of the light and it should be used where its ornamental quality can be appreciated. Flat lattice is useful for attaching to something else, or in a situation where structural strength is not required. It can be used as a plant support, screen, fence topper, decorative window element in walls, and as a general garden accent.

Edge lattice. Here, the wood is on its edge (rather than lying flat). This not only looks more substantial but is also considerably stronger than flat lattice. The depth of the wood can downplay the intricacy of the pattern and cause shadows to be less varied and interesting. Edge lattice is appropriate for railings, gates, fences, plant support (where the plant is fairly substantial), and in situations where more privacy is desired (the thick profile will increase what the trellis can screen).

Basic panel lattice. Panel lattice is similar to flat lattice, but it can be altered from the basic diamond or crosshatch lathe style. Panels can be made in a huge variety of patterns that can add to the style of the garden. Some are made small and in patterns that are appropriate as bed edging, large walls, or even garden sculpture. Free-form shapes and patterns allow for endless design options.

Framed screens. Trellises can take on new uses as garden art if they are beautifully built, framed, and displayed. Panels can also be hinged together to form a movable screen, similar to something that might be used indoors, to provide shade, shelter, and privacy, or to hide unsightly areas

Spindle lattice. Remove one direction of the lattice (either horizontal or vertical) and you are left with spindle lattice. Spindle lattice will provide a lot less privacy than other lattice options but is a popular option for fence toppers.

Wall lattice can be as simple as a standard fan-shaped structure to hold up plants, or it can get quite extravagant, as in the uses of classic French *treillage*. In formal courtyard gardens it is common to find huge walls covered in elaborate trelliswork that embellishes the architecture and even plays with perspective. Mirrors are also frequently added to play with depth.

Wabi Sabi Industrial

transitory

a perfectly beautiful

imperfect - eaten - has
discoloured - pa

less green, coloured & wet
licked by rain & face sap

dishevelled by rain & wind
broken

distressed shape - organic
grew of its own accord

crumpled & bowned

If you haven't figured it out yet, I heartily encourage mixing it up. Wabi sabi and industrial styling really are two very different things—each quite worth exploring on their own. But they have similarities that, in my mind, make them natural partners. Both celebrate beauty in the simple, everyday utility items of our lives. And both exude an unexpected warmth that comes from time and patina. Industrial ephemera largely recall days gone by, when our society was more closely tied to manufacturing. Wabi sabi, which is based in ancient Japanese philosophy, encourages finding beauty and peace in simplicity. Wabi is to be unmaterialistic and humble by choice. Sabi means "in the bloom of time"—a phrase I personally love, as it makes me think not just of gardens, but also of being beautifully pregnant or gracefully aging, and it alludes to having patience for everything to work out. Neither wabi sabi nor industrial style has time for ostentation, pretense, or artifice. Industrial style loses these things for the sake of practicality and hardworking, proletarian usefulness. Wabi sabi rejects them in a near spiritual desire to live outside of the mainstream—to enjoy a life that finds beauty in imperfection and sagacity in nature. Industrial style requires upcycling (they just don't make things like they used to) and wabi sabi accepts the natural process of growth, decay, and death in a simple, slow, uncluttered, and authentic way. Find the joy in utilitarian surfaces, stvripped-back architecture, and salvaged objects. Together they give rise to a style that is simple, clean, modest, and effortlessly chic.

imperfect

modest

asymmetry

aged

Stone speaks

Cracks and crevices—the marks of time, weather, and loving use—can be seen in stone. Uniquely made by nature rather than industrial manufacturing processes, stone universally symbolizes longevity and memory. When used in design, it is an anchor for everything around it and brings with it an austere beauty.

Salvaged beauty

Shun conspicuous consumerism and opt for unassuming materials. Gritty beauty is found in recycled metals, weathered wood, and ceramics. When these pieces find a home among plants in the garden, they instill a sense of constancy. Be careful to keep things clean and orderly; this look isn't messy or slovenly.

Unadorned form & function

Clarity of thought and space is just one benefit of a wabi sabi way of life. Keep things simple and clean as an act of respect. Furniture and plants that are lovingly cared for can evolve a patina and age gracefully. Keep it uncluttered so you can appreciate the details.

Thoreauvian wabi

As Thoreau removed the weight of material concerns when he went into the woods, he subjected himself to a chosen poverty. Recreate a similar place of garden solitude with a little hut and beautifully made basic furniture, like this table and a hanging shelf. Little more than fresh-picked vegetables and the sound of a gentle rain or rustling breeze are required.

Bleached oak dining table

Contemporary stoneware pots

Reclaimed sabi

While wabi is a cultivated poverty, sabi is the celebration of the old and faded. Well-worn items carry with them the characteristics of their previous use and impart that charm to the newfound purpose. Industrial chairs, seats made from old metal implements, decoratively reused sign letters, and a repurposed stone trough come together to forge a strong, masculine sensibility.

Manufacturing barrel seat

Granite stone trough

Industrial lounge

Stones, softened with time into smooth, comfortable shapes, and recycled traffic lights pair with an intricately mechanical stool. Fabric containers give flexibility to planting as they can be placed nearly anywhere, including on the wall. Earthy tones of brown, black, gray, deep green, and rust congeal in an industrial vibe.

Industrial patio furniture

Bag planter

Earthen elegance

Simple construction lets the materials take center stage. A clean-lined, modern wood table and casual wire chair keep the furniture straightforward and functional. A petrified wood stool and ceramic chimes add an elemental heartiness that is unapologetically terrestrial.

Simple wood table

Petrified wood stool

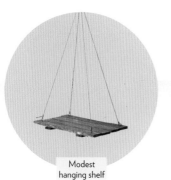

Modest
hanging shelf

Tiny house

Red
metal chair

Recycled
sign letters

ATTRACTING BATS

Bats are among our most desirable garden cohabitants. They are voracious mosquito eaters and their excrement (guano) is one of the best fertilizers a gardener could ask for. Bats have an undeserved reputation for being scary, but the reality is that there are very few that feast on blood (none in North America), they are nothing like rodents, and they don't contract rabies any more often than other animals you might encounter in your yard. These helpful mammals are beautiful to watch in the twilight hours, as they dance around the sky ingesting countless pests. To encourage them, it is worth banishing pesticides and installing bat boxes on a south-facing surface.

Tractor
seat stool

Clay pebble
stones

Vintage school
bus light

Metal
mesh chair

Orange
butterfly chair

Stoneware bells

Shelved gardens

In tight spaces, create a visual treat by using shelves. Shelved gardens allow for a whole variety of styles to be mixed and matched. Terra-cotta pots are a classic choice because a collection will look beautiful together even though each piece will, over time, take on its own special verdigris. Just as with a bigger garden, there will be microclimates (for example, the plants on the lower shelves might get less light but more water) that should be considered. By keeping one thing constant (type of plant, flower color, or container) it is relatively simple to give the whole garden a chic sense of cohesion.

Succulents on shelves

Crocuses in lawn

Moss

Lemon thyme

Imperfect lawns

Lawn perfection is, to my mind, an unnecessary measure of exactness that is largely promoted by chemical companies. I love a May lawn that is covered like a pimply teen with happy yellow dandelion spots. Earlier in the spring I enjoy crocus and other bulbs that pop up through the barely green grass.

Perfect lawns are not as good for the environment as weedy lawns. Aside from the fact that they don't require perpetual spraying and chemical maintenance, imperfect lawns also feature common plants (clover, plantain, and dandelions) that are very useful to beneficial bugs such as butterflies, ladybugs, and bees. Such generally unwanted plants also have other benefits: many are edible and they can also divert pests from nearby ornamentals or vegetables.

Enjoy the imperfection and recognize that sometimes going with the flow of nature can be just as satisfying as engaging it in battle.

Autumn leaves

Seed heads

Late-season sunflower

Decayed beauty

Everyone can see beauty in the flush of new leaves and the flourish of flowers. But as the seasons pass and the garden changes, finding new beauty in a collection of silvered leaves and seed pods blanketed in hoarfrost is an active aesthetic challenge. Texture and tactile sensation *can* be just as pleasing as floriferous beauty. By recognizing that there is just as much ephemeral beauty in decay as there is in growth, we can choose plants not just for their flower color and bloom time. If a plant does not die back to the ground completely, observe and enjoy how it fades in the fall, weathers the winter, and comes back again in the spring.

Greenhouse garden

Sensual feasts

The atmosphere of a great garden is generally composed of far more than just beds, borders, paths, and hardscaping. The things that make it special are the morning sun, the musty smell of geraniums, or the warm, damp feeling of walking into a greenhouse full of plants. Rubbing your fingers on soft leaves and new growth are tangible joys to be relished.

Dan's reconstructed garden niche

Recycled wood covers the wall of the garden, and numbered pots help customers select succulents for purchase.

"I love the things that are used. Objects retain and transport the energy of what they once were, and you can feel that." — Dan Kowalski

Strung-together cut bamboo is draped over a tree for added texture.

Sculptures were part of the original garden, built at the start of the nineteenth century.

Dan's garden is adjacent to his San Francisco design shop, Fl!pp. When he took over the building, there were remnants of a garden left by the original owner (a turn-of-the-century longshoreman) scattered throughout a narrow, alley-like space. A found collection of stone and concrete statues was resurrected and restored; the pieces still grace the garden. But the wooden wall is the main focal point. It was constructed of redwood wall lathes that were salvaged when some of the interior walls were torn down. The design of the asymmetrical, lined pattern was an idea sparked by a collapsed barn in nearby Sonoma County, and the wall does an excellent job of keeping the focus at eye level, avoiding a closed-in feeling that could come with the imposing building behind the garden. Dan is a former watchmaker and the garden is a direct reflection of his fascination with working objects and interesting relics. The ever-evolving assemblage celebrates fun and funky objects that always have a backstory.

A blue tin peanut-oil jar from India has also served as a lantern and candle holder. Succulents and gold-painted pots complete the vignette.

MAKING A CONCRETE CONTAINER

Materials
- Four wood panels, cut to size of desired container
- Four 2-in. × 2-in. pieces of wood, cut to height of container
- Cooking spray
- Pre-mix concrete
- Chicken wire or wire mesh panel
- A wine cork
- A piece of Sonotube whose diameter equals the desired interior radius, cut to height of container

1. Assemble the wood panels into a square using the 2 × 2 pieces of wood as blocks to hold the box together on the outside of the mold. Place the box on top of a piece of wood (does not need to be attached).

2. Spray the outside of the Sonotube and the inside of the box with cooking spray.

3. Mix the concrete per package instructions (it should not be crumbly) and fill the base of the box about 2½ inches (6.5 centimeters) deep.

4. Create a drainage hole in the container by adding a wine cork in the bottom. Embed it (standing up) in the wet concrete so that it can be removed later when the concrete dries.

5. Cut a rectangle of wire mesh that is about 4 inches (10 centimeters) shorter than the desired height of the container. Bend and trim it into a rectangular sleeve that will sit between the Sonotube and the walls of the container. Do not let this touch the walls or you will see it in your final product. This mesh gives structural strength to the container; the bigger the container, the more important its structural strength.

6. Fill the box with the remaining concrete, making sure the mixture settles around all the corners as well as the mesh and the Sonotube. Do not fill the Sonotube. Let dry for a few days.

7. When the concrete has cured, remove the wooden box and peel the Sonotube out of the middle of the container (you will likely not be able to reuse it). You can finish the outside with a variety of finishes or leave it plain. I chose a clear concrete glaze to give the container a dull versus wet and shiny contrast finish, but paint can be applied in any way that appeals to you.

LIGHTING WITH A TWIST

Materials
- Spool of polyester macramé cord
- Lamp shade frame
- Decorative Edison-style light bulb
- Indoor/outdoor light socket with plug attached

The goal of this project is to cover your lamp shade frame with an interesting and textural surface and added decorative details, provided by the macramé cord. Since your shade will undoubtedly be shaped differently than the one I used, this will require getting creative. Take some time before you start and imagine how you want the finished product to look. Do you want to highlight the shape of the shade? Perhaps you want to fill in some of the space by wrapping in a way that will fill in holes between the legs of the shade. You may also want to use knots as decorative features on the light fixture. I chose to leave the sides open, but you can form rosettes at the joints with extra wrapping, then add loops at the bottom that resemble a chandelier. Follow your own tastes!

1. Cut a long piece of cord—as long as you can easily manage in one hand. Ball it up so you can hold it comfortably in one hand and the ball fits between the prongs of the shade. This will help you wrap quickly and avoid knots in your cord as you wrap.

2. Knot your cord where you want to begin wrapping. The knot should be in a place where you can hide it or make a feature of it. Some macramé cords are fusible and you can use an iron to melt the cord together at the beginning and avoid having a knot.

3. Start wrapping the cord around the frame. It is easiest if you wrap about ten times, then stop to tighten and eliminate the slack from the wraps that were just formed. Making sure the wrapping is consistently tight will help your fixture last longer and ensure an even and polished look.

4. Wrap the fixture, adding knots where desired and creating designs by wrapping over and under adjacent prongs if desired (I didn't do this, as my fixture was small and I wanted to see the light). Rosettes can be made by wrapping around a joint in a repeated over-and-under circular fashion, until a large flower shape is created. Try to end a string at a joint as this will allow you to hide the knot more easily and start a fresh length of string.

5. When all wrapping is complete, tuck ends of cords to the inside of the fixture and out of sight, trimming where necessary.

LIFESTYLE

When a garden becomes part of how we live, the simple source for things we enjoy and life's little luxuries, then it has gone beyond being just another part of our homestead. Whether cooking, playing, creating something to share, or making a peaceful sanctuary that holds personal meaning, the gardeners who favor the following garden styles are motivated by individual passions and commitments—life choices, familial circumstances, and ways of living.

122

PRETTY POTAGER

134

ORGANIC MODERN

" The muted grays, white plaster, and textural plantings combine to lower one's blood pressure upon impact."
— Molly Wood

146

PLUSH YOGA

Homegrown Rock 'n' Roll

What do you get when you blend youthful irreverence, a desire to connect with community, and the need for a simple lifestyle that is tied to the land? Homegrown Rock 'n' Roll. Urban farmers, allotmenteers, so-called gentlemen (and women) farmers, hardworking hippies, and even the burgeoning cadre of horticultural experts who specialize in hydroponics and aquaponics are all making gardens in this style. Their common ground is a desire to use the land in a way that supports growing, cooking, crafting, brewing, preserving, building, and creating.

Classical garden design enthusiasts might look at this style and find little to enthuse about, with its chaotic sensibility and general lack of structure. But therein lies the beauty. It is all about resourcefulness—simple, homey charm that provides cottage industrialists with a way to live that answers to no one and no thing, except the flow of the seasons.

Homegrown gardens are cropping up everywhere. They are on urban rooftops and in vacant dirt spots; they stretch into the suburbs and countrysides. A grassroots movement that rails against industrialized agriculture and environmental degradation while promoting sustainability, local commerce and food safety drives it. Rock 'n' roll gardeners aren't just digging in the dirt as a satisfying pastime or a way to cultivate beauty; they are doing it as part of a political movement and a social statement. Consequently, these gardens look very different. They aren't afraid to boast oddball materials, they often welcome weeds, bugs, wildlife, and barnyard characters as friends that play a part in a greater cycle of the garden, and they generally embrace the chaos that comes with the whole package.

authentic

irreverent

allotment

simple

self-sufficient

BE BEE FRIENDLY

There is no doubt that bees are struggling for survival and researchers are desperately trying to determine the exact cause of colony collapse disorder and why it is happening more often. A single source may not be the culprit and it most likely seems that the root problem will be a complex matter. Current research points to the use of both neonicotinoid-type products (pesticides) and fungicides. By ceasing your use of these products and keeping yourself educated on new research, you can help reverse the trend.

Be a producer

Don't just grow your own vegetables—keep chickens and other small animals and get involved in the full life cycle of the products they provide. Host beehives and cultivate honey and wax products. Forage, tap trees for sap, and stretch the season by growing year-round in a hoophouse.

Live outside

Being intimate with your landscape means really living in the garden in a way that most folks do not. Homegrowers often have summer kitchens, outdoor showers and tubs, and other modified ways of extending their everyday living quarters into nature. Establish a devil-may-care attitude toward your garden; a jovial rakishness will help you see opportunities. This isn't about following the rules; it is about working with what you have and enjoying every minute of it. The beauty of these gardens comes from the element of surprise and the ingenuity that arises out of necessity.

Eco style

Why make the effort if you are going to break the hosepipe ban, or spend tons of money on denuding the land with chemicals and synthetic fertilizers? This is eco-friendly gardening at its peak. Be an early adopter of solar, geothermal, and off-the-grid technology wherever you can. Not to be subversive, but to do your part. And certainly plan to keep all your garden accessories green.

Use it up, wear it out, make it do, or do without

The creed of our grandparents is alive and well. Before you discard anything, think about how it might find a new life. Avoid consumption and consumerism. Incorporate ideas such as lasagna gardening, which uses the cardboard packaging so prolific in our online shopping lives and transforms it into a soil builder and a tool for weed control. Buckets, stock tanks, and recycled feed bags find lives as planting vessels, bathtubs, fish homes, and even shade curtains. Anything goes, so be imaginative.

Wooden
nesting box

Hen house

Wire egg
basket

Chicken waterer

Beehive

Bee skep

Butterfly on
butterfly bush

Bug house

Enamel
wash basin

Polytunnel

Watering hose

Potting table

Rhubarb forcer

Hanging
drying racks

Raised bed
joint

Colorful
plant support

Chickens

Adding chickens to the garden is not a huge undertaking, but it does require some special considerations. A chicken house will make sure the hens have a place to lay eggs and will also provide them some protection. If you are letting your poultry roam free, you will not require a sizable run. Most homegrowers make this decision based on local factors such as housing ordinances and the prevalence of predators. Year-round watering (and accommodations in areas where it freezes) is also an important element of coop design. Nesting boxes come in all shapes and sizes and can be a fun way to add character to your garden. If you are raising chicks, it will take a season before they start to lay—but be prepared with collecting baskets, because when they start producing eggs, it is a daily harvest.

Bees & bugs

Garden and farm life is anything but pristine and clean. In fact, it is deliciously disheveled, dirty, and at one with all the little creatures that come along. With the onslaught of marketing from garden chemical sellers, one could start to believe that bugs are bad, but nothing could be less true. Welcome bees and bugs into the garden—they will work their little butts off making it a better place—with custom homes that also make for interesting textural art, functional hives, and old-fashioned skeps. Make sure they have plenty to eat by planting to attract bees and butterflies.

Greenhouse operations

Homegrown gardens have to operate as high-capacity machines. Every part works with the others to make the micro farm a sustainable enterprise. The pieces can be scaled to serve a single family or to feed and supply a small community. Scale up production or just extend the season with a hoophouse or greenhouse. These structures should be functionally appointed inside. Potting tables, hoses, water collection tanks, and industrial sinks are all required fittings.

Production beds

Efficiently growing vegetables for home use or for selling requires special attention to tools and harvesting methods. Raised beds with simple construction (such as mortise-and-tenon versions made from untreated cedar) will last a long time and need little maintenance. Drying racks that hold recently harvested goods allow for removal of dirt and encourage things like onion and garlic tops to dry. Sturdy planting cages are a must for far more than tomatoes, and terra-cotta forcers will help protect sensitive plants and encourage tender (and tasty) early spring growth.

CHICKEN-FRIENDLY GARDENS

In addition to the fresh eggs they produce, chickens keep bugs and weeds in check, producing rich fertilizer along the way. They are charming and playful but do require some special considerations to stay healthy and happy.

- At a bare minimum, you will need a coop, a run or space for the chickens to roam, and a place to compost the bedding material.

- Plant conifers and evergreens. The area beneath them will provide a year-round area for dust baths.

- Plant fruit producers such as blueberries, mulberries, and apples that chickens like to eat.

- Use logs to gather insects. Overturn a log after a few days to provide a bug feast for your chickens.

- If you are letting your chickens roam free-range, be aware that annuals and many plants will be the victims of scratching and foraging. Make a choice and plan your garden accordingly.

Natural partners

Companion planting takes advantage of the natural friendships that plants have with each other. Some plants help their neighbors by enabling the uptake of more nutrients, others repel common pests or provide mulching weed control; some even provide literal support by holding each other up.

Zinnia

Cosmos

Gomphrena   Cornflower

Mint

Sage

Rosemary

Marigold

OPPORTUNISTIC GARDENING

The rock 'n' roll gardener has little notion that plants are used for design and generally takes the approach of planting only what is useful, trying to squeeze as much of it in as possible. Plants aren't just for fresh eating; they are also used in home remedies and tinctures, preserved as jams for later use, given as gifts, or utilized in bigger projects. Gourds, for instance, can be made into bowls, birdhouses, or other crafts. Farm-raised ingredients can be baked into delicacies for the farmers' market. Woody shrubs can serve as fences and be woven into baskets or used as the basis of other twigcraft. In this anything-goes, resourceful garden, even wildcrafting (harvesting uncultivated plants for food or medicine) is part of the celebration. Make dandelion wine, wild rose hip jam, or other treats from the volunteers in the garden.

Cut flowers

A patch of blooms for cutting is among the simplest ways to enjoy the bounty of a garden. Doing nothing more than sprinkling some seeds on the ground can grow many of the best cut flowers, providing beautiful home decoration and an opportunity to pass arranged blooms onto others at the local market.

Chamomile

Edible *flowers*

Consumable blossoms add much more interest to cooking than just novel plate decoration—most blooms have interesting flavor, too. Nasturtiums are peppery, hyssop tastes like licorice, bee balm is similar to Earl Grey tea, and chamomile has a faint apple taste. Use them in cooking and preserving uniquely flavored specialties.

Nasturtium

Bee balm

A shed serves as backdrop to a mixed vegetable, herb, and cutting garden.

Jon & Mary's market garden

Free-range chicken

Armed with a goal of showing how commercial horticulture can help amateur gardeners, Jon Wheatley and Mary Payne shaped a garden that features an orchard with beehives, cut flowers, fruit, vegetables, and even nursery stock, as well as a dovecote, free-range hens, and ducks. Their hoophouse grows a range of exotic vegetables such as oca and anu (both tuberous root vegetables from the Andes), Chinese artichokes (which look shockingly similar to white worms but are purported to be a delicacy in France), and balsam pear (which looks nothing like a tree pear), popular in Indian curries.

"We wanted to incorporate elements of commercial horticulture ... strawberries for 'pick your own' crops ... even watercress growing in the water-wheel pool."
— Mary Payne

A polytunnel extends the growing season and is packed with edibles. Gladiolus, dahlia, and agapanthus blooms are ready for cutting.

SUMMER KITCHENS

Cooking and eating outside is one of the great joys of summer, and it doesn't have to be a difficult or expensive luxury. I can't argue against the convenience of an easily lit gas grill, but the often off-putting price point begs a rationalization for how often you will put this implement to use. Perhaps, if you live in a place where an outdoor kitchen can be a year-round resource, it makes good sense, but most must recognize an extreme seasonality and should opt instead for a simpler summer kitchen. A summer kitchen should allow you to do the following:

- **Easily cook a meal outside.** A chef's kitchen is not required to wash and prepare a salad straight from the garden, blanch fresh-picked green beans, grill meats, and enjoy it all with a locally produced aperitif.
- **Highlight tastes exclusive to outdoor cooking.** Gas is handy, but charcoal tastes better. For me it is a matter of redundancy: Why have a second kitchen if it doesn't bring its own flavor to the table?
- **Allow for the things a regular kitchen does not.** Things like boiling sap procured from maple or other sweet syrup trees (and letting the copious amounts of steam escape into the atmosphere), processing a bountiful harvest into canned goodies for winter (where the discarded bits can be easily shooed into the compost bin), and imparting food with the smoky character and flavors of open-flame cooking.
- **Provide a beautiful place to eat that is handy to the garden.**

KITCHEN MUST-HAVES

- **A surface.** Countertops can be any sort of table—even an old door atop a couple of saw horses or a repurposed bar cart. Cinder blocks can also become simple structures for mounting a faucet and a catch bowl.

- **Heat.** Try to locate the countertop near electricity so that a hot plate (like the kind you once used in a dorm room) can be used. Alternatively, consider putting a camp stove to use—these simple and inexpensive cooking devices don't have to be reserved just for wilderness adventures.

- **A grill.** I prefer the simplicity and flavor of charcoal, but if you want to spend more and have the hassle of tanks or service lines, then go for gas.

- **Running water.** This can be achieved with a hose, or if you prefer something a little fancier, hook up to a neatly mounted tap.

AQUAPONICS VS. HYDROPONICS

It would be easy to think these are the same thing, but in fact they are quite different. The only commonality is that both use water as a growing medium and they both are increasingly available in systems for home gardeners. Fish make a profound difference. In an aquaponic system, their waste provides the nutrients that feed the plants, whereas in a hydroponic system, the nutrients are controlled by humans. One is a living ecosystem, and the other is not, but both present the future of high-yield agricultural production.

	Aquaponics (with fish)	Hydroponics (no fish)
Size	Must be able to accommodate fish, plants, and system. Many home systems resemble (in size and construction) raised beds.	Can be as small as a jar in a window, or scaled to be much larger.
Special Requirements	Temperatures need to be controlled for fish safety and plant health. If you live in a cold area this means you will likely need a hoophouse or greenhouse.	Does not require a greenhouse (though it can be used), but temperature must be sharply controlled to keep plants healthy.
Plant Food	Nutrients come from fish waste.	Nutrients come from human-administered solutions.
Organic Status	One-hundred percent organic system (that is dependent on a living ecosystem).	One-hundred percent organic system (that is dependent on nutrient solutions administered by the gardener). These can be very expensive.
Pests	The fish control most common problems (for example, root rot) and insect pests.	The system needs to maintain sterility to achieve pest control.
Production	Recent studies show that advancing technology in aquaponics is making it even more productive than hydroponics.	Hydroponic growers can produce as much as ten times more produce per square yard with seventy percent less water than traditional in-ground gardening.
Bonus	You can eat the fish!	

Playful Pop

A s far back as my family can remember, we were gardeners, farmers, and ranchers. As a garden writer and designer, I count myself still involved in the family tradition but wonder, like many parents, if I am doing a good enough job to connect my tech-savvy, modern kids to the natural world around them. I reason that at the very least, making an outdoor space in which to enjoy family meals, fresh-picked veggies, and some fun games is a good start toward making sure they understand by immersion the necessity of our greater ecosystem.

I can't say that a Playful Pop garden must have a certain list of things, but I can tell you that it must be charmingly colorful and happy. Its art should reference our modern lives, and be thoughtful enough to engage parents, kids, and any other creature who shares the garden. My favorite gardens approach family design in a way that is well planned, beautiful, and not something that you have to get rid of after a couple of years because it has been outgrown—rather, it can grow, age, and evolve as gracefully as we all hope to.

ABSTRACT background

colorful

lighthearted

family

cheery

gatherings

Built-in activities

There is no excuse for voluntarily installing large, soon-to-fade heaps of plastic in the landscape. These smelly, ugly, unimaginative contraptions will vastly outlast your family's interest and will likely never match your style—and then what? Using natural materials and opting instead for features that are attractive and fun for adults and children alike will not only improve the mood of the garden but also impart a sense of permanence that will encourage togetherness and timeless play.

ENDURING AND ENDEARING FAMILY GARDEN FEATURES

- Ball game venues
- Bocce court
- Hammock
- Hanging tire
- Hillside slide (suitable for all sizes of people)
- Horseshoe pits
- Lawn croquet
- Outdoor theaters
- Playhouse (that can later become a storage shed)
- Pool (consider chlorine-free, naturally filtered)
- Rill
- Sandpit
- Splash pads
- Tents
- Tree house
- Tree swing
- Water fountain
- Willow houses and tunnels
- Zip line

Natural pools

An adjacent, plant-filled filtration area, which works without the addition of chemicals, filters this garden pool. Natural pools offer an environmentally friendly and chemical-free alternative to standard pools. They can be naturalistic in style or quite modern.

Happy color

Adults aren't drawn to mixed-up bright colors in the same way children are, but a happy medium can be found when creating a family space. Try picking one or perhaps two complementary but outrageous colors (rather than a whole rainbow) for a scheme that will hold a child's attention while also appealing to adult sensibilities. You can also embrace pop art influences (like graffiti) to bring an edgy youthfulness to the design.

REASONABLE SAFETY

Gardens should be an interactive experience. Flowers should be smelled, grass should be rolled in, and trees should be climbed. Of course, no parent wants their child to be hurt, but trying to spare them from every mishap is counterproductive to fostering the ability to take risks and explore wisely. Garden organically to spare humans and animals from harmful chemicals; consider bark, sand, or gravel for areas where children might be inclined to fall, and implement features that are of comfortable heights. Either avoid toxic and thorny plants where kids are likely to play or teach them about the plants so that they understand the dangers.

The natural nest

Banish plastic from the family garden and opt instead for the subtle beauty of wood. Children outgrow toys so fast; it's conscientious to consider the long life span of the toy compared to the short attention span of a kid. Classic outdoor play equipment (such as wooden swings and sand pits that can be repurposed later) is beautiful and timeless and will hold the attention of little and big people alike. Furniture that is made to seat more than one person and places for family pets make sure that togetherness is the primary purpose of the garden gathering place.

Cedar sandbox
with built-in bench

Irreverent party place

Get a little kooky with color. Why not mix baby blue, soft pink, red, green, and white? A knee-high meadow with a mower-carved space seems the perfect place for an impromptu evening gathering around a mobile fireplace. Lightweight lounge chairs and sitting pillows in fun colors provide comfort; picnic blankets can serve as the floor. Real chickens could be scratching nearby for entertainment, or substitute fun sculptural fowl for lighthearted relief.

Fire drum

Adventuresome mod

A sleek barbeque whose legs detach for tabletop grilling is the perfect multi-tasking, take-anywhere solution. Pair it with a sturdy, modern Adirondack chair made of recycled materials and you have an ideal spot to watch friends and family go whizzing by on the zip line. Zip lines are easy and unobtrusive garden toys that can be strung between trees or structures. Bright accessories (like this birdhouse) can be any color, and give the garden a little playful decoration.

Zip line

Kinfolk comfort

A tiny garden can happily house something for everyone. Using primary colors, a smart picnic table coordinates beautifully with a sophisticated grill and contrasts with a cherry-red lantern. Nearby, a teepee provides an easily stored playhouse. If there are no children, opt instead for a lace teepee and chandelier, which have a certain bohemian sexiness that would set off the more sleek elements. Who hasn't made up or played a silly dice game to pass the time with friends? Lawn dice can be used in an oversized team version of Yahtzee (keep score on a chalkboard) or any other party game.

Play teepee

Rope swing

Green-roofed
doghouse

Family-sized
sunbed

Wooden planter

Low rocking chair

Playful
floor cushions

Chicken sculptures

Flexible
vegetable pot

Black contemporary
Adirondack chair

Modern planter

Height-adjustable
charcoal grill

Electric-pink
birdhouse

Lawn dice

Blue charcoal
barbeque

Oak and
metal table

Red ceramic light

Sectioned horsetail

Hollyhock

Allium fairy wands

Plants for play

Many plants have built-in toy qualities. Not only will they be gorgeous in the garden, kids will find them easily converted (with playtime imagination and ingenuity) into fun toys. Full-flowering hollyhocks make lovely dressed dolls when picked and upturned. Long-bladed grasses provide all that is needed for weaving mats or making hand whistles. Cornhusk dolls were first made for Native American children. Pulling apart the sections of horsetail (*Equisetum*) can be fun all on its own, or it can be the root of all sorts of pretend games. Carnivorous plants like the Venus flytrap (*Dionaea muscipula*) can be fed bugs. It is a little-known fact that fairy wands are in fact the dried remains of giant allium flowers.

PERFECTLY PET FRIENDLY

Help your pet enjoy your garden as much as you do. Most animal welfare organizations publish extensive lists of plants that can be toxic to pets. If your animal is inclined to nibble, it might be worth taking extra precautions when growing these varieties. Every animal is different, and a problem for some is often not a concern for others.

Both cats and dogs avoid moist dirt and are less likely to dig when the ground is wet. So keep things well watered and consider having a bog area around water features that house fish (aka cat treats).

Cats. Plant things that cats love to eat, roll around in, and play with. (Make sure to cover sandboxes, as cats will be drawn to them as litter boxes. Not only is it disgusting, cat feces also carry parasites harmful to pregnant women.) Some cat favorites: catmint (*Nepeta* ×*faassenii*) and catnip (*N. cataria*); pennyroyal (*Mentha pulegium*); lemon grass (*Cymbopogon citratus*); cat grass (*Dactylis glomerata*); and valerian (*Valeriana officinalis*).

Dogs. Your dog will see your garden as his domain. Work with him to make patrol routes that avoid your favorite plants. Densely planted areas, masses of one plant, and raised beds can encourage dogs to go around. Avoid coco shell mulch—it contains high concentrations of theobromine, the dog-toxic substance in chocolate. If your dog is prone to eating these types of things, it could be damaging or lethal.

Pragmatic plants

Tough plants will be able to survive the rough and tumble that comes along with gardens full of kids, pets, and errant sports balls. Employ euonymus, vinca, ivy, and cotoneaster in areas where you expect high traffic and trampling feet. Easy growers such as sunflowers, buddleja, hardy geraniums, squash, sweet peas, marigolds, and nasturtiums are good for teaching children about gardening and growing.

Ivy

Cotoneaster

Vinca

Bamboo forests and giant plants

Playing with scale and light and can make a garden feel magical not just for children but for adults, too. I think of it as the *Alice in Wonderland* effect: by surrounding yourself with oddly scaled plants or groves of giant bamboo, your own sense of size in the landscape can feel different. Oversized leaves can make you feel disproportionately small by comparison. Grow areas of gunnera, butterbur, and rhubarb for this effect. Rodgersia, hosta, and mullein (with its large but furry and soft leaves) can also be planted to enhance the play on scale. Bamboo, crape myrtle, and rhododendron all create magical groves that are fun to play in.

Bamboo

Hosta

Rodgersia

Mullein

Black bamboo

A tire swing is simple and elegant. Colorful lanterns keep the mood light without being junky.

Charlotte's festive family retreat

"I love the apple trees — they provide great shade and a lovely place to dine."
— Charlotte Rice

Children's toys can be made into garden accessories.

A white house is the perfect backyard background.

Bright furniture in a classic bistro style is both cheerful and fun.

Charlotte and her husband sell home goods that they hope will "color you happy when you are washing, cleaning, baking, or relaxing in your home." The store was born around the same time as their first child, and they wanted to slow down and take more time to enjoy life. They moved from France to Denmark, and their hundred-year-old home and garden came with a pool, a sandbox, and an in-ground trampoline, which is a favorite of their young family. They cleared and added a simple ground-level wooden terrace so they could dine outside by the water. But the real personality comes from the colorful accessories, reminiscent of their products, which make the garden feel welcoming and truly family friendly.

Lanterns and candles in vivid shades
light the way to the yard.

DECK ESSENTIALS

Decks are handy for providing a level platform over nearly any terrain. They can be right up to the house in the form of porches, or placed further into the landscape as boardwalks or a platform for enjoying the surrounding nature.

Construction materials fall into one of four basic categories: painted fir, hardwoods, synthetic material, or pressure-treated wood. Choosing which to use comes with a set of considerations including upfront costs, long-term maintenance, expected usage, and available colors, finishes, and textures.

Painted fir. Consider this option only for covered porches, as a painted wood finish simply isn't practical if the surface is exposed to weather. It is warm and inviting when topped off with area rugs, rocking chairs, and all the fixings of a romantically creaky old porch. It works well for historic wood homes and helps infuse an old-time feel. Plan on repainting every five to eight years, depending on wear and tear.

Hardwoods. Ipe, teak, redwood, cedar, mahogany, walnut, and other woods are more or less accessible depending on where you live (but Internet supplies abound, so make sure to check this option, too). Scarcity and natural weather resistance drive up the price and you would be wise to compare the options that are locally achievable for longevity and maintenance. Ipe, for example, is extremely weather resistant and if you like the look of silver wood, it needs no maintenance (retaining its freshly cut, deep brown coloring, however, may require annual sanding and oiling). Conversely, redwood or cedar, while also good choices for a deck, do not have the same longevity as ipe (redwood and cedar will last ten to twenty years, ipe will last at least fifty). Take the time to learn about the source of the product you select; sustainable and responsible harvesting practices along with forest regeneration plans are key to maintaining this industry and resource.

Synthetic decking is a particularly good choice if you live near the ocean or in a place where humidity and water are a major consideration. It can also work if you forgo the fake wood graining and opt for a streamlined, high-style version to pair with modern architecture. UV resistance and fading can be problematic; if you are considering this product, do your research on the brand's quality and long-term reviews. It is nice that many of these products are being manufactured with recycled materials, but for most gardens, I prefer natural materials and don't recommend faking it with unnatural wood graining just for the benefit of low maintenance.

Treated wood. Treated wood decks are popular because they are relatively long lasting and the materials are very affordable. Commonly referred to as pressure-treated, the product is made by treating softwoods (often pine varieties) with chemicals that dramatically increase their life span. Some of the chemicals used in the past were found to be harmful to surrounding soil and not something you want small children to crawl over, but modern versions have been proved safer. Paint companies have developed lines of stains that can transform treated wood from the oddly tinted green color of the preserving treatments into much more stylish shades—grays, browns, and even teals, pinks, and purples; so you can feel free to express your personal style.

Cottage Au Courant

sweet

Cottage gardens hold near-universal appeal, as they are often the gardens of our parents and grandparents. Born of necessity, the cottage garden was the original homesteader's paradise. Always an overflowing, informal place where chickens might mingle with kids and bikes and vegetable patches, as well as the occasional artistic work of a neighbor or the homeowner, the cottage garden remains a lively place where there is always something going on.

Nothing marks a cottage garden more clearly than lots of purposeful plants grown for your own unique uses and desires. Do you love strawberry rhubarb crisp, blowsy flowers, and the smell of lavender (as I do)? Well then, your first priority should be to figure out where a rhubarb plant will thrive (for some reason, I have always had the best luck at the base of a wall or fence) and start planning around it. You may as well line a path to get to it with lavender and peonies, and use strawberries as ground cover. But perhaps you will find the rhubarb grows best right smack in the middle of your existing lawn, and if this is the case, you will have to resolve a way to make it look like something other than a strange, leafy weed in the middle of a grassy desert. So you must anchor it, plant around it, create a logical and practical reason to go to it, and a beautiful way to enjoy it once to you arrive. And suddenly you have the start of a cottage garden plan. This grow-it-because-you-love-it attitude is the basis of this style and you can use the practical attributes of what you love most to map a layout that will fully emerge with time.

informal

quirky

engaging

meandering

Controlled chaos

Keeping the cottage garden modern, or *au courant*, requires a healthy avoidance of messiness and chaos, which can easily take over. Repeat plants—avoiding as much as possible the idea of one of each. Tie the garden together with color or a strong redundancy in materials. Treat your cottage garden like any other room in your actual cottage or home. Make sure there is a tidy put-away place for everything—from plants and garden tools, to bikes and toys and chickens or small livestock. If everything has a place, the garden will be full but retain a calming sense of organization.

Resourcefulness rules

Found objects turned focal-point sculpture, edging made from repurposed objects, and plants traded over the fence should always find an easy home in a cottage garden.

Don't be fussy, rigid, or sleek

There are some rules (though not many) to follow when planning and shaping your modern cottage garden. Let paths meander as they need to. Let travel routes and destinations evolve from either necessity or desire. Necessity might dictate quick access to the compost heap and a straight line to the front door; desire might lazily navigate you to the base of a beautiful tree or a sunny spot offering the perfect view of a favorite flower.

Cultivate abundance

Indeed, abundance is the soul of this garden style. Encourage plants to self-seed, migrate around the garden, and bump elbows with each other. Don't fret when one thing starts tumbling down over another; in fact, celebrate unexpected successes.

BRINGING TOGETHER OUTDOOR FURNITURE & ACCESSORIES

Good garden furniture should retain a timeless style that is easy to mix and match. When choosing a piece, find something that appeals to your senses but also fits the overall tone you are trying to achieve. Relate the object's features in at least one way to something else in the garden—if possible, in more than one way. Does the piece have a color, texture, or shape—or maybe a similarity of scale, elegance, ethnicity, or pattern—that ties it to other accessories, plants, or furniture? Look for these shared qualities in disparate items, and your collections will have a much greater depth and be far more interesting than if you tried to make everything a perfect match.

Modern
Adirondack chair

Galvanized containers

Blue bistro chair

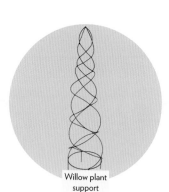

Willow plant
support

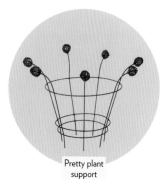

Pretty plant
support

Wicker chair

Pink hanging
planter

Colorful bunting

Glider sofa

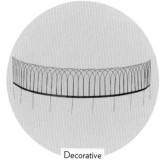

Decorative
bed edging

Checkerboard planting

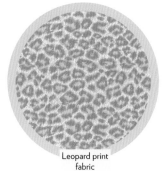

Leopard print
fabric

Urban harlequin

Modern takes on classic furniture, industrial-looking containers, and playful checkerboard paving toughen up the feminine lines of the cottage and can help to organize space. But don't lose the classic charm of the style. A cheeky (but subdued) leopard print fabric for accent is unexpected, yet works with the urban styling.

Bee skep

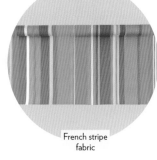

French stripe
fabric

French country

Avoid ornate pieces to keep the look airy and modern. And remember, what looked good in your grandmother's garden will likely look good in this garden—be it French bistro chairs or something found at your local resale shop. Often all that's needed is a slick of new paint in a fresh hue. Recurring shapes help the garden come together. Bee skeps, willow plant supports, and similarly cone-like shrubs will lend a nice rhythm. Add classic French striped cushions to the chairs in a cheery set of colors for a spark that keeps the rhythm from putting you to sleep.

Modern pink
fabric

Vintage flower-
picking basket

Pretty in pink

Since the cottage is all about casual and homey, feel free to mix and match shapes (furniture sets are beyond boring), but avoid a lot of bulky pieces that can overwhelm. Opt instead for easily moved furniture—you want to always keep your options open so you can make like a cat and follow the sun, or perch yourself near the prettiest, best-smelling thing in bloom. From hanging planters to wicker chairs, the cottage garden is full of charm and functional quirk. Play with a single color theme to define a space, bring personality, and set off plants. A flower-picking basket and eccentric plant supports will help you grow and enjoy fresh cuttable flowers such as peonies.

Wooden arbor

Kantha blanket

Summer party

A walk through the arbor and down the path to the comfortable glider sofa is made all the better with layers of beautiful details such as wire bed edging and festive bunting overhead. Bunting is an easy garden craft and can add flair when strung between trees or across a lawn. Cut it in scallop shapes rather than traditional triangles for an unexpected twist. Layers of exotic *kantha* blankets continue the pattern theme and will make the glider sofa all the more cozy.

Foxglove

Hydrangea

Nigella

Plants with a purpose

Populate your cottage garden with plants you love or for which you have special uses. Homegrown bouquets of cut flower favorites are particularly rewarding fruits of your labor, as are tinctures from herbs and special preserves.

Lavender

Daisy

Peony

COTTAGE GARDEN WISDOM

- A cottage garden requires maintenance. You will need to harvest, weed, thin, stake, deadhead, and prune plants. Although it's not low maintenance, this garden will keep you in tune with the seasons like no other.

- To lessen the work, choose fewer varieties of plants and fewer types of things.

- Splitting plants is a great way to get to know other gardeners and neighbors. Use your bounty to share, trade, and improve not just your plot but the gardens of those around you.

- With the rise of farmers' markets there may be less need to cultivate your own food or flowers, but plant diversity is important to the planet, so even as you strive to keep the total number of varieties and plants down, use your cottage garden to cultivate the obscure and unusual.

Four-season fancies

Juniper

Snowdrops

Perennials and self-seeding flowers are common in the cottage garden, but they should be anchored with evergreen shrubs or trees that will provide a backdrop to the early spring ephemerals, give height to the garden, and provide interest in winter.

Wild bluebells

Trout lily

Boundaries & borders

Cottage gardens typically have a defined boundary—the white picket fence is a classic—but think about using plant materials instead. A low boxwood hedge will work, but perhaps more interesting is a hedge of santolina, lavender, catmint, germander, or dianthus. Varieties of grass, holly, pieris, or (if it is perennial where you live) rosemary can provide somewhat taller hedging options.

Informal hedge

Santolina

Dianthus

Orange poppy

Daisy

Groupers

Plant in multiples, then have multiple clumps to keep messiness at bay. As you do with textiles, take care to choose complementary and harmonizing colors and styles. Embrace ornamental grasses or native plants that are atypical of the historic cottager's garden. Unexpected twists on a style give a place personality. Try picking a couple favorite plant pairings (I love white daisies and bright orange poppies) and repeat the combo all around the garden.

Ramblers & softeners

Consider adding clematis, roses, or other climbing plants to soften the vertical architecture of the garden. Let them romantically meander as they wish.

Clematis

Marquette's fresh cottage garden

In an updated cottage garden, the typical riot of color and plants can be kept tidy with a controlled color palette, a balanced layout, and trimmed hedges.

Every cottage garden needs a cat.

> "Inspiration came from the style of the house. From that grew a cottage garden with boxwood-bordered beds, perennials, and a white picket fence."
>
> —Marquette Clay

Marquette created this garden to go with his cottage-style house in Oklahoma City. The site is not particularly roomy, but by editing and making good use of what was available, he managed to make the garden feel quite expansive. The many shades of evergreen (provided by wintergreen and Japanese boxwoods, foster holly, *Thuja* 'Green Giant', lilyturf, and fescue sod) not only provide structure but give a restful, year-round color palette—important in this region, where autumns and winters can seem long. Add a fresh green door, green container plantings, and just a few splashes of purple-leaved plants, and the edited cottage garden stays serene and peaceful.

Rounded stone ornaments add rhythm.

FABRICS: CHOOSING & LAYERING PATTERNS

The cottage garden (and many other styles, too) calls for layers of patterns. Mixing old-fashioned decoration with crisp new patterns for a look that seems to have just happened that way—complementing each other but not matchy-matchy—is a little tricky, but it can be mastered with guidance and experimentation.

1. Start with a pattern that you love and just can't wait to use. This is your foundation. Using the colors that dominate the piece, pair with at least one solid or small print that coordinates with one of these colors.

2. Next, bring in another pattern that is different. If your piece is floral, then find a geometric piece, or a stripe; but make sure this pattern uses at least one of the same colors as your starting point.

3. Finally, bring in another pattern like your original. It should have the same colorway but at a wildly different scale. For example, if you have a big floral, go for a tiny floral, or if you started with fat stripes, go for skinny stripes.

CHOOSING FABRICS

Good exterior fabrics include not only those specified as "outdoor" (usually meaning they have been chemically treated or are made from plastic- or poly-based materials to ensure they will weather the weather), but also fabrics that are naturally rot and mildew resistant. Jute and linen, for example, whether new or found in more primitive form (such as grain and flour sacks), do not mildew when dried naturally and stored in clean, dry places. Heavy cotton duck cloth is also a good natural alternative to treated fabrics. Here are some other general things to keep in mind.

- **Use a mix of fabrics in individual elements.** For example, with pillows and cushions, choose different patterns for the front and back.

- **Decide how dynamic you want your mix to be.** You can stay within a closely guarded set of colors and achieve something that is tame and soothing, but if you want a more vibrant effect, introduce a small amount of a contrasting color. Not sure? Give both a try and see which you prefer.

- **Don't go too far with the mix.** Top out at five to seven different pieces of material; beyond that, you risk a design mess.

- **Make sure your dominant colors match.** Or, if you are familiar with color theory and want to get a little trickier, make sure they harmonize (use a color wheel if you need—harmonizing colors touch each other on the wheel).

- **Match materials in style and weight.** They should seem of the same period or genre. You will find it hard to make a heavy velvet go with a lightweight Hawaiian print.

MAKE YOUR OWN OILCLOTH PLACEMATS

While there is an ever-increasing selection of fabrics that can be used for outside design, it is still fun to create something original. Using paint or dyeing techniques will help you achieve a unique pattern; waterproofing makes it useful for both indoor and outdoor use.

NOTES ON OILCLOTH

- The fabric can be used for tablecloths, outdoor rugs, outdoor screens, banners, and upholstery (though I don't think this final option is the most comfortable).

- A slight yellow tint is unavoidable and permanent in the fabric due to the linseed oil; take this into consideration when choosing lighter fabrics. The yellow tint will lighten as the linseed oil dries. Also, pay attention to the quality of the linseed oil; finer and organic oils tend to be lighter in color and will not significantly alter the color of your fabric.

- Batik, stamping, fabric paint, sun-printing, and other fabric-altering techniques can be used to create a personalized oilcloth pattern.

Materials

Heavy cotton duck, canvas, or linen fabric (I used white linen)
Drying frame (I used a laundry drying rack)
Linseed oil and paintbrush
Oil paint or oil dyes if you want to create your own design

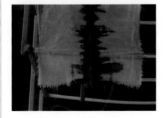

1. Prepare the dyes per package instructions for coloring your fabric.

2. Cut the fabric to the shape of your placemats. I initially tore off two rectangles from my fabric that were twice the size of my placemats. This allowed me to easily wrap them together when dyeing, for a consistent dye stripe across the final product. If you are using canvas or linen and want a frayed edge, start your tear with a small snip of the scissors, then pull the fabric apart.

3. Fold edges together where you wish to add color and tie tightly with string (rubber bands wound tightly around the balled fabric will also work) to create an uneven stripe (I went for deep purple) down the center of the placemats. You could apply this technique to any similar project.

4. Lay the placemats out on a piece of butcher paper (wax side up) and with long brush strokes, cover each piece of fabric on the good side with linseed oil. Make sure that the fabric is saturated, but keep excess to a minimum. When each piece is fully painted, soak up extra oil with paper towels or remaining pieces. So long as the piece was fully saturated, a second coat is not needed unless you desire a stiffer piece of fabric. (More layers of linseed oil will increase the stiffness of the fabric.)

5. Hang the placemats to dry. Take special care to not leave wet pieces in a pile as they can be very flammable. Additionally, make sure that while they are hanging to dry, layers are not overlapping or touching.

Pretty Potager

vegetables

Personally, I don't feel that a house is a home unless the garden produces something for the kitchen table. The French, of course, sympathize with me, and, as might be expected, their potagers (a fancy term for kitchen gardens) provide endless ideas of what to plant and how to make it more than just functional—in fact, downright pretty. Ornamental kitchen gardens expand on the practice of farming and turn production rows into artistic expressions that are as pleasing as any flower garden.

It isn't a huge leap to understand how the gardeners of the French Renaissance, with all their shapely patterns drawn in plants, saw the patterns of production-focused farm rows and began to combine the two. Flowers, both edible and not, as well as herbs and shrubbery, were used to enhance the veggie patch so that the food was aesthetically pleasing. And we all know that when something looks good, it tastes better.

organized

productive

mixed

ornamental

Get some rhythm

Gardens are like singers: if they don't have rhythm, they are going to be boring. Happily, garden rhythm doesn't require natural-born talent—it is easily achieved by repeating plants at regular intervals. So, if you need to grow lots of kale to make lovely green smoothies, don't plant them all in one spot—spread them out so all that big greenness is highlighting other plants. Or use them as edging for a bigger bed. Spreading things out also has the added benefit of confusing insect pests; they may not find all the separated plants as easily as they might attack one large grouping.

Establish a focal point

Farmers have no need for focal points, but kitchen gardeners do. Focal points give you something interesting around which you can organize the rest of the garden. They also provide an attractive distraction from the fact that many times, vegetable plants just aren't the most interesting.

Add structure

Experiment with interesting bed shapes and structural materials. Try crescents, circles, crosses, and L shapes in addition to the standard squares and rectangles. Within the beds, plants can be laid out in zigzags, diagonal stripes, or more complex patterns. I particularly like checkerboard patterns, which can be done with all different colors of leafy greens. French Renaissance garden patterns are a great inspiration resource, as are Celtic designs.

Don't forget the non-plant components of the garden. Paths can be made of just about any material, but gravel, brick, and bark all look good and are fairly low maintenance. Plant supports, plant pots, rainwater barrels, and composters can all be attractive, too, and needn't cost a fortune. Recycled and handmade products have a charm all their own; instead of hiding them away at the back of the shed, why not make them an integral part of the design for your beautiful potager?

Draw lines

Old-fashioned, clipped-hedge knot gardens seem to be just a little pretentious for modern life, but they can be quite fun for the potager. There is little difference between taking the time to plant a perfectly straight line of carrots and spending equal time planting a well-executed curlicue of feathery carrot tops. Weave it all together to create knots, or make other planted patterns. Anything can be used, but my favorites include lavender, boxwood, and little lettuces.

Raised beds and containers

Raised beds can be constructed of all sorts of materials. If you are in an urban area and perhaps garden on a balcony, the fabric bag style would probably be the easiest to install and manage. If you don't like the look, you could use woven wattle to hide the grow bag. Wood is the most common material for larger area beds and I prefer simple mortise-and-tenon construction. There are, however, myriad options for attaching the wood to form the bed. Adding a hinged glass door makes it into a cold frame, which works like a mini-greenhouse and will help you extend the gardening season. Wattle, logs, stone, stumps, sandbags, and other objects can also be used.

Flexible plant container

Raised bed frame

Supporting characters

Many edible plants tend to get weighed down with their own production and are healthier and happier if you can provide them with some structure in which to grow. Pea towers, trellises, and tomato cages can all be formalized and made into striking features in the garden. Willow, twigs, and plant materials that can be woven together give a rustic, homegrown touch and work well to hold up lightweight vines. Modern metal frames and sturdy wood tuteurs (obelisk-like trellises) are more substantial and permanent features. You can even fashion fun supports from heavy-gauge wire to use in your container plantings.

Wicker sweet pea frames

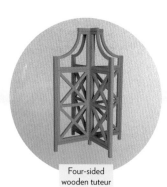

Four-sided wooden tuteur

Focal stars

A potager nearly always has a formal layout that allows for focal points at either the center or the ends of framed views in the garden. Trees, fountains, tuteurs, containers, pretty sheds, strawberry towers, a table and chairs, or even a striking plant such as a towering globe artichoke can all be placed in the center of the garden.

Modern wooden trellis square

Forged iron obelisk

Tools and implements

There are plenty of tools with which you can arm yourself, but some are basic essentials for every vegetable gardener. A solid shovel, a hand rake, and a dibbler (which will help you plant seeds) are just about all I ever need. Solid natural twine can be used to solve most problems. When starting seeds, some sort of hardening off (that is, slowly easing the plants out of the warmth of your home and into the chilly outdoors) is usually necessary, and cold frames or small cloches are easy to use. When it comes time to harvest, sturdy and easy-to-carry trugs will keep your hands free for picking. If you have a fruit tree, a larger, backpack-style picking basket can be very useful.

Basic garden hand tools

Harvesting trug

Wood cold frame

Wicker grow bag cover

Wrought iron tuteur

Topiary plant support

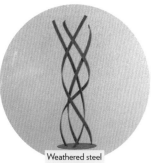

Weathered steel sculpture

Table and chairs

Natural garden twine

Backpack for picking fruit

Victorian cloche

RAISED BEDS OR NOT?

My husband has considerable difficulty with the idea of paying for dirt. While I understand his inborn resistance, it is a decision that I come to after a lot of thought about the best way to manage my garden. I use raised beds and a lot of the soil inside them was imported. Choosing to use raised beds has its costs, but for the price of the beds and the soil to fill them, you get a variety of benefits.

- **Soil control.** If you have terrible soil (rocky, clay, highly acidic—mine is all of the above, plus sandy, chalky, and polluted) you can, with a lot of work, correct the issues. Or you can just build a raised bed and import good soil, which is often much easier.

- **Height control.** Raised beds can be elevated enough to make the bend-over labor of gardening a lot less strenuous. Higher beds (above 18 inches or 46 centimeters) will also be less likely to fill with weeds as their seeds tend to travel in ground currents that raised gardens are usually above.

- **Temperature control.** Raised beds warm earlier in spring, allowing you to plant sooner than if the garden were in-ground. Soil is also at its best then, which can mean higher yields.

- **Pest control.** Slugs and snails generally do not like to climb the sides of raised beds, so damage from these pests is less prevalent. You can also put chicken wire beneath the beds to prevent gophers and moles from eating plants from the bottom up.

Butter lettuce

Strawberries

Beets

Tomatoes

Eggplant

Everyday all-stars

Of course, the original reason for a potager is to supply the kitchen, so don't forget the vegetable standbys and herbs. Some might plant five kinds of carrots; I am of the mind that five kinds of basil are more important. Or perhaps five kinds of thyme or tomatoes or potatoes (I can't decide). Whatever your vice, choose your favorites and explore varieties you have never seen in the grocery store. I plant my herbs in pots so as the season wanes, I can move my favorites up near the back door, where I can continue to harvest right up until the first frost.

Ornamental vegetables

I like to draw the eye around the garden by placing deep-colored and exciting-looking vegetables in prime locations. The white midribs and green leaves of Swiss chard are dramatic, as are the huge, burly, prehistoric-looking leaves of *Brassica oleracea* 'Lacinato' (a variety of kale). Reds and purples are easy to work into vegetable gardens, and I find the furry seed heads of quinoa and amaranth to be fun ways to add surprise.

Chive flowers

Quinoa

Okra flowers

Purple kale

Amaranth

COVER CROPS & CROP ROTATION

What you plant, as well as where and when, can have a big impact on your kitchen garden's success. Cover crops (also known as green manure), which are typically planted in the fall, help build the soil for future plantings. After the garden is done for the season, cover crops such as clover, rye, or fava beans are planted so that they can overwinter and be turned under in the spring. These plants fix nitrogen in the atmosphere and impart it to the soil. Their roots soften the dirt, and when they are turned in, the organic matter improves the resources for new plants.

For similar reasons, it is wise to rotate plantings from season to season. Some plants deplete soil of nutrients, others build the soil up; by rotating you can keep your garden healthier. As an added benefit, this rotation means that a new design can be created every year, and no disaster will ever last too long.

Espaliered apple trees perform very well in the garden. The regular pruning required to train the trees encourages strong fruit production.

Trained trees and plants

Many plants can be trained to grow in precise ways and shapes. Fruit trees do very well when trained to grow flat against walls in patterns know as espalier, fan, and cordon. Getting the most produce per square foot or meter is the inevitable goal of vegetable gardening and this often leads to forcing plants upward. Cucumbers and some squash can be trained onto a trellis so that their ground space needs are reduced. Supports and trellises are great opportunities to employ beautifully crafted structures or elements that exhibit your personal style.

Boxwood

Marigold

Beauty boosters

If you are going to make your kitchen garden a place that is as pretty as any other pleasure garden, you are going to have to approach the subject as equal parts designer and farmer. Don't hesitate to add plants for no other purpose than to make other things around them shine. Not only will you want to be in this garden, but good insects will appreciate the variety, and bees will be drawn to the additional pollination sources. When making your plan, think about harvests and how neighboring plants might fill in gaps after you pick.

Daylily

Nepeta

Brooke's secluded front yard potager

"I've never had success growing pumpkins for Halloween, but my tomatoes love me." — Brooke Giannetti

A table, birdcage, and potted herb garden create a focal point at one end of the garden.

Fragrant herbs and flowers are planted along walks and edges.

Comfy chairs and a lime tree provide a second focal point.

With three kids and six chickens to feed, Brooke wanted a place where she could grow food, both with and for her family. Working within a tiny city lot that lacked sun in the backyard, she followed the light and was able to convince her husband to rip up her front lawn to construct and plant a kitchen garden. The area is shielded from the street by a fence and shrubs, so the whole thing feels quite secret. Starting with only a bit of knowledge gleaned from a local organic nurseryman who sold seedlings to her and her daughters, Brooke has been quite successful. In their first season, her family (chickens included) enjoyed strawberries, lettuce, tomatoes, zucchini, and carrots. Recognizing that a garden of any sort is a ceaseless set of new challenges, her future gardens will experiment with the addition of edible flowers and tweaks to make things easier (such as moving the hose bib closer to the garden beds).

SEED SENSE

Let's make some sense of the annual seed-buying ritual. If you've never done it, and are anything like me, those seemingly inexpensive little packets add up far quicker than expected. In no time, I consistently purchase much more than I need or can possibly use. Seed buying is just so hopeful that it is easy to be impractical. Over the years, I have made a few rules for myself that you might find useful when seed shopping.

I only buy seeds from places I know and trust. I also try to source from suppliers whose ethics and growing conditions closely match my own. Get off the mailing lists of other catalogs; they will only tempt you into overspending and failure.

Assess what you have. Lots of seeds last for a long time and others not so much. Whatever you didn't use from the previous year should be assessed for its viability; seed viability charts abound online and are easy to reference. Pitch what isn't going to grow well and don't buy things you already have.

Be realistic about your space. Most vegetables need full sun and good water. Sort out exactly how much of this type of space you have available for your potager, then make a casual map of the area.

Be honest about your commitment. Personally, I hate starting seeds indoors. I have a terrible time preventing seedlings from getting leggy, and my cat insists on nibbling the shoots. It isn't worth the battles, so everything that can't be directly sown (planted directly in the soil outside) is purchased as seedlings later. That eliminates tomatoes, peppers, and eggplants from my seed-buying list.

Make your wish list, then prioritize it. I select things that taste noticeably better when fresh from the garden (such as spring peas and interesting varieties of lettuce), in addition to things I can't easily get in the market (such as ground cherries and wasabi arugula). You might have different priorities, but come up with some way to rank your wish list for importance.

Buy with realistic expectations. How much space will the plants truly need? I never have room for it all, but I nonetheless buy a few extra packets with the vision of creating a new garden area. Sometimes it happens and sometimes not, but at least I haven't bought piles of extra packets that I can't fit in.

Share with friends. Many packets have far more seeds than I need, so giving extras to neighbors is an easy way to ensure that if my crop fails, they will probably share their excess with me.

SOIL, COMPOST, MULCH

The ground in which you grow your plants is as important as any other single element in the success of your garden. This earthy underworld rarely gets the attention or credit it deserves for the good it does. It is always wise to have an inexpensive soil analysis done to understand exactly what you are working with. From there you can figure out what you might want to grow, and if you need to make amendments. However, all gardeners—no matter what the state of their soil—can benefit from the addition of compost and mulch.

A couple of notes about compost and mulch. Make sure compost is mature and clean; compost that is too hot can kill plants, and no one wants compost filled with weed seeds or waste treated with pesticides. Mulching can mean plant-killing critters will survive the winter, so be prepared. Also, rake mulch into a doughnut-like ring around trees to avoid smothering the trunk and to allow water to collect.

	Compost	Mulch
What is it?	A time-released fertilizer and insulator	A time-released fertilizer (if it is organic and not a synthetic product) and insulator
What is it made of?	Livestock and poultry manure (if available), kitchen scraps, yard litter, garden waste, and paper products	Natural or synthetic substances—everything from crushed rock and plastic sheeting to wood chips, discarded newspapers, and straw
What does it do?	Enhances the surrounding earth, feeding countless microorganisms, earthworms, and fungi that make healthy soil	Minimizes gardening chores by smothering weeds, conserving moisture, eliminating erosion, aerating packed soils, and protecting tender plants from frost, evaporation, and heat stress
How do you use it?	Spread as a topcoat, or work into the ground when planting; add to soil in early spring or late fall	Spread as a topcoat, usually at least 2 inches (about 5 centimeters) thick in early spring or late fall

Organic Modern

As I get older and wiser, I'm increasingly drawn to simpler joys. I want less, and when I have less, I find I have less stress (I'm smiling thinking about trying to say that five times fast). A few years ago I planted okra in my garden. I frequently plant stuff just to learn about it. I discovered that unfortunately, there are too few recipes I really love that use okra, but I also learned that the plants and their hibiscus-like blooms are worthy of a far finer fate than a stodgy row in the veg patch. At the end of the season I had no idea what to do with the giant pods that I had harvested too late, so I strung them together to let them dry. As they did so, their corners split and made them even more beautiful. Now this homemade garden garland, draped over an old painting that sits on my mantel, is one of my favorite decorations. This is the essence of the Organic Modern style.

Gathering up rustic and natural materials, bits and pieces with a story and unpretentious beauty, and combining them in a simple but sophisticated way is the joy of this type of garden. Keep it clean and uncluttered, filled with light and vegetation. Use taxidermy, wall gardens, and plant sculptures to establish little vignettes. Combine hard with soft, and layer in warm neutrals. Mix and match styles and textures; don't worry about symmetry, but do keep lines straight and clean. Think about how your design decisions impact the world around you. Follow these guidelines and you will be well on your way to your own version of modern organic serenity.

light

green

natural

clean

rustic

Light & white

Texture and form can shine through when the palette is kept simple. Look for pieces with interesting details that will prevent the mostly mono-chromatic color schemes from becoming boring.

Eclecticism

Mix a variety of styles in furniture and accessories as well as planting and layout. The key is to find commonality between elements, perhaps in shape, color, or material, so that everything can hang together successfully. Mix rustic Adirondack chairs with sleek, oversized concrete pavers. Asian-influenced lanterns and a painted apple crate add detail and bring the look together with this hi-low mix.

Neutrals & naturals

Clean lines and pale colors help to keep the feeling light and clean.
Don't be afraid to add in metals or other less rustic pieces to keep the modern aspect.

Eco cred

Use sustainable materials as well as organic and unrefined textiles, and make sure your garden is ecologically responsible. Consider rain barrels and rain gardens, gray water recycling systems, and local or recycled materials. Australian designer Marnie Lewis uses Australian cypress in this garden; it is harvested from sustainably managed forests, is naturally termite resistant, and doesn't leach tannins.

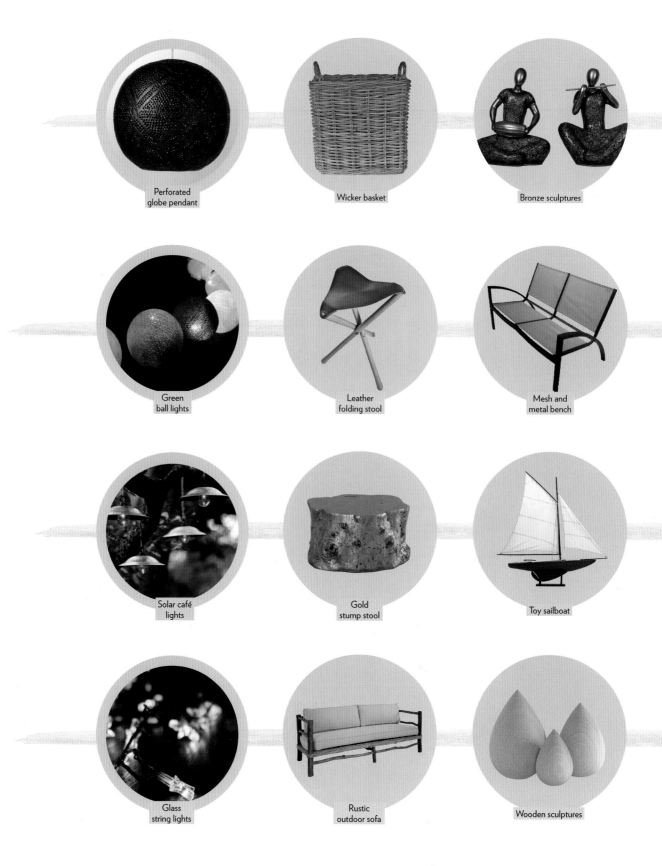

Perforated
globe pendant

Wicker basket

Bronze sculptures

Green
ball lights

Leather
folding stool

Mesh and
metal bench

Solar café
lights

Gold
stump stool

Toy sailboat

Glass
string lights

Rustic
outdoor sofa

Wooden sculptures

Wood and
metal bench

Wall-mounted
plants

Bronze beauty

Able to handle the elements and still look good, bronze is commonly used for municipal park sculpture. Bronze sculpture can be very expensive, but if you scale down the size, you can employ the beauty of bronze in garden statuary or furniture details. Contrast the weight and permanence of the metal with airy, wall-mounted plants and lightweight wicker baskets.

Potted olive

Wood slat
planter

Fresh and warm

Find color commonality among different materials to unify the look. The warm, russet hues of the leather stool, wooden planter, and terra-cotta pots balance the fresh, cool greens of the bench and lights.

Bistro chairs

Gilded urn

Gilded Tuileries

Paris's Tuileries garden is casual and relaxed, but reimagined with a touch of gilded glamour it becomes edgy and exciting. Classic bistro furniture, solar-powered café lights, and boats that playfully glide in the fountain make sure that the inspiration is obvious. Gilded urns and a matching golden stump amp up the collection and guarantee a très modern, chic vibe.

Fire bowl

Chunky woven
planter basket

Smooth serenity

Unify disparate materials by matching their finishes. Smooth textures and rounded shapes juxtaposed against the rougher textures of the woven planter and the twiggy sofa prevent boredom. Serenity is found in soothing hues and raw materials.

Saxifraga exarata

Crassula macowaniana

Saxifraga aizoides

Crevice gardens

These little miracles of nature can be found in the most intriguing spaces. Almost always, on close inspection, it is hard to sort out what exactly the roots of the plant are feeding on, and how the whole thing can even exist in the first place. Rather pedestrian versions (pun intended) are found in the crevices between pavers, where weeds somehow thrive. But with patience and diligence, it is possible to establish creeping thyme or moss, or some other more desirable, traffic-tolerant plant. The crevice can also be vertical, in a rock wall, or in the pothole of a stone. No matter where they choose to settle, these small gardens are always surprising and pleasing for their sheer audacity.

The plants that occupy crevices are typically tough, tolerant, and opportunistic.

Scree gardens

Geranium Rozanne ('Gerwat')

Scree can be made up of gravel, small stones, or even sand. Scree gardens are particularly useful during transitions. A gravel patio, for instance, can form an economical seating area. A scree garden will help to blend gravel areas into planting areas. With just a few plants here and there, the edges are blurred and the plants can take center stage. Use just a few plant varieties and repeat them in combinations; ultimately you'll achieve the effect of the garden having casually happened that way. Plants for scree gardens tend to be small, often alpine or sculptural.

Nepeta cataria

Rhododendron eriocarpum

Eschscholzia californica

Diascia barberae

Thymus

Dianthus 'Pink Baby'

Wall display of *Platycerium bifurcatum*

Sculptural plants

Modern design tends to require keeping things as spare and curated as possible, meaning that herbaceous borders are not going to work for this style. There may only be room for a few plants, so they must make the most of themselves. Plants that not only provide green, but also are interesting in shape, form, or texture add another layer to the design. Consider succulents, grasses, wall-mounted specimens (such as *Platycerium bifurcatum* or staghorn fern), and caudiciform (stem-like) plants such as ponytail palms for added living sculpture.

Beaucarnea recurvata

Fish swimming in *Stipa tenuissima*

TERRARIUMS

I like to create terrariums that represent a magical world I could live in if I were the size of my thumb. These miniature gardens, made of tiny plants and encased in glass, are always eye-catchers and are great tabletop gardens both indoors and out (though I would never leave a terrarium outside for a cold winter).

There are a variety of options for making a terrarium. They can be completely enclosed (the most tricky) or, at the other end of the spectrum, more of a tray garden. Whichever you choose, make sure you do a little research to get the soil and climate details right. Here are a few additional tips I rarely see mentioned.

- **Follow the planting mix for the plants you desire.** You will regret forgoing the charcoal layer in an enclosed terrarium when you're later scrubbing moldy, slimy plants from the inside of your container.

- **Apply the same plant care basics as for full-sized gardens.** Plants that need similar conditions should be put together. Don't assemble a garden in which humidity-loving tropicals are trying to hang out with desert-loving cacti. Someone in your grouping will not be happy.

- **Think small and then go smaller.** Even 4-inch (10-centimeter) pots are likely too big; aim for plants in 2-inch (5.1-centimeter) pots or smaller. You will have less waste and frustration.

- **Add other miniatures.** I enjoy hiding tiny animal figurines and silly Lego people; use your imagination.

Molly's peaceful sanctuary

Serenity was the foremost goal in creating this peaceful garden. The garden—built for a woman who had a strong sense of personal style—was dressed in much the same way as the client's interiors. A sophisticated palette of muted gray and white plaster was carried from the inside out, in an effort to blur the lines between house and garden. Molly wanted to keep the focus internal and designed to highlight the light and sky. Subtle colors lend a soothing aura but they also provide a strong backdrop against which the plants can really pop. Other organic elements, such as the elm wood table and the stone fountain, are also appreciated in this clean and organized garden.

Each piece is noticed because none competes with another. Succulents, including aeonium and echeveria, surround the fountain.

"The muted grays, white plaster, and textural plantings combine to lower one's blood pressure upon impact." — Molly Wood

LOVELY LIGHTING

For most people, garden time is spent after work and during evening hours, so it is well worth the planning to make your garden as attractive at night as it is during the day. There are many choices for casting a lovely glow on your garden, so choose a mix that serves the special needs of your property.

Type of light

Directional lights or down lighters

Spreading and diffusing lights

In-ground or well lights

Spotlights and accent lights

Sconces, wall mounts, flush mounts, ceiling lanterns, and hanging lanterns

Bollards and posts

String lights

Novelty lights

Step lights

Water lights

Candles and torches

Properties	How to use
These powerful lights have sleeves to direct illumination, eliminate glare, and reduce light pollution.	Station lights in trees to point down and illuminate a patio, or attach to the side of the house to provide ambient lighting from above. Use to direct light—for instance, on the front of a structure.
A low-level lighting that points down to create a small puddle of illumination.	Best used on paths, in planting beds, and around walkways, some diffusing lights can also be mounted into stone walls and spill light down the wall's face.
Fixtures are buried in the ground, so that the top sits flush with the soil. They should be set low enough to avoid a run-in with the mower.	Use to up-light trees and plants, or to wash light across a wall or facade.
Similar to directional lights and down lighters, spotlights can provide powerful illumination for a whole area or direct attention to one place.	Use to cross-light or create an effect called moonlighting. Cross-lighting helps to reduce shadows. Moonlighting simulates its namesake by grouping light sources so that they all shine from one direction. Cool, blue-tinted bulbs may also be substituted for warm-tinted bulbs.
Usually decorative and intended to complement a home's exterior and garden; these accent lights are offered in a wide variety of styles.	Select fixtures that complement each other as well as the surrounding architecture to give exterior settings special character.
Freestanding lights that are typically used to illuminate pathways, steps, walkways, decks, and patios.	The construction of bollards and posts provides opportunities to produce shadow patterns and details only enjoyed at night. Direct downward at a low angle to illuminate a surface.
Easy-to-find (especially during the holidays) basic lights that usually have a series of tiny but evenly spaced lights along a string of wire. Commercial-grade versions are more durable and allow strings to be connected in succession.	Most popular for holiday displays, string lights can also be used year-round. Larger bulb shapes and a wide variety of bulb covers can help establish different styles. They are easily tacked to surfaces, hung from structures, or creatively applied to forms.
Outdoor lamps, internally lit containers and shapes, and lights that have been fashioned to look like other things offer decorative style in addition to lighting.	Novelty lighting gives a garden some playful personality. New designs are constantly being introduced, so keep an eye out for styles that will add flair to your garden.
Small and narrow, step lights can be unobtrusively installed underneath the overhang of a step or inside the lip of a fountain.	For safety's sake, steps and stairs should always be lit. Step lights can be used in a variety of applications where it is desirable for the fixture to be nearly invisible.
Used for underwater illumination, water lights are most often built into the sides of pools. They are also commonly used in fountains and sometimes ponds.	For interest, add colored bulbs or filters, and consider timers that will rotate colors to change the mood of the light.
These traditional light sources capitalize on the magic of fire as illumination.	Candles offer the prettiest and most romantic garden lighting. There are candles and lanterns that help keep insects away; others provide pleasing fragrance.

Plush Yoga

earth

Most of the time, when I enter a garden, my mind begins to settle. Unless, of course, that garden is my own, where often all I can see is the extensive and exhausting list of things I need to do.

For the majority of people, though, entering a garden begins a mental passage from one state of mind to another and, in those gardens that are specifically designed for relaxation, meditation, and the pursuit of serenity, the experience is magnified.

Through the ages, cultures of all sorts have used symbolism, geometry, color theory, and a whole host of design tricks to shape surroundings that elicit emotion, provide platforms for calmness and self-reflection, and help bodies and minds heal from the injury of everyday living. I've always thought that if your garden is comfortable and thoughtfully laid out, providing places to nap, eat, and rest, you have a pretty great start.

However, taking cues from modern and ancient beliefs and methods, you can up the ante on creating a place that soothes the soul. Earth-based religions such as Buddhism, Hinduism, paganism, and Taoism, as well as principles of feng shui, yogic philosophy, and astrology can all provide a wealth of ideas for symbolic gestures and design intentions. Your meditation might be walking and thus requires a labyrinth, or maybe you are in need of a place to practice yoga or tai chi. It might be a place to perform the ritual ceremonies of prayer, or simply a place of contemplation, but a garden such as this is always a place to quiet your thoughts and gain an increased awareness of the rustling wind and green leaves that surround you.

peace

fire

balance

meditation

Hallowed space

Close the garden in and actively shut out the rest of the world. This type of garden benefits from an enhanced entrance, through which you must pass in order to arrive in a revered place. The Japanese *torii*, for example, is a gate that separates the profane from the sacrosanct. Similarly, this sunken garden creates a protected room surrounded by earth. An entrance and a transition symbolize passage between mindsets, making it significant and notable.

Make it personal

Close your eyes and imagine a place where you feel safe, calm, comfortable, and at peace. What does that look and feel like? That vivid mental image is your special place. While you are there, take a look around and make note of your surroundings. For some, it is the ocean, or a garden, or a childhood home. For me, it is a cabin in the mountains set in a grove of quaking aspens. Bring an element of your mental special place to your real garden. It will help you to connect with your own peace.

Go natural

When getting in touch with your inner self and the world around you, nothing seems more counterintuitive than filling the area with unnatural plastic and synthetic materials. Ground yourself in the elemental qualities of raw materials such as stone and wood.

$$\frac{a+b}{a} = \frac{a}{b} = \varphi \approx 1.61803$$

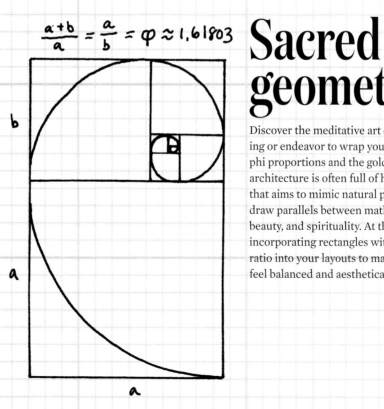

Sacred geometry

Discover the meditative art of mandala making or endeavor to wrap your head around phi proportions and the golden mean. Sacred architecture is often full of hidden geometry that aims to mimic natural patterns and draw parallels between math, science, art, beauty, and spirituality. At the very least, try incorporating rectangles with the golden ratio into your layouts to make the design feel balanced and aesthetically pleasing.

Air

Air gardens are full of movement and light. The wind rustles through trees and plants and they sway and dance. There are open views of the sky, chimes played by the wind, and tiny creatures happily buzzing about. Incorporate things that encourage thought and ideas. Grasses and prayer flags are lovely additions to air gardens.

Blowing grass

Prayer flags

Water

Flowing lines (nothing straight) and quiet contemplation characterize a water garden. The trickling sounds of a stream, fountain, or pond filled with koi will quiet outside noises. Moss and lush dampness will ground the space. Lotus flowers, symbolic of water and its flow, can be used in all sort of decorative motifs. Whites soothe, both in flowers and furniture; grottoes, caves, and earthy, damp places provide a calming coolness.

Koi

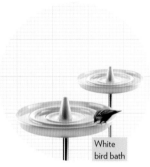

White bird bath

Fire

Fire gardens aspire to be sun traps. They have fireplaces, are dressed in red, and maybe even embrace thorny plants. They are passionate and ready for action. Actual fire elements can come in a variety of forms, from torches to fire bowls to incense burners.

Modern torches

Candles

Earth

Ground yourself in earthy gardens. Orchards and vegetable patches are obvious examples, but so too are those that incorporate elements such as twig art, wood, trees, and earthenware like hypertufa. A sunken area, where the earth literally surrounds you, can be a place that feels particularly stable and secure.

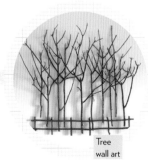

Tree wall art

Tree trunk bowls

Mason
bee house

Dinner
triangle

Lotus
candle holder

Stone, fire,
and water feature

Clay incense
burner

Meridian
fire bowl

Hypertufa
planter

Woven
trellis

FIRE OPTIONS

There are three main ways to bring the warmth and soul of fire to a garden; your preferences and circumstances may favor one over the others.

- **Open natural wood fire.** The same basic approach the Neanderthals used. It is, however, banned in many places for air quality and fire safety reasons. Wood fires can be made in all sorts of vessels or even on the ground within a fire ring.

- **Gel.** Often used in urban areas, gel fires are a lot like a can of cooking Sterno. They come in a variety of forms and because of the cleanliness of the fire (no sooty smoke), the flexibility of placement, and the ability to control the size of the flame, they lend themselves to application where a modern look is desired, or perhaps a tiny fire feature is needed. Considered a green option, these fires are easy to light, require no venting, and can be enhanced by scented aromatics.

- **Gas fire.** Typically piped into a home's gas main and thus can be lit with the flip of a switch. The installation expense is not insignificant, however, and the realities of running gas lines to your garden can also be a design challenge. The upside is that you don't need to refuel.

Plant the chakras

In metaphysical traditions, chakras are the centers of *prana*, life force, or vital energy. Chakras are frequently mapped to the human body and are often described in colors. Planting by the chakras would therefore be to choose plants according to color and similar symbolism to the chakra.

Hydrangea

Eryngium

Agapanthus

Communication and the color blue are associated with the fifth chakra. This can be symbolized in plants, but also with the flow of a water feature.

Sedum

Moss

Euphorbia

The **heart** chakra is green and evokes harmony, peace, and love. If I were to make a meditation garden for myself, I would focus on this alone, forgoing all floral brightness for the peace and calm of simple green.

Iris

Heuchera

Liatris

Indigo and deep purple represent the chakra of the **third eye** or the brow. Complex or highly geometric plants represent the focus on intuition and thinking.

Tickseed

Witch hazel

Portulaca

Manipura or the chakra of the solar plexus is yellow. It supports our personality, humor, and ability to have a good laugh. Select plants for their sunny disposition.

Cotinus

Coleus

Japanese maple

The **root** chakra is colored red. You do not need to pick purely by flower; red can be found in leaves and berries as well.

The **crown** chakra centers on spirituality and divinity and encompasses all the colors, so it is generally depicted as white. Play with translucence and light reflection to make this symbolic reference.

Daylily

Rose

Poppy

The **sacral** chakra is focused on sensuality and self-esteem and is colored orange. Consider plants that not only have the color but also a romantic perfume.

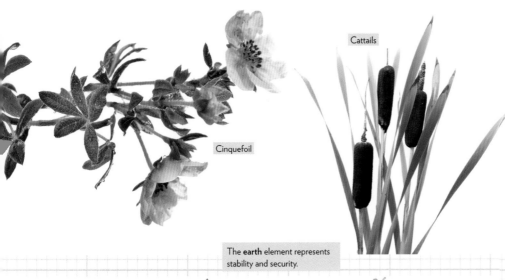

Cinquefoil

Cattails

Honeysuckle

The **earth** element represents stability and security.

Mint

Marjoram

Sage

The **air** element represents wisdom and knowledge.

Basil

Strawberry

Rosemary

Fire is associated with passion.

Willow

Yarrow

Iris

The **water** element is associated with intuition and emotions.

Plant the elements

Growing a plant from seed, nurturing its growth, and experiencing its full blooming expression is similar to the yogic practice of setting an intention, nurturing the practice, and finally loving and accepting one's own personal expression. Additionally, gardening, like yoga, connects us to all things.

Earth, air, fire, and water are frequently associated with the compass points (earth: north; air: east; fire: south; and water: west). To have a true elemental garden, you must choose plants that have associations with each of the elements and plant them generally in the appropriate direction. This is a bit tedious to my mind, but the idea of recognizing the associations of plants when choosing what you grow is a nice way to give your garden special meaning. If you are the creative type, you can make all sorts of associations, but here are some of the plant and element connections that have been carried through history.

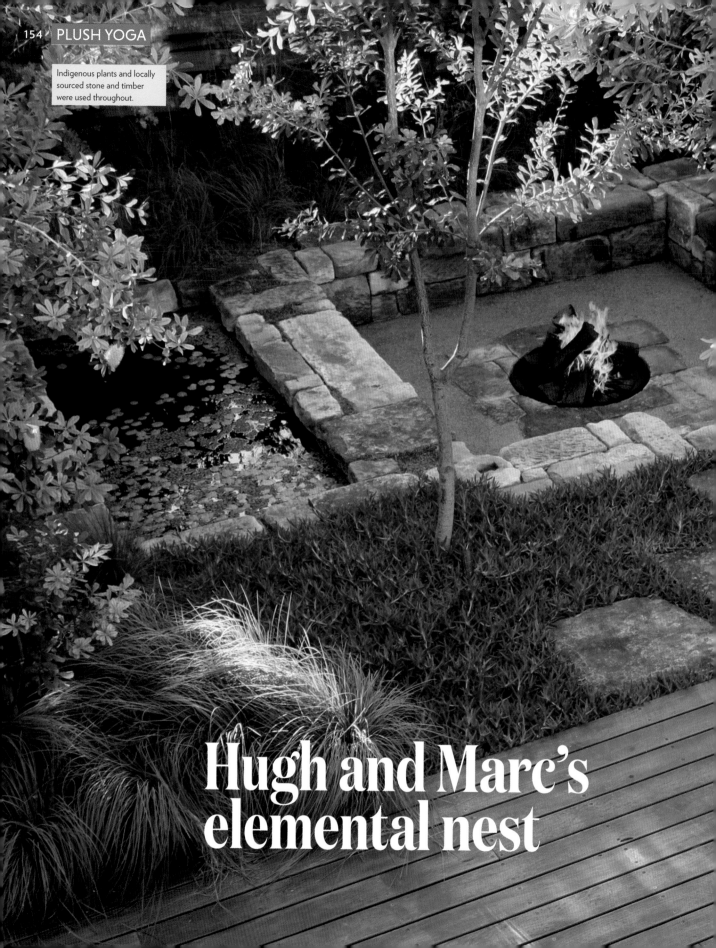

Indigenous plants and locally sourced stone and timber were used throughout.

Hugh and Marc's elemental nest

Relaxed, unstructured plants keep the mood calm.

Set between buildings in urban Bondi Beach, New South Wales, Australia, Hugh and Marc took the uncommon step of constructing the garden before tackling the interior of their apartment. It is rare to have such a gem of a space, and they wished to replace the patch of sloped lawn (sporting a clothesline in the middle) with something that recalled the original landscape. After the exterior was established, Hugh and Marc let the interiors be guided by the design of the outdoor space.

Gardens are scarce in their area. But Hugh appreciated native landscapes of the region and sought to recreate what is locally referred to as a "Bondi gully" in the space between buildings. The area was once long sweeps of beach dotted with gum trees and stunted brush. Streams, fern gullies, palm groves, and beautiful blue lagoons sat just behind the sand. This garden is natural and relaxed, recalling a feeling of being in the bush. The materials are all locally sourced and the plants chosen were indigenous whenever possible. Marc is the yogi of the pair and there is a subtle gesture to the elements, with the fire pit and the water feature placed side by side.

"We painted the interior of the apartment black, so at night all you can see is the garden, no internal walls." —Hugh Main

MINI GABION DIY

Gabions, which are metal mesh baskets that hold rocks or concrete, have historically been a tool employed by the likes of civil engineers. But these industrial building blocks have come into vogue for uses beyond securing structures and edifices.

Today, gabion cages are regularly put to use in garden design as an alternative to other retaining wall materials. Additionally, smaller versions can become footings for arbors, benches, planters, or even the foundations of modern water features. On a small scale, you can create a candle holder or base of a planted centerpiece that captures the gabion look and construction.

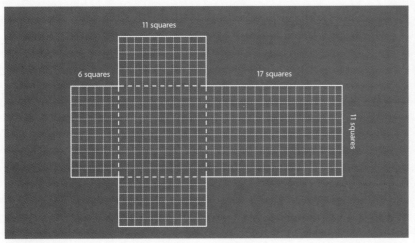

Materials

1 sheet of ½-inch- (1.3-centimeter-) square metal mesh (called hardware cloth or hail screen)

Wire cutters

Narrow gauge wire (that can be easily wound like thread)

Filler (I used moss and black beach pebbles, but you can use sea shells or rocks of any sort—even feathers).

1. Cut the screen into two pieces. One will measure 6 squares wide by 22 squares long. The other will be T-shaped in the measurements shown (see diagram).

2. Roll the rectangular piece in a circle so at least one set of squares is overlapping; secure by threading the wire through the seam.

3. Fold the T-shaped piece into a box, leaving one flap open. Secure the sides with wire. You will have a short lip hanging over the lid to help secure the top after the gabion is filled.

4. Insert the center circle into the box and secure it with wire.

5. You can either fill the gabion at this point, or wait until after you have cut the center circle out. (I couldn't wait, so I filled it first, then cut.)

6. The finished gabion can be filled with just about anything.

ENVIRONMENT

" We have two
of our old
Citroens buried
where the
house used
to be. They
have become
the most
important
habitats for
wildlife."
-John Little

If you are anything like me, you crave certain types of landscapes. I yearn for the big skies, open prairies, and dramatic mountains of Colorado and Montana. But perhaps you prefer something that is more wooded or enclosed by dense planting. Maybe you're drawn to northern and hardy, or flowing and free? Let the terrain and the garden styles in these chapters help you embrace and create your own geography.

196

TROPICAL NOIR

208

HANDSOME PRAIRIE

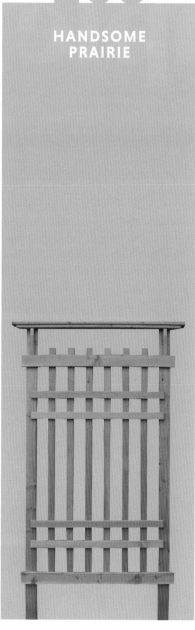

Forest Temple

P lease don't assume that I expect you to plant a forest or build a temple. Rather, I propose that you think of Forest Temple as a design reference for tree people, fairy lovers, and wood nymphs reincarnated. It is for those who love to be under a canopy rather than out in the open; who find comfort and peace in being surrounded by trees and greenery. Forest Temple style is a divine answer to a vacant or overgrown urban lot, a courtyard, greenhouse garden, tiny green patch—wherever you can fit one—and of course, any garden which naturally incorporates the woods. I've even experienced one, once, on the roof of a department store in central London.

A woodland sanctuary gives the sense of being just barely cultivated, and it often has haphazard planting. This isn't your style if you want cut flowers—it is a garden where, instead, you will be able to enjoy the fleeting beauty of an ephemeral, or a single stem here and there. Such gardens can be made from scratch or they can be managed to enhance something that already exists. Regardless of their origins, these appealing spaces exude a warmth and patina borrowed from nature. Woodland plants, textural trees, walls of green, dangling vines, mossy pots, the smell of earth, and the faint sound of trickling water set the mood and fill the senses in this garden.

understory

verdant

solace

canopy

fantasy

Barely contained wildness

When gardeners carve out a piece of wild or uncultivated land to begin the process of transforming it, they must realize that, should they ever abandon their efforts, it is only a matter of time before Mother Nature takes it back and makes it feral again. Her wild ways always prevail. The Forest Temple takes this into account, honors it, and doesn't fight back too hard. Concepts of permaculture and forest gardening provide the guiding principles. In general, keep things low maintenance. Study ecosystems so that you can create and enhance them. Learn what would grow naturally together and use those plants to devise a heightened version of what could have happened naturally. Use native plants to honor the site and work with the trees instead of against them.

Sculpture, follies, art, and architecture

These elements provide destinations within the garden. The forest is a place to hide and discover. Meandering paths with treasures waiting to be found add surprise. Even if the garden is confined to a container, think about hiding something that isn't readily visible—I like to think of it as a reward for those who take the time to look a little closer. Beautiful classical sculpture is always appropriate as the pay-off for a ramble down unknown paths, but other artwork or whimsical additions can enhance the destination as well. A finely honed urn or statue in the middle of the cultivated wild is a surprising and pleasing paradox.

Glamping & foraging

Let glamping (glamorous camping) be your inspiration for outbuildings, features, and accessories. Cultivate forest food treasures such as mushrooms and ramps and instead of harvesting from your garden, call yourself a forager (it sounds much more romantic and rugged).

Twig bench

Gothic lantern

MIRRORS

Under a canopy, things can feel overly dark. Use mirrors in the garden to reflect light and greenery. Don't worry about them steaming up or getting a little dirty; it will add to the mystique.

Reclaimed stools

Twiggy hand light

Bentwood bench

Ceramic moss pots

Faux bois planter

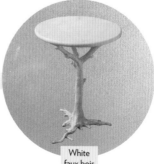
White faux bois

Head planter

Driftwood birdhouse

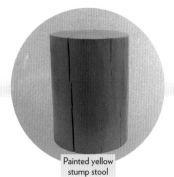

Painted yellow stump stool

Woodland fairy tale

For those with fantasies of being Snow White and living in the Enchanted Forest, try combining gothic-detailed lanterns and twig furniture (that looks like it could magically come alive and grab you at any moment). Stump stools are practical extra seating options as well as easy impromptu tables and plant stands. Show your little bird friends how much you appreciate them with their own charming abode.

Camp stove

Plaid wool blanket

Sylvan survival

Few textiles are really appropriate for this garden, unless you need a warm blanket while sitting around the campfire. Cut wood, wood chips, branches, and wood stools all come together to make stepping stones, trails, impromptu seating, and decoration. Consider a camp kitchen as a permanent garden feature—it is less expensive than a typical outdoor grill and far more delightful.

Stone water feature

Cement planters

Secret history

Invoke mystery and intrigue with the sound of trickling water whose source you can't quite see. Concrete (both natural and textured) contains the same grays and browns as the forest floor and has the ability to get just as mossy. Industrial materials set within the forest convey a sense that someone has been there. Who knows when they might next return?

Birch bark container

Square block stump seats

Secluded retreat

The objects that works best with this garden looks like they were built right there with what was growing on-site and, in fact, if you don't watch out, the surrounding tangle might just eat them right back up. Pieces are rustic but artistic and often made of twigs, sticks, and twisted vines, or have faux bois decoration. Aged sculpture is unexpected but charming and highlights the fact this is indeed an intentional garden.

Brook wakerobin

Maidenhair fern

Epimedium

Layer woodland plants

For this planting style to work, it is important to think in layers. First, have a leafy canopy in place. This provides the shade and the sense of protection and enclosure that defines a forested setting. If you don't have full-grown trees, then maybe woody vines such as grape or rose can be trained over a pergola to form the canopy. It is also possible that the canopy is the overhang of an upper level deck or balcony, the roof of a greenhouse, or, if small enough, the dappled shade provided by a container-planted tree.

Elegant climber

Vertical gardens and green walls

Capture the flourishing essence of wilderness by growing your garden upward, even though you may use plants from the forest floor (mosses and ferns, for example) to populate a living wall of flora. Many vertical gardens are in places that lack regular and consistent light, conditions similar to the understory.

Green wall

FOREST TEMPLE WISDOM

Because the joy in this type of garden comes from the natural rambling, it is okay to let it look a little reckless. Save yourself some backbreaking maintenance labor by accepting that your wild space will have a strong will of its own, and at least a few weeds should be welcomed.

Remember that once the leaves are gone from trees, your garden will look entirely different. Rather than walls of green, you will have architecturally interesting branches and

stems—and the option to grow early-season plants that will enjoy the fleeting sun available before spring leaves set on.

Don't try to keep plants separated. Encourage them to not only ramble, but get right up in each other's business. Roses or other vines growing through nearby trees, shrubs, and other features should be encouraged; it adds to the natural tapestry.

Red trillium

Fern

White bloodroot

Astilbe

Once the canopy is in place, add texture with hanging plants and medium-sized trees. Dwarf conifers and mid-sized shrubs (blueberries, for example) can fill out the lower middle layer. Fill the floor of the garden with woodland plants, ferns, vines, and moss. Moon flowers, roses, epimedium, and vining plants will tie the layers together as they snake through and climb or wander. Trillium, astilbe, and a healthy selection of the lower ground plants (roots and tubers) that give seasonal ephemeral beauty will provide fleeting sparkles of color. Try colchicums, bloodroot, and snowdrops for early spring interest, before the trees leaf out.

Pink sorrel

Perennial edibles

If you want this garden to feed you (literally rather than figuratively), there are many harvestable versions of plants that will thrive here. Inoculated mushroom logs are always fun and can be used as a focal point in a small garden. Wild berries and perennial vegetables such as sorrel, asparagus, lovage, or wild leeks can fill out the garden.

Mini & string gardens

If you have only the tiniest of spaces, have fun with string gardens, which can stylistically emulate the layers of a wooded thicket. Or, think of a container planting as your own private forest. Create a fairy garden with scaled-down human elements.

String garden

A canopy creates an enclosed haven in the musty, gritty understory.

"Think of this at an abandoned Victorian garden with a new owner who is attempting to introduce a Japanese aesthetic."
— Clive Rundle

Clive Rundle's tumbledown Victorian garden

Bronze and stone statuary: proof that this is a cultivated place.

Nothing makes me happier than seeing a true expression of someone in something they create. Whether it is art, clothes, architecture, or a garden, the realization of an individual vision is what makes being a designer fun. So even though you might look at this garden and not see the design beauty, I assure you it is there. It is the vision of Forest Temple. Clive Rundle is a fashion designer whose reputation for fantastic runway shows makes him the star of Johannesburg's fashion week in South Africa. His garden, started from scratch and fifteen years in the perfecting, is a cultivated and refined study in enigmatic neglect.

The sense of untouched splendor is purely by design.

An avenue of flowering cherries and raised beds beckons.

CHOOSING A TREE

There is a lot of information online and in books that can help you sort out the best tree for your situation, but I find things can quickly get overwhelming when you walk into a nursery and start shopping. Here is what I recommend for finding the right tree without too much stress and worry.

EVERGREEN OR DECIDUOUS?

Evergreens stay green year-round; often their leaves are needles. A deciduous tree loses its foliage in the winter. When considering this, think about your willingness to deal with leaves and other things that fall from trees (seed pods, pinecones, and sap to name a few). Before choosing between evergreen and deciduous, ask yourself these questions.

- What is your view of the tree, and what is behind and in front of it in the various seasons?
- Are you trying to hide something unpleasant?
- Is that nasty little something there year-round?
- Will a green backdrop make something else in front of it really shine?

FIGURE OUT THE DETAILS

Flowers and fruit. These add color and attract butterflies, birds, and other wildlife.

Color. Red, orange, yellow, and purple are all colors that add beauty in the fall, but trees come in a variety of hues that last beyond autumn.

Tolerance. Will the tree put up with you and will it tolerate your garden? If it needs wet feet, and you aren't going to water it, then it isn't going to like you. If you live where it gets cold in the winters, palms may not be your best bet. Check the requirements of the tree and make sure you can reasonably provide it a happy home.

WHAT SHAPE AND SCALE?

Considering these issues will help you narrow the options. Think about the space you have and how different forms and sizes will relate to the tree's surroundings. For example, very large trees are often better behind a home (where they will provide a backdrop to the architecture) than in the front yard. Consider whether your tree should be small, medium, or large. Also, decide on the shape: weeping, umbrella, oval, pyramidal, round, mound, triangular, spreading, vase-shaped, or narrow?

Short and stout trees: *Up to 25 feet (7.6 meters) tall and 40 feet (12.2 meters) wide.* They can grow above the roof of a single-story house but often give the visual effect of an enormous shrub. They don't interfere with overhead utility lines but they need lots of room. **Examples:** Japanese maple, magnolia, rhododendron, yew

Short and skinny trees: *Up to 25 feet (7.6 meters) tall and less than 30 feet (9.1 meters) wide.* These are great for small areas and many have ornamental qualities or can be productive (they often give you fruits, nuts, and flowers). **Examples:** serviceberry (*Amelanchier*), dogwood, willow, most fruit trees

Medium and wide trees: *Approximately 25 (7.6 meters) to 45 feet (13.7 meters) tall and more than 30 feet (9.1 meters) wide.* These are the smallest of shade trees. Consider planting them on the south side (in the northern hemisphere) of your home to provide shade in the summer. Also be aware that these will need to be kept away from overhead power lines. **Examples:** ash, hornbeam, Babylonian weeping willow, many varieties of sorbus

Medium and skinny trees: *Approximately 25 (7.6 meters) to 45 feet (13.7 meters) tall and more than 30 feet (9.1 meters) wide.* These are commonly used along property lines, driveways, or in tight places. They can be great for windbreaks or more formal gardens. **Examples:** birch, cypress, ginkgo, laurel, most maples

Tall and large trees: *Taller than 45 feet (13.7 meters) and more than 30 feet (9.1 meters) wide.* These are the shade trees of city parks, and they can provide the most shade for homes and driveways. While they are generally long-lived, they also take a long time to reach full size. **Examples:** chestnut, eucalyptus, oak, tulip tree (*Liriodendron*)

Tall and thin trees: *Taller than 45 feet (13.7 meters) and less than 30 feet (9.1 meters) wide.* These are great for shade in areas that do not have a lot of room. **Examples:** locust, columnar or fastigiate varieties of large trees

Sacred Meadow

open

I think wildflower meadows have the same mystery and excitement as a very tall corn maze or a vast wheat field—but they are much more stylish. The plants have a way of embracing you and sharing their sense of being wild. If you have ever experienced the joy of walking through a wheat or rapeseed field, you know that it is hard not to stretch out your arms and run your fingertips over the tops of the plants. Similarly, the vastness of a cornfield can make a person feel quite insignificant, but also cocooned. I am drawn to these emotive places and look to Sacred Meadow style for my own garden inspiration.

Increasing drought, water shortages, and busy lives make lawns and their high maintenance not only less sustainable but impractical for modern existence. I also think the old-fashioned notion of a perfect lawn being a highly desirable status symbol is thankfully slipping away. Really, we all just need to agree that turf grass is nothing more than a ground cover that we can evaluate critically against other planting options. Quite the opposite of a manicured lawn, a meadow teems with life and variety and is a lively alternative that requires less of our controlling input.

These magical places provide plenty of opportunity for creativity and design. They support edible and medicinal plants, beneficial bugs, and pollinators, and they infuse us with their uninhibited spirit.

beckoning

native

tapestry

free

There is more than one way to establish a meadow. If you have a lawn in place, you can encourage it to grow wilder by allowing in local, non-invasive meadow plants over time. Targeted mowing and maintenance plans will discourage the turf and encourage the wild plants. Additionally underplanting it with bulbs and other perennials will hasten the conversion. Completely bare soil can be seeded with formulated wildflower mixes or planted with small selections for greater control over the initial plant placement. To decide which approach is best, analyze what you already have and what you plan to accomplish. No matter how it is made, though, a meadow is largely meant to self-manage and change over time.

Seeded, planted, renovated

Natural water

In the wild, most meadows have some sort of water flowing through them. Rivers, streams, bogs, and ponds give the meadow character and allow for opportunities to change up the planting mix. If you're lucky, these water features may occur naturally in your space—if not, you can simulate them with pumps that recycle water. Such features can also be adapted into rain gardens (maximized for rainwater capture).

Pretty paths

Just like the planting mix, the paths through this type of garden may migrate over time, too. Mown trails can change every couple of months if you want and generally should be drawn to entice visitors to delve deeper into the garden. Gravel, mulch, or stone can also be good path options. Catwalk paths (deck-like elevated walkways) are fun for wet meadows and enhance the sensory experience by changing the point of view and adding excitement. Narrow paths are dramatic and mysterious. Wide ones are good where you need to see what's coming or if you wish to avoid edge-hugging plants flopping in and blocking the way.

Mobile lounge

A meadow garden is constantly changing. Even morning and evening light can be strikingly different as the rays dance with grasses and plants. The nuanced nature of this garden style might be best enjoyed from a different spot every day. Go mobile with your meadow lounge by employing pieces that can easily be rolled from place to place. A compact garden oven will keep everyone warm while providing a place to grill. A bright floral pouf reflects surrounding plants.

Wheeled bench

Freestanding outdoor oven

Edgy lace

Bring to mind a wild meadow that might be in an abandoned but romanticized industrial yard or perhaps along railroad tracks. Contrasting weight and materials makes the idea of lace work in the garden without having to give up grunge excitement. Lightweight, carefree softness is found in a delicate umbrella and a romantic circle bench, but intricately patterned concrete blocks ground the ensemble and give structure. Industrial planters are simple and clean enough to work with the details of lace and wild flowers.

Circle bench

Green lace garden parasol

Mixed wild

Blended elements come together to create an eclectic setting. Smooth-shaped pots and fire pits in black and white finishes play well with more fanciful monochrome details. Awnings are a great place to introduce pattern, but outbuildings can also be painted in fun colors or striking stripes. More intricately patterned cushions add an offbeat contrast and neutral background colors bring it all together.

Bamboo chair

Fire bowl

The carefree painter

Mixing patterns and prints and piling on extra details ensure that no one is bored. Why not give the camper van a life beyond the annual holiday and park it in an attractive field garden—ready for year-round use? Modern lines, classic furniture shapes, natural touches, and a painter's palette are the perfect idea sparks for a garden meadow.

Teak baroque chair

Camper garden room

Outdoor pouf

BRING ON THE BUTTERFLIES

Butterflies are drawn to meadows by the plants that provide nectar for food and homes for their transitioning stages of development. Variety in plants will also encourage variety in butterflies. Meadows that are sunny and protected from wind will be filled with these beautiful insects.

To lure butterflies, consider including aster, black-eyed Susan, columbine, coreopsis, daisies, dianthus, echinacea, scabiosa, penstemon, and yarrow in your meadow. Herbs such as borage, bee balm, and sage are also great sources of nectar.

Caterpillars feed on some of the same plants but additionally like mallow, hollyhock, common rue, sunflowers, fennel, dill, and milkweed.

Laser-cut
steel screen

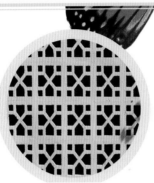

Breeze blocks

Industrial
metal planters

Gypsy poufs

Striped awnings

Grass-filled
ceramic pots

Painterly cushion

Succulent
wall art

Coral-colored
planter

Acorus (dwarf)

Bouteloua gracilis 'Blonde Ambition'

Hakonechloa macra 'Aureola'

Anthoxanthum odoratum

Pennisetum setaceum

Assorted grasses & no-mow lawns

Grasses form the backbone of the meadow. They come in all heights and have a variety of characteristics, including unexpected color. Low grasses let taller flowers shine and provide fill, while tall grasses offer a backdrop and can be great accents. Grasses can also be used as ground covers—those with a low-growing, matting habit are great for paths and no-mow lawns, and those with a more open habit help control weeds while letting other grasses and accents shine through.

Teasel

Northern evening primrose

Borage

Wild garlic

Herbs & medicinals

The diversity that is naturally built into a meadow garden provides a habitat for beneficial insects and pollinators. Native meadows have long been the medicine cabinet of native tribes and ancient healers and are still fertile resources for modern-day herbalists. Planting or foraging for meadow herbs will reward you not only with tasty ingredients for meals, but also with the foundations of many home remedies.

Daisies

Agave

Red daylilies

Bulbs & brighteners

While grasses are the heart of the meadow garden, excitement comes from the unexpected and the colorful. Think about how an agave sits heavily in a sea of grass, or how a strappy agapanthus looks solid compared to an airy mix. These contradictions are engaging and can be produced by contrasting the weightiness of a plant's foliage against the grass. Bright colors and masses of flowers can also give visual weight; good options include daisy-like plants from the aster family. Also, try using bulbs such as allium and tall, flowering plants like gaura and hemerocallis; their blooms will seem to sit on top of the grasses.

MEADOW MAINTENANCE

A meadow does not need watering, fertilizing, or grading so don't be tempted to make it more complicated than it needs to be.

- **Don't improve the soil.** Poor, wet, clay, acidic—whatever your ailment, there are plants that will thrive there. Make sure you remove invasive plants, but look at what is growing naturally and build on that.

- **When you mow your meadow, mow it high** (leaving at least 5 inches or 13 centimeters of growth). Mowing creates mulch, encourages plants that you want, and spreads desirable seed. Also, pay close attention to when you mow. To encourage annuals and biennials, wait until after they set seed; to discourage a plant, mow before it matures. Local extension experts or organizations such as PlantLife in the UK can help you understand the plants that grow in your area.

- **Enhance a meadow by planting native perennials or additional wildflower seed.** Try to find locally sourced seed so that it will have the best chance of surviving and thriving in your climate.

A birch grove grew from seedlings gifted by friends, and creates a dappled overhead view.

John & Fiona's habitat campground garden

"We have two of our old Citroens buried where the house used to be. They have become the most important habitats for wildlife."
—John Little

John runs a company that specializes in green roofs, school gardens, urban habitats, and building with sustainable materials. With this sort of work, having your own private place to experiment is essential. The goal of the garden was twofold for John and his wife, Fiona: devise as many different habitat niches as possible, and establish a space for parties and for friends to camp and stay. Strong influences came from recycling centers and finding waste; through this project John has discovered that some of his favorite features (the crushed concrete stream that runs from the house to the pond, for example) and the best wildlife habitats come from the creative reuse of unlikely resources.

Native dark mullein gives extra height to meadow plantings.

Fireweed, tansy, perforate St. John's wort, meadow cranesbill, fennel, and European teasel are a lively mix.

PRACTICAL PATH MAKING

I can quickly get all metaphorical on the discussion of paths because I believe it's important to be mindful about the directions we take and what happens along the way. There are many sorts of garden paths. Some are planned to the finest detail and others just sort of happen. If your garden already has some form and structure, it is an interesting exercise to think about how you get to all the places you go and the way the route makes you feel. This is a quick way to help you understand what you are hoping to get out of your garden and how you might continue to improve what is already there.

TYPES OF PATHS

Grassy. Just because a path doesn't have formal edges doesn't mean it isn't a path. Grassy paths can go straight down the middle of a lawn, or they might take a curvy route that is slowed by plantings and beds that must be navigated. For the sake of maintenance, make sure you can easily mow the path. Consider your mowing device and don't make turns too tight or widths too narrow, but otherwise there are no rules. Let it get wider and narrower, divert to enjoy something special, or force a slow route by being indirect. Often this sort of path evolves over time as grassy areas are slowly carved away to make room for more plants, leaving meandering routes.

Paved. If you are going to make the investment to pave a path, you need to think through all the details so you can get it right the first time. Foremost, it is imperative that you research the proper way to install whatever paving you choose in your climate. Don't shortchange the footing depths or recommended gravel and sand layers, or you will most certainly regret it a few years later when you have heaved and uneven, weedy surfaces. Consider making paths wider at special places and at the beginning and end. This will help denote places where you might want to spend a bit more time or invite others to do so. And if in doubt, always err on the side of wide—you won't regret it.

Gravel. Paths made of gravel are loose and forgiving. Edging can go away as gravel can generally flow into the planted edge and also serve as mulch. If you care to formalize this type of path, as you might see in large formal gardens, you must compact many jagged-edged layers of gravel together so the surface becomes more stable; for this, professional installation is a good choice.

Conversely, a loose gravel path is an easy DIY task. First, place many (at least a dozen) layers of newspaper (a few less if you opt for cardboard or a commercial weed barrier) to form a weed barrier. Then install gravel over the top. The more gravel, the better, but never less than 3 to 4 inches (7.6 to 10 centimeters). I find that an annual spring treatment of an organic pre-emergent over the gravel paths will also help weed troubles tremendously.

Mowed. Romantic and ephemeral, the mowed path is here and then gone. Not quite the same as a grassy path, a mowed path is one that is created in a moment with a swipe of the mower through a field or meadow. The edge is simply the remaining tall plants. It can change and shift with the seasons and years. If you have a large garden, it is lovely to let an open area become a bit more wild and natural, leaving the option to create new mowed paths.

Natural. Sometimes paths just happen. They might be the result of animals choosing a preferred route, or possibly neighborhood children finding their way. It may also happen that a path arises from runoff and water in the form of a river bed. I am of the opinion that these sorts of paths should not be arbitrarily ignored or destroyed, but studied and worked with. If you try to move or eliminate them, they almost always turn up somewhere else—usually in a place even less desirable. Study natural paths and the reasons they are there and make sure you understand their origin before trying to alter them.

Stepping stone. Stones for walking upon can be precarious, but that is why we love them. Whether they traverse a full flower bed or bridge a small stream of water, they always give rise to a bit of suspense. No one wants to fall off or make a misstep, and consequently a stepping stone path focuses our journey over the individual steps. While this is lovely over water or through a flower bed, where we might already be looking down, it is less than ideal when we want to be able to enjoy a view or feel more leisurely.

Stepping stone

Natural

Grassy

Mowed

PATH DIY HINTS

- If you aren't sure about the route your path should take, use garden hoses to lay out the edges so you can adjust the shape and course. Live with it for a few days and adjust as needed before you commit.

- If you plan to do the project yourself, but have a lot of excavating to do to get the recommended drainage layers in place, consider hiring a contractor just to excavate and prep the area. You can lay the pavers and do the finish work, but leaving the foundational elements to the pros will save effort, time, and money.

- Make sure your path is wide enough. If you want it to be formal—perhaps to a front door—make sure that two people can walk side by side. This means making it at least 4 feet (1.2 meters) wide. Consider making it even wider where you expect more people or where people might gather.

- How you run the direction of your pavers matters. If, for example, you are building a brick path, laying the pavers end to end running in the direction of movement along the path, it will result in a path that subliminally hurries people along. But if you lay them perpendicular to the direction of movement, they will slow people down. Depending on the journey you're envisioning, one may be a better choice than the other.

- Every path should have a purpose, even if it is just to circumnavigate the landscape. Consider the journey and what might lie around each corner. Use a path to build surprise and suspense by making sure it tells a story. Only reveal small pieces of the narrative at a time.

Gravel

Brick-paved

Earthy Contemporary

I used to struggle to understand the nuanced difference between contemporary and modern design. But there is a difference worth understanding. Contemporary is now (like, right now), it is of the moment, and it is constantly changing. Conversely, modern is a notable design movement that started in the 1950s and was marked by a dramatic break from the ornate interiors and home decoration that had been the fashion prior. Long, low, clean lines, neutrality with color pops here and there, and big expanses define modern. We like to call the movement and style mid-century modern these days, which is fine, but really it is just modern.

The thing about modern is that it is still relatively new and its sensibilities pervade what we call contemporary. My favorite explanation is from blogger Lindsay Nealon: "Yesterday's contemporary is today's vintage. And tomorrow's contemporary is still unknown."

So when we talk about contemporary—we have to get ourselves on the same page—currently it is heavily influenced by modern design, meaning that it is full of long, straight lines and a tendency to be restrained in intricate details. But it is also a few other things. It is looser and more livable, it is earthy, it is reflective of the fact that we are into mixing things up (we call this eclectic) and that we are constantly evolving and experimenting.

livable

juxtaposed

Geometric layouts & details

Straight-line paths made of square or circular pavers are typically modern. Spheres, cylinders, cones, and cubes can be reflected in everything from furniture and sculpture to plants. This type of mathematically based orderliness can be a soothing and relaxing contrast to our chaotic lives. Use geometry, but keep it current by not being a slave to it, and let in elements that catch your fancy. Create contrast with a wild and floriferous planting below a strictly rigid line of trees. Or juxtapose ornate and old-fashioned furnishings—refurbished in an up-to-date color—and use them as a focal point in an otherwise spare garden. This patio was built with stacked, square-cut stones, but it is softened with gravel and casual, irreverent planting.

Less is more

Use as few kinds of materials, colors, and plants as you can and then get creative by making a big statement with what you have. Try to carry something into the garden from indoors. Extend the color and style of the flooring in your open-plan kitchen to the decking just outside. You can also make a connection by using similar tiles of other details, such as stainless steel accents. These types of gardens are a reflection of our lives—we don't have as much time to garden as we might like, so keep it easy by keeping less.

Contemporary materials

Chunky wood, metals (both shiny and rusted), and concrete are cost effective, easy to use, and readily available—so put them to good use, in as many ways as you can imagine. Turn industrial screens into a trellis, decorate walls with slices of railway sleepers, use rebar to screen off an area, or make your own custom containers from concrete and hypertufa techniques. Combine these with other materials such as glass, sheet metals, and plastics to forge new finishes, shapes, and options for your garden.

Punchy color

Play with color and use it to tie things together or to make a point. Contemporary gardens often use lines of brightly colored plants to draw lines or shapes on the landscape. Give an otherwise neutral (as in greens and browns) garden a shot of colorful surprise by dropping in a magenta set of bench cushions or punctuating a path with a bright red maple. Smooth cobbles come in colors ranging from black to brown to white, and these can also be used to form blocks of colorful contrast. It is common for interior finishes to be carried outside. Try this out by using a single color in plants and flowers outside, then painting an adjacent interior room the same color. Unusual hues work well on walls and other hardscaping features. Be brave (especially if it's just paint), and create a strong color theme for your garden.

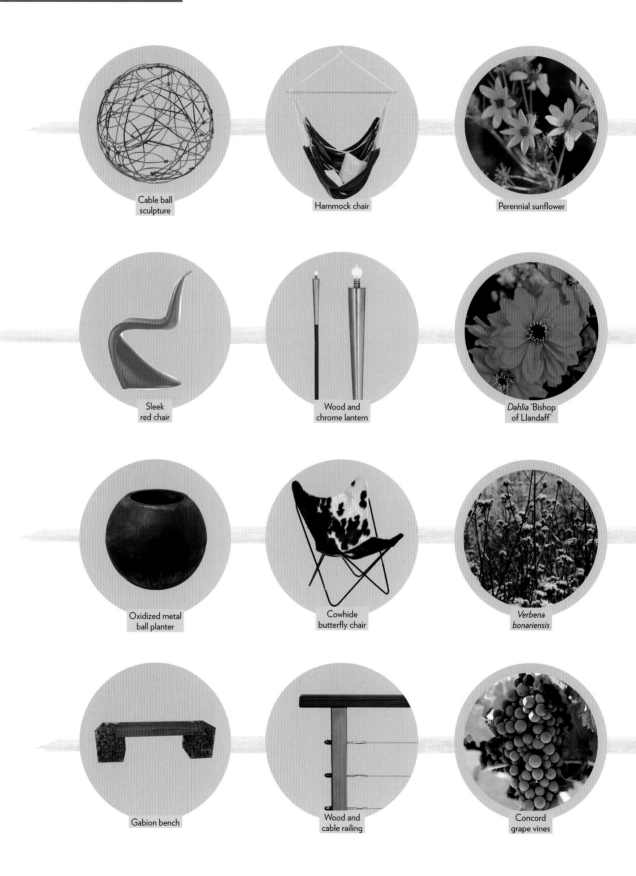

Cable ball
sculpture

Hammock chair

Perennial sunflower

Sleek
red chair

Wood and
chrome lantern

Dahlia 'Bishop
of Llandaff'

Oxidized metal
ball planter

Cowhide
butterfly chair

*Verbena
bonariensis*

Gabion bench

Wood and
cable railing

Concord
grape vines

Ceramic owl

Lightweight
concrete furniture

Concrete

Combine the subtle gray of concrete with casual and sunny yellow flowers for a sophisticated but relaxed garden. Concrete is not only physically weighty but can also be visually heavy; contrasting it with a floppy, soft hanging seat will keep it all from being too austere. Wire balls repeat the color palette with simple shapes, but a funky owl sculpture makes sure no one takes anything too seriously.

Reflecting balls

Stainless steel
water wall

Shiny

Shiny surfaces and deep reds create drama. Use stainless steel gazing balls and sheeting water walls to reflect light into the dark, deep red–flowered *Dahlia* 'Bishop of Llandaff'. Stainless steel surfaces can be maintained with a regular application of mineral oil that will clean and seal the surface.

Corten
steel fireplace

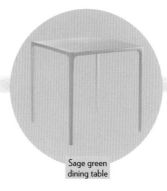

Sage green
dining table

Rusty

The heavy, dark, rusty fire pit and similarly shaped planter are balanced by the lightness of *Verbena bonariensis*. Mass plantings of airy plants such as verbena can produce a frothy, ethereal effect that will help prevent the heavy materials and structures from dominating. The sage green table and lightweight, wire-framed butterfly chair add counterbalance, detail, and color.

Big beads
fabric

Contemporary
wood chair

Chunky wood

Squares and circles mingle in furniture shapes, materials, fabrics, and even plants. Comfortably generous furniture is livable and contemporary. The bench's gabion basket construction offers an opportunity to customize the texture and color of the filling. Black pebbles are perfect for this collection, but you could substitute shells, different-colored stones, or another material entirely. Cable railings help to lighten the look of a wooden barrier. Delicious, ready-to-eat globes of grapes dangling from an overhead pergola seem like the perfect complement to a cozy nook softened by outdoor upholstery with a chic dot pattern.

Cordyline

Euphorbia

Miscanthus stems

Color-block plants

It is fun to play with colors and pairings when planning a garden, but in contemporary gardens there is a heightened sense of color importance. Plants are often used like paints to make bold strokes on the landscape. Turn to modern art for exciting color pairings and maybe even use a painting to spur design ideas for a planting bed. To make these sweeps you will need many plants together—think double digits per grouping.

Canna leaves

Phormium

Blue fescue fills similarly colored pots

Single-plant containers

Keep things ultrasimple with the single plant, single container pairing. Don't fret about trying to find the suite of plants that will all live in the same little microclimate—just use one and fill the container with it. When mixing and matching plants with containers, try to follow the rule of thirds. That is, two-thirds of the total height is container, one-third plant. Or the other way around. Tall grass or canna in shorter containers works well, as does agave, phormium, or another shorter, sculptural plant in a tall container. Finding just the right container is important for making the combo work; take your time shopping.

Tree sculptures

Use sculptural trees as focal points. You can individually place trees that have striking features—for example, stewartia or crape myrtles—but also try planting them in groves. Pleached trees (planted in a row, then pruned and trained at the tops to form an elevated hedge) and strikingly columnar or tall, thin trees also look good lined up like soldiers.

Boxwood

Disk-leaved hebe

Blue fescue

Tidy plants

Messiness becomes all the more noticeable in a garden that prides itself on being orderly. Tidy plants such as hebe, pittosporum, and boxwood are easy choices for creating shapes without lots of stray leaves and flowers, or completely unruly growth habits.

Pruned trees provide shade.

Contemporary colors bring cottage details up to date and are reflected in the landscape.

Fernando & Karin's seaside hideaway

"I enjoy the whimsy of the circular path leading to a bubbling fountain. The entryway of flat boulders is amazing. It's like living in my own little world." — Karin Ballarena

Grasses surround a ceramic water feature. The catchment area is concealed beneath the fountain's base.

A stone entry path through the garden welcomes guests.

At night, low plants glow with the warmth of ground lighting.

This is the family the garden built. As a designer and a builder respectively, Doyle McCullar and Fernando Ballarena frequently worked together to build gardens. When Karin called Doyle (after she saw a garden on TV that he and Fernando had created), she was looking for help with the garden of her coastal cottage. Doyle designed this garden as a lush, contemporary landscape, and when Fernando showed up to build it, a connection was made. Fernando and Karin (now married) share the cottage, the contemporary seaside garden that Doyle designed, and a new life together.

COASTAL CONSIDERATIONS

TOUGH COASTAL PLANTS

Trees
- crape myrtle (*Lagerstroemia* spp.)
- cypress (*Cupressus* spp. and *Chamaecyparis* spp., among others)
- eucalyptus (*Eucalyptus* spp.)
- plane tree (*Platanus* spp.)
- strawberry tree (*Arbutus unedo*)
- willow (*Salix* spp.)

Shrubs
- buddleja (*Buddleja* spp.)
- elaeagnus (*Elaeagnus* spp.)
- escallonia (*Escallonia* spp.)
- heath and heather (*Erica* spp. and *Calluna* spp.)
- hebe (*Hebe* spp.)
- lavender (*Lavandula* spp.)
- pittosporum (*Pittosporum* spp.)
- plumbago (*Plumbago* spp.)
- potentilla (*Potentilla* spp.)
- rhododendron (*Rhododendron* spp.)

Grasses
- bamboo (*Bambusa* spp.)
- black mondo (*Ophiopogon planiscapus* 'Nigrescens')
- liriope (*Liriope* spp.)
- miscanthus (*Miscanthus*)
- native dune grass (explore in your area)

Perennials
- anise hyssop (*Agastache* spp.)
- euphorbia (*Euphorbia* spp.)
- hardy geranium (*Geranium* spp.)
- honeysuckle (*Lonicera* spp.)
- kniphofia (*Kniphofia* spp.)
- persicaria (*Persicaria* spp.)
- phlomis (*Phlomis* spp.)
- sage (*Salvia* spp.)
- sedum (*Sedum* spp.)
- senecio (*Senecio* spp.)
- stachys (*Stachys* spp.)

Making a garden near the ocean presents particular challenges. The soil is almost never good; typically it is quite sandy, with little organic matter to help hold water and provide nutrients. Then there is the wind. Coastal breezes and eruptive storms sap plants of moisture and can whip them into tatters. Add the constant saltwater misting and it's easy to understand how plants can just give up. That doesn't mean *you* have to give up, though. There are ways to deal with the realities of coastal elements.

Improve your soil. Don't go down just 5 to 6 inches (13 to 15 centimeters). Dig deeper—try for at least 10 inches (25 centimeters). Adding compost and organic matter will provide nutrients and help the soil retain water. If you are close enough to the water, drag seaweed straight onto the garden for mulch and nutrients.

Plant low and en masse. Wind will pass more smoothly over low plants, and taller plants that are grouped together will not only support each other, but begin to act as a wind modifier. Wind breaks can be strategically planted to help nearby plants that are less tolerant of a strong and constant breeze.

Give your plants an occasional bath. Washing off the salt residue with overhead watering will help prevent leaves from burning in the salt and sun.

Work with what you have. Don't fight the location too hard. It's no fun to take on an unwinnable battle. Instead, choose tough plants that are able to handle the conditions.

RAILROAD TIES & SLEEPERS

Excluding cinderblocks, railroad ties (or sleepers) are among the easiest and least expensive materials for making a whole host of garden features. You can bury them to make paths, edging, and steps; stack them single-high to make planter beds; or keep piling them up to make retaining walls. They are relatively easy to work with and are well within reason for a do-it-yourself project. But there are some considerations before you get started.

Know the material. Where did your sleepers come from? Were they in fact used as railroad ties? If so, you should think hard about whether or not you want them in your garden. True railroad timbers have been treated with creosote, which is carcinogenic and dangerous to people and animals. Don't plant food crops near them, as these chemicals will leach into the soil and your vegetables. If you insist on recycling the real thing, make sure it is only in a place where there won't be any contact with human flesh, either directly or indirectly.

Check into preservative use. Even if your sleepers are not actual railroad timbers, you still need to be sure you understand what preservatives have been used on them. Newer landscape timbers (produced after roughly 2003) have probably been pressure treated with ACQ (alkaline copper quaternary), which is an arsenic-free substance and generally considered safe. Prior to 2003, a different chemical soup called CCA (chromated copper arsenate) was used in wood treatment and this leached arsenic into nearby soil. Try to avoid CCA-treated timbers.

How were materials treated? Make sure your timbers have indeed been pressure treated and not simply painted with a treatment. Often, if the price is extremely attractive, the preservative has only been topically applied and the timbers will quickly rot. Pressure treating forces the preservative deep into the wood through a soaking process so that the treatment permeates the wood and is more than skin deep.

How are you going to put the timbers together? Treated wood (particularly with ACQ) can be very hard on nails and bolts. The copper in the wood corrodes steel as much as five times faster than wood without. Use double-galvanized or stainless steel fasteners to ensure the longevity of your project.

There are multiple techniques for securing timbers.

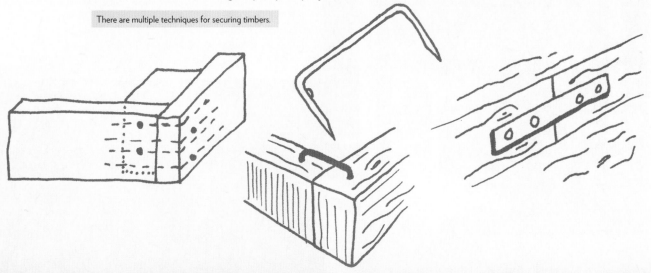

Tropical Noir

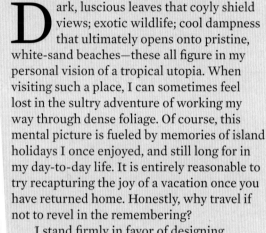

indigenous

D ark, luscious leaves that coyly shield views; exotic wildlife; cool dampness that ultimately opens onto pristine, white-sand beaches—these all figure in my personal vision of a tropical utopia. When visiting such a place, I can sometimes feel lost in the sultry adventure of working my way through dense foliage. Of course, this mental picture is fueled by memories of island holidays I once enjoyed, and still long for in my day-to-day life. It is entirely reasonable to try recapturing the joy of a vacation once you have returned home. Honestly, why travel if not to revel in the remembering?

I stand firmly in favor of designing gardens that make sense for the climate and culture of a place. But I see nothing wrong with incorporating ideas from wherever they may come and distilling them into something that uniquely fits your world. Big leaves that cast long shadows are right in the tropics, but they can also be right in more temperate places. Tropical gardens luxuriously transport guests to a place that holds intrigue and encourages a relaxed party. If you can make it work in your climate (and that is what this chapter is about), then why not? So let your garden feel otherworldly and give yourself a secret haven where you can escape and sip kitschy, fruity cocktails whenever you want.

mysterious

bold

exotic

jungle

Get hot with color

Tropical style is bold and bright. It easily incorporates wild colors that range from dazzling pinks and bright purples to sunny yellows and citrus greens. When planning greenery, furniture, and accessories, mix together colors that might normally stretch the limits of sensibility. Try lavender and coral pink, aqua and deep lilac, lemon and fuchsia. Keep the intensity of the colors the same and you almost can't go wrong. In this garden, walls painted sunset pink, tropical orange, and hot coral clearly set the tropical mood.

Plan to entertain

Sipping glamorous (or kitsch) cocktails and whiling away the days requires gracious seating and lounging areas. Make sure that large cushions (emblazoned with island motifs or tropical plants) keep guests comfortable. Sandy floors, grassy paths, weathered wood, and hammocks strung between trees all lit with a nearby tiki torch or two will set the laid-back vibe. No one wants to be rushed away and no one wants to know that the rest of the world is carrying on outside of this place.

Plant densely

Tame the jungle by building layer upon layer of texture and color and form. Tropical gardens require that from the canopy down to the vine-covered floor there is something to look at, and that it is all orchestrated to maximize space and celebrate the often absurdly large-scaled features of exotic plants.

OUTDOOR SHOWERS

The steamy heat of the jungle or a hot day mowing can make anyone wish for the cooling rinse of a shower. Outdoor showers aren't just for those who live beachside; they can be a great addition to any garden.

- Site your shower near the house so that towels and supplies are handy, and heading inside afterward is convenient.

- Remember to balance the need for privacy with a sense of outdoor openness. Fully explore all the viewing angles of the shower to ensure the protection you desire.

- Get imaginative with materials. Stone, decking, and permanent structures can be built, or keep it simple and buy a kit that can be moved around the garden.

- Decide if you want a cool shower that is just for quick rinsing, or if you prefer the full hot/cold experience. You can also pick one temperature (warm), in order to keep the fixtures simple. By mixing the hot and cold water with an inside valve that can be shut off, and attaching a short length of hose, you can make the shower easy to winterize—just remove and drain during the freezing season.

Bahamian naturalist

Classic tropical furniture and materials generally highlight teak, rattan, jute, wicker, and bamboo. These materials can be used in furniture, accessories, and structures. Keep the colors natural with a burst of something bright (such as red lights) to stave off boredom.

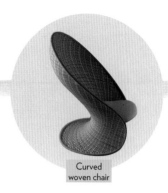

Curved woven chair

Modern tiki

Hawaiian and Polynesian elements combined with modern casual furniture prevent the look from becoming too thematic. Add in gauzy mosquito net curtains and textiles with a retro-modern feel to complete the look.

Wooden beach chair

Rain forest resort

Sexy resorts that beckon couples to spend weeks together wearing nothing but bathing gear are often graced with the warmth of dark tropical woods. Mood and diffused lighting, provided by candle lanterns and fixtures, add to the vibe. Big tropical prints are a relief from all the overtly dark tones.

Dark wicker chaise

Laid-back leafy

Overstuffed, beanbag-like furniture in tropical hues encourages lounging. Give relaxed furniture a bit of structure by accessorizing with a funky floral fabric in tropical colors. Match characteristics; the buff-colored container keeps it smart by playing to classical tropical motifs (such as the pineapple) in a modern way.

Soft stuffed chair

Red industrial
lantern

Stone bowls

Green
tropical fabric

Grass umbrella

Colorful lanterns

Mosquito curtain

Polynesian-
inspired pattern

Tiki totem

Outdoor
floor lamp

Rattan hurricane
lanterns

Hibiscus
print fabric

Drum-like
planter

Geometric
bird feeder

Bamboo and
burlap lantern

Vintage tropical
print fabric

Buff pineapple
planter

CREATE A COLD-HARDY JUNGLE

Cool rain forests, otherwise known as montane rain forests, are just like the warm, moist tropical places we readily think of, but they are in cool, temperate areas. These naturally occurring environments prove it's not such a stretch to consider planting or designing with a tropical look in cool climates.

- Tropical plants—many of which we temperate-climate dwellers know as houseplants—are fast growers. They cannot be left to face the winter alone, but their fast growth can make them easy successes if you move them into the garden just for the summer.

- Plan to protect tender plants in the winter. This likely means digging them up and storing them indoors.

- Plant windbreaks to establish warmer microclimates in your garden.

- Use deep-black-colored compost, which will help warm up your soil faster.

- Use container plants (and set them within planting beds among hardy evergreens), to keep the garden easy to manage at season's end when it all must be removed and protected.

- Big leaves and tropical-looking plants exist beyond the tropics. Don't be afraid to opt for hardy-to-your-zone plants that have similar features. There are cold-tolerant palms, ferns, and cannas. And gunnera, rhubarb, butterbur, and others can easily fill in for less-tolerant exotics.

Staghorn fern

Epiphytic plants

Orchid

Epiphytic plants rely on other plants for support. They are not parasitic, but they are capable of rooting themselves to the other plant species, which helps them gather the nutrients they need. The rain forest is home to nearly half the known epiphytic plant species. Orchids, dangling Spanish moss, *tillandsia* (airplants), mosses, lichens, ferns, and bromeliads are all examples. These plants help form the layered textures of the tropical garden when grown over other garden plants.

Bromeliad flower

A sizable tree stump supports epiphytic plantings.

Tillandsia and moss

Tree ferns

Banana tree

Taro leaves

Big leaves

The bold foliage of large-leaved plants such as taro, canna, Chinese fan palm, elephant ear, and banana is anything but dainty. These monstrous plants give texture and spine to the tropical garden. Use them liberally and plant them in clusters of three or more for exotic pageantry.

Vivacious beauties

Tropical plants often have unapologetically big, garish, flowering features. *Strelitzia* (bird of paradise), hibiscus, and chenille plant are some of the most eye-catching and easily found of the bold-flowering tropical plants.

Bird of paradise

Hibiscus

Chenille plant

Artfully placed parasols in a poinsettia tree shade the entertaining area.

Kevin's tiny tropics

Shrimp plant

" My selections of plants and flowers all echo the roots of where I have lived. I suppose you cannot escape your past — not even in your garden."
—Kevin Beer

When Kevin started creating his small tropical garden in Hollywood, he had little to work with. The only existing plants were a very old and large poinsettia tree, two succulents, and a rose bush. The concrete patio was edged with a thin strip of dirt. Now reminiscent of the jungles of Louisiana where Kevin grew up, the garden has been filled with tropical flair made possible by extensive dumpster diving. Kevin is a professional collector, picker, and designer, so hunting down Hawaiian details for the garden was all part of the fun. There are surfboards, tiki totems, and colorful lanterns. The narrow dirt strip is maximized by layering in succulents, banana palms, bougainvillea, and cacti that give both height and eye-level detail. A turquoise fence sets it all off and complements the hot colors of the tropics.

Draping tendrils, unusual repetition, and vintage icons amp up the moodiness. Layered details make this tiny garden feel much larger.

UNDERSTANDING FOUNTAIN FUNDAMENTALS

The gurgling water of a fountain can change a garden's entire mood. The sound, the cooling mist, and the wildlife that will flock to it are the universal side effects of a fountain feature. No matter what your garden style or price point, there is a fountain for you. The best, however, come from the imagination, and use any variety of objects and materials that can bring water to life.

The basic fountain is always the same. You will need a waterproof tub to line the base of the fountain, which is where the water will settle when the fountain is not running. This is usually buried, but if you plan to build something aboveground then you will need to cover this.

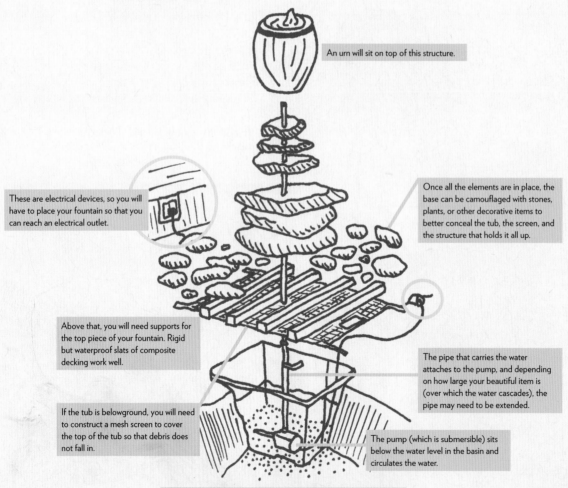

An urn will sit on top of this structure.

These are electrical devices, so you will have to place your fountain so that you can reach an electrical outlet.

Once all the elements are in place, the base can be camouflaged with stones, plants, or other decorative items to better conceal the tub, the screen, and the structure that holds it all up.

Above that, you will need supports for the top piece of your fountain. Rigid but waterproof slats of composite decking work well.

The pipe that carries the water attaches to the pump, and depending on how large your beautiful item is (over which the water cascades), the pipe may need to be extended.

If the tub is belowground, you will need to construct a mesh screen to cover the top of the tub so that debris does not fall in.

The pump (which is submersible) sits below the water level in the basin and circulates the water.

A fountain is three simple things: water (which flows in a continuous, recycled circle), a pump (which makes it move), and the beautiful part (a sculpture or other object over which the water flows).

BRINGING HOUSEPLANTS OUTSIDE & BACK IN AGAIN

Tropical indoor plants can be valuable tools in creating a lush outdoor garden. The plant that is very small when potted in a ceramic vessel on your coffee table can become a massive garden focal point if taken outside and encouraged in the garden through the summer.

Take care when making the transition from indoors to outdoors. Doing this in haste will very likely put the plant in shock and perhaps kill it. The transition process is called hardening off and it applies not only to houseplants but to any tender seedlings that were started indoors.

Hardening off plants
- Start by bringing plants outside for an hour or so at a time. Slowly increase the duration over a couple weeks until the plants are out all day long.
- Avoid direct, intense sun at first, even if the plant requires full sun.
- Avoid windy spots which can upset the plant and dry out the soil.
- Avoid exposing the plants to excessive rain.
- Only leave plants out permanently once the threat of frost has passed.

Moving plants inside and overwintering
- Buy pots with castors or get wheeled platforms that allow you to easily move large specimens around.
- Some plants are easier to let die back when the frost comes (taro root and elephant ears, for instance). The bulbs can then be dug up, cleaned off, and stored in a cool, dry place until spring.
- Other plants can be saved from year to year by taking and rooting cuttings from existing plants, or in the case of pelargoniums (common annuals often referred to as geraniums), bringing them inside and encouraging dormancy for the winter. Coleus, begonias, and pelargoniums are all good candidates for overwintering.
- A dolly can be helpful for moving plants.
- Not everything will be beautiful all year. Many plants are preordained to set seed at the end of the season and die back. But some (particularly those you brought outside in the first place) will be very happy to join you back in the warmth of the house come winter.
- Watch out for aphids and other bugs and perhaps even repot plants in clean, fertile soil to help them maintain their strength to fight off pests.
- Sunlight, air circulation, and water are essential to keeping healthy indoor plants.

Handsome Prairie

Big skies and wide-open spaces call for a garden that augments and embraces what is naturally arresting. There is no chance you will win if you try to outdo Mother Nature, so you may as well get her on your side. Some gardens, particularly those of the prairie style, are mostly about bumping up what already exists. It is kind of like putting on a little blush to bring out your cheekbones, or wood polish to enhance the grain on a timeworn table. Prairie gardens appreciate the views that already exist and don't try to interrupt them; these gardens organize plants (typically souped-up versions of what once might have been wild and native on the site). Above all, prairie spaces embrace the wild and the free.

These gardens hug homes that are casual, simple, and age well. The horizontal lines of the landscape found their way into many details of the Prairie School of architectural design and likewise, the architecture gives us a jumping-off point for the construct of the garden. But whether your prairie design is farmhouse style, arts and crafts, craftsman, or something else, the idea is to evoke simple, earth-based elegance. Deep porches, solid construction, and fine craftsmanship are all characteristics that carry into the garden.

country

crafted

forthright

horizons

hearty

Pleasing porches

A porch on which to sit and gaze out over the distant horizon is not required, but if we want to be true to the American roots of this style, it is certainly a feature that will feel at home. Deep (at least 6 to 7 feet, 1.8 to 2.1 meters) and wide (across the entire front of the house and even wrapping around the side) leaves plenty of room for romantic swings and comfortable furniture. If a porch isn't compatible with your home's architecture, consider a patio that has sweeping views.

Honest, indigenous materials

The materials at hand are the materials that work best. You might use stone fence posts made from local limestone, or naturally shaped flagstones from a nearby quarry to make paths and patios. Brick is generally locally produced and bears the characteristics of the nearby clay and shale that went into its creation. Use handcrafted stone and woodwork in a way that honors the material.

The low sweep & flow

Trees are generally used as frames or enhancing interruptions to a more expansive view; plants are grown low to maintain openness. Grasses and plants that sway in the breeze combine with sweeping, arced paths, for a landscape that has movement and feels casual.

BUILD AN ECOSYSTEM

Native grasslands worldwide are dwindling. In North America, less than one percent of the Great Plains exists as it once was, as most has been given over to farming. Meadow and prairie ecosystems minimize climate change and support more species than wooded areas and almost as many as rain forests, yet we tend to not worry about their loss in the same way.

Creating a garden using the plants that once dominated the grasslands local to your region can help restore habitat for birds and butterflies and prevent the loss of species.

Reclaimed
wood bench

Navy blue
olive jar

Repurposed
denim daybed

Wire planters

Turquoise
olive jar

Stag pillow

THE OLIVE JAR

Olive jars provide a classic
shape and can be used
in a variety of ways in a
garden scheme. Consider
the possibilities:

- Fountain
- Planter
- Elevated focal point
- Large vase for seasonal
  displays
- Turned on its side as
  sculpture

Red olive jar

Copper
landscape light

Yellow
olive jar

Bronze
garden lamp

Melamine
picnic plate

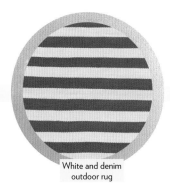

White and denim
outdoor rug

Designer denim

Simple colors and materials recall the hardworking roots of this style. White houses, red barns, and blue jeans are never flashy or formal and they provide a perfect backdrop to plants with a splash of color. Ticking stripes are easy but elegant textiles that happily pair with a rustic bench made of recycled wood. Melamine picnic ware is great for outdoor dining—it isn't fragile, is dishwasher safe, and comes in lots of cheery patterns.

Union Jack
floor pillow

Lace pennants

Rustic romance

Bring the romance of lace into the garden by using eyelet details. When mixed with soft colors and utilitarian details such as burlap, strapping, and wire filigree, it can be pretty and feminine but remain outdoor appropriate.

Mission style
patio chair

Craftsman trellis

Creative craftsman

Use generously sized but well-proportioned furniture with strong geometric lines and little ornamentation. Burnished browns and rich woods are paired with white to keep it fresh. The red pot provides a flash of historically accurate color.

Porch swing

Wright-inspired
birdhouse

Right Wright

The low, flat lines of the glowing light fixture and the similar shape of the Frank Lloyd Wright–inspired birdhouse recall prairie style architecture. Golden containers and porch swings make sure the look remains bright and happy. Yellow-tinted lights (which make me think of sunsets) will help bring to life this warm mood.

Grow grasses

There is a reason they are called grasslands: wherever grasses grow, they tend to dominate. Grasses come in a wide variety, ranging from short and bushy to free flowing, colored, tall, and erect—even dramatically plumed. They tend to have a very dense root system that helps them survive in dry periods and hold their ground in heavy rains. Prairies need grasses to help keep dirt in place; without grasses, the natural weather patterns would erode topsoil.

NOT NECESSARILY NATIVE

There is a constant debate about natives. What is native and what isn't? How picky should one be in trying to plant with natives?

Making an effort to plant natives that have historically been part of your area's landscape helps preserve and restore important habitat and ecosystems.

That said, slavish rule-following isn't the essence of environmental preservation, and it also isn't going to net you a very pretty garden. Native plants have a tendency to be less distinctive than those that have been bred and grown specifically for garden use. There are, of course, many exceptions, but you shouldn't feel bound to plant a native species when a cultivar (the same species, but specifically bred for enhanced garden characteristics) could be more engaging. You can plant the pure native, or you can be mindful of the native environment and then plant things you enjoy and that will do well in your garden.

Staghorn sumac

Eastern red cedar

Wild trees

Prairie trees are like oases that you can sometimes see from miles away. They always seem to indicate that a little seasonal water is nearby, or perhaps a regular stream. Planting wild trees in your garden will help blend your private space with the wider landscape.

Pawpaw

Cottonwood

Create sweeping drifts

Plant single species in large drifts to follow the contour of the land. This will highlight undulations or form ripples and shapes where there aren't any. Less showy plants can gain impact when grouped in large clusters that interweave with other groups. Ones and twos won't cut it to achieve the woven-together look; plant in bigger sweeps of five or more plants.

Adam's prairie muse

"It's through trial and error that the garden improves and I grow as a designer."
—Adam Woodruff

Plantings blur boundaries between the wild and the domestic while complementing surrounding vistas. Thomas Yano's graceful bronze and brass sculptures lend vertical interest and a series of focal points.

Grasses play a big role, providing movement and the foundation through which shrubs, perennials, and bulbs emerge.

Developing a hilltop house and pool with expansive views into a garden that blends with the surrounding landscape has been an evolving project. Adam Woodruff was first asked by the homeowners to help them create a Tuscanesque garden, but in working together they found that particular aesthetic didn't make sense for the site. With Piet Oudolf's Lurie Garden in nearby Chicago as a guiding influence, a stylized prairie garden emerged. As plants grew and filled in, the original blocks of planting were thinned to shape a more dynamic and diverse garden, and now, the existing pool and expansive patio fuse beautifully into the landscape.

WHY IS PERMACULTURE IMPORTANT?

**DON'T FIGHT MOTHER NATURE,
LESS IS MORE,
AND IF IT AIN'T BROKE, DON'T FIX IT.**

These might all sound like clichéd rules for living, but they are among the basic and useful tenets of permaculture design, a philosophy that prescribes working with rather than against nature. The basic idea is to develop agricultural ecosystems that are sustainable and self-sufficient. The probability of a home gardener following permaculture principles to the letter is unlikely in my opinion, because within the philosophy there is an extreme lack of regard for aesthetics. And don't we all want to live in a beautiful place?

But when planning your garden, borrowing ideas from permaculture can establish a way of gardening that is more productive and less labor intensive. The following are some of the most easily and commonly applied permaculture principles.

Use native plants. Choices that are well adapted to your local area will have an easier time surviving without your support, the use of chemicals, or the resources of additional water or fertilizer.

Learn the characteristics of plants you choose. This goes beyond just how nice they look. Many plants can serve many purposes. Take bamboo: planted as a screen for the neighbor's ugly fence, it can also provide you with harvestable stakes to support your tomatoes.

Encourage diversity in your garden. Specifically, don't put all your eggs in one basket. (Permaculture is so full of clichés!) By encouraging diversity in all its forms, the ecosystem you create will be able to withstand the ups and downs inherent with gardening.

Mimic nature and its natural patterns. Don't try to overtake what is naturally occurring; instead, go with it. Learn about companion plants that help each other out. This is one way of copying a natural pattern.

Group plants into guilds. A guild is a collection of plants with compatible roots and canopies that might be stacked in layers to form an edge. As you learn more about your site, you'll discover groups of plants that work well together. The three sisters garden of the Native Americans that paired corn, beans, and vining squash is a great example of a guild.

Identify microclimates and take advantage of them. Dark and cold corners, windswept places in full sun, and poorly draining areas in your yard present unique opportunities. Try to find plants that naturally love these conditions and let them thrive.

LAYING OUT PLANTS: A STYLE GUIDE

WHEN YOU'RE READY TO PLANT

Try sketching a plan beforehand. Use books and visual interest. By working on paper and using your mind's eye, you will view the garden differently and more creatively than when you are walking through the garden center or have your hands in the dirt. Combine all the visions (on the ground, on paper, and in your mind's eye) in the most practical way when you are planting your garden—don't be a slave to the plan.

Unload all the plants and set them where you intend to plant them before digging anything in. Make sure you are happy with the composition while it is still easy to move things around. As you are adjusting your layout on the ground, keep in mind how the plants will mature. Leave space for those that will grow larger, and make sure the taller plants will not shade or block the view of shorter specimens.

Traditional. Generally, traditional beds are organized to be viewed from one side. They have a defined front and back and are best placed against a wall, fence, property line, or structure. Tall plants go in back and layers and tiers of plants are added as the composition is built toward the front, always keeping in mind that something will be fading while something else is coming into bloom. In the grandest of herbaceous borders, the same plants are often grouped in small clusters or they can spread out; cohesion is gained by repeating them. The whole look is meant to create a deep wall of plants that provides a full gardening season of color and show.

Drifts and sweeps. More casual, drifts and sweeps gather larger swathes of plants together and build interest with these interwoven groupings. This type of garden may not have a front and a back and therefore height is less of a concern when placing groupings. It also isn't a requirement that taller plants are in back. The goal is a flowing composition where large clumps of plants reflect and relate to other large clumps, and the whole thing is inviting and casual.

Meadows. Planting in a meadow style almost always requires that plants be within a similar height range, as they are all mixed in together. Singles of plants are spread throughout the whole composition and it is only the trees or twiggy shrubs that break the topmost plant-height plane. Formal and informal plants can be mixed and it is quite trendy to place clipped boxwood shapes among a more wild mix of plants. This is a hypercultivated re-creation of nature and can be tricky to maintain as plants grow and spread on their own.

Sparse and spread out. Common in the desert, this style relies on shapely and colorful specimen plants. Garden plantings are widely spaced, so that gravel or other types of paths can move among them. The format is extremely loose and open. Bed edges don't exist and a garden with this style of planting generally has the greatest sense of emulating nature.

WORLD

222

ARTY ISLAM

"The sensuous elements of a garden were very important on a number of levels."

—Lucy Sommers

234

SCANDINAVIAN WILD

246

SOPHISTICATED TAJ

Gardens that mean something to us must be distinct expressions of who we are, including our interests and our heritage. A landscape created to meet homeowners association requirements or someone else's preferences will never satisfy our yearnings for a personal retreat. Use the following worldly styles as inspiration—to tap into the experiences, ancestral traditions, and cultural ties that resonate with you and can help define your outdoor haven.

258
XERIC HACIENDA

270
LOW COUNTRY SHAMAN

" Even though our home faces the ocean, we are always in the back because it is the nicest." —Jakob Roepstorff

282
BUCOLIC ZEN

Arty Islam

Who wouldn't want to describe their garden as heaven on earth? A private paradise? I certainly would and I can't even begin to describe the places flattery would get you if you described my garden this way. Islamic garden design, if followed with some sense of accuracy, will certainly give you a template for an earthly paradise. Guided by the Quran (Islam's holy book), this garden is a metaphor for a belief system that literally defines paradise as a garden—something to aspire to in the afterlife, but to create here on earth.

A garden style that originates in a desert is going to carry some semblance of those climatic origins. Consequently, this isn't going to be the leafy, lush Eden of western concepts. It is instead guided heavily by the realities of making an oasis in a moisture-starved climate. The process of organizing water, and moving it around, guides the basic design. In the Quran, four rivers, one each of water, milk, honey, and wine, are described to run freely in Heaven. Translated to Earth, these rivers must symbolically all revert to water (sadly; I for one would love a garden where I can sip from a river of wine while my kids romp in their own favorites of milk and honey—but I digress). The rivers, which run in four different directions, and also serve to bring life-giving water to the garden, form the four-quadrant sectioning of this formal garden style. The *Char Bagh* garden—rectilinear in shape, quartered, and laid out in a strict grid—is the natural geometric plan to emerge from the necessity of irrigation.

palace

patterns

يا الرزق من دعاء

symbolism

mystical

sensual

Let the water flow

Persian gardens evolved from the regional practicalities of irrigation. These desert paradise gardens were an extension of an organized effort to get water to plants. The geometric lines of irrigation systems guided the layout of gardens, and the water transportation mechanisms remained as features. Rills move water from place to place and provide cooling. Fountains make water audible; the sound can drown out mental preoccupations. Pools reflect and multiply the surrounding architecture. In Islamic tradition, water is symbolic of the soul, and its constant flowing reminds us of the soul's ability to renew itself. Many Islamic gardens have nothing but water; it is essential.

Protective walls

The gardens of paradise are sequestered. These personal places of respite are not for the proud gardener who wishes to show off to anyone who walks by. The walled garden is a private place where sensual experiences can take place. Make the most of it by including features that are lovely to touch, smell, and see. Use the walls as a backing for a soothing pavilion or colonnade that provides shade.

Char Bagh tradition

In Islam, basic truths (traditions) guide all artistic endeavors. To follow a traditional layout requires one to honor conventional material choices. Char Bagh gardens have four quadrants that are separated by the four heavenly rivers (water, milk, honey, and wine) described in the Quran. This rectangular quadrant garden layout also always has water moving through it. Traditional materials such as stone and tile decorate the garden, and mosaics feature intricate geometric patterns.

Calligraphic, abstract & geometric pattern

Calligraphic pattern, which is a hand-drawn art, is used to represent the divine without using images. This abstract representation of the Quran and God is carried through in other repeating patterns. A highly prized art form, it is cherished for its beauty and is applied to every possible surface.

Tranquil refuge

Persian gardens are for repose, respite, and relaxation.
Unlike Western gardens, they are not made to walk around
in, but rather as a place to enter, sit, and not get up until you
are ready to leave. The pale palette is serene but the ottoman
and the stool lend intricate detail. Use stencils in Islamic
patterns to add mosaics and textural interest to walls, floors,
and anything that can be painted. Sturdy but simple and
comfortable furniture anchors the garden and follows along
with the straight lines of the typical layout.

Garden sofa

Brown
ceramic stool

Eclectic private paradise

An eclectic twist can be applied to any style. Surface
textures don't match, but warmth and color are common
threads, as are details of traditional Islamic gardens. An
octagonal central fountain is common to the Char Bagh
garden. Contrast its aged stone texture with the modern
metal table perforated in a Moravian star pattern, and an
oversized, kitschy, star-shaped floor cushion. Mix and match
containers of potted citrus trees to play with more texture.

Perforated red
bench and table

Stone fountain

Funky fez

Let the ornate mint teacups of Morocco inspire a colorful
design. Aged gold finishes bring together the outdoor bench
and traditional lanterns; throw cushions continue the nod to
bold colors. Traditional terra-cotta planters or corrugated
metal pots with their earthy patinas are perfect places to
house hardy palms.

Sleek bench

Marrakesh lanterns

Cool casbah

Repeated geometric and abstract patterns create intricate
and complex designs. These patterns symbolize the infinite
nature of the divine and are a way of depicting spirituality.
The outdoor rug and the fountain tiles reflect this sort
of design, as does the perforated metal of the lantern.
Combining the patterns and mosaics makes for an indulgent
appeal. The metal chairs and complementary pots planted
with traditional papyrus provide a lush place to relax.

Red
metal chair

Pierced lantern

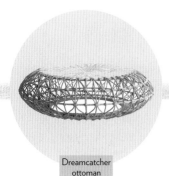

Dreamcatcher
ottoman

White olive
urn planter

Crocheted
star pillow

Potted
citrus tree

HELPFUL HABITATS

Our quest for tidy gardens and a general overuse of garden chemicals has threatened the existence of many of the most tiny garden creatures. Bees, wasps, dragonflies, beetles, lacewings, ladybugs, and others are necessary for pollination and other pest control. By providing a habitat for helpful insects, we can encourage them to live in our gardens, repopulate, and generally keep everything under control. Man-made habitats are fun to make and can take on beautiful artistic forms. Pieces of bark, pinecones, sticks, bricks, terra-cotta tiles, bamboo, seed pods, and other gathered elements can be layered together, forming nooks and crannies for comfortable bug living. An online search of insect habitats will provide plenty of ideas for making your own.

Casablanca
market teacups

Potted palm

Colorful pillow

Tile fountain

Potted papyrus

Casbah
outdoor rug

Rosemary

Pomegranate

Rose

Traditional plants

Horticulture is the least valued element of the Islamic garden and often plants are not even included. There are, however, many plants specifically named in ancient texts that are repeated again and again. Delphinium, myrtle, lavender, bay, roses, pomegranate trees, and rosemary are all traditional options that appeal to a variety of senses.

Delphinium

Potted pops of color

Scatter containers both large and small throughout the garden and plant them with colorful flowers. Terra-cotta pots filled with geraniums are classic but mix them up with different container styles and varied plants and blooms.

Geraniums

Fruit & palm trees

What would the Garden of Eden be without a fruit tree? Standard (which means that they have been pruned to have lollipop heads) citrus trees are common in the Islamic gardens of paradise, as are potted palms. If you aren't up for seasonally moving your trees indoors in colder climates, you can opt instead for locally appropriate fruit trees. Many palms are also used as houseplants, so consider moving your collection to the garden for the summer; this often provides an invigorating boost of light that encourages them to grow stronger.

Citrus tree

Agave

Desert plants

Agave and prickly pear cactus

Desert plants which are well suited to being displayed as specimens rather than as part of bigger planting schemes will be at home in this style of garden. Experiment with different varieties of yucca, agave, and cactus.

Yucca

Barrel cactus

Artist Michael Gough created the mosaic's intricate pattern and ceramic artist Delfina Bottesini produced the tiles. The pebbled area is beautiful and therapeutic; the clients were interested in reflexology.

Lucy's Persian oasis

Soft plant colors (lemon yellow, cream, lavender, green) contrast with the mosaic's stark black and white.

"The sensuous elements of a garden were very important on a number of levels."
—Lucy Sommers

He wanted shade, she wanted sun—and they both wanted a vegetable patch and a summerhouse. Getting her clients to give up a few contradicting pieces that just didn't fit (goodbye, summerhouse and food garden), designer Lucy Sommers was able to find a yin and yang balance in this Islamic-inclined design. Persian carpets that reflect the garden are often commissioned (so that the beauty can be enjoyed indoors during the winter months), but in this case the carpet is pebble and outdoors, and can be enjoyed year-round. Using the square-inside-a-circle theme that is symbolic in Islam for an earthly Heaven, the garden was built around an existing apple tree. Water adds reflective qualities, and loose plantings, contained by more formal planting structures, surround the courtyard. There are sunny and shady areas, plus a desired romantic French influence (see the delicate, lacy garden chairs), a patch of grass, space for his and hers meditation places, and all the reflective symbolism of a traditional Islamic garden.

Scented (marzipan) water hawthorn planted in the pool produces subtle fragrance. Meditation spaces bookend the pool.

STYLE: FORMAL OR INFORMAL?

Formal	Informal
Follows straight lines and geometric shapes	Follows the natural terrain and uses curved lines
Shapes may copy details from related architecture	Shapes mimic nature (and there are no perfectly straight lines of great length in nature)
Symmetry is a focal point	Balance comes from plant characteristics such as shape, color, size, and texture
Best viewed from above	View from above or walk within—works both ways
Historically found around castles and palaces	A more modern approach to gardening
High maintenance	High to low maintenance depending on plant choices

DIY LIGHT FIXTURES

1. Prepare balls by painting them.

2. Decorate to your taste. I used paint pens.

3. Using a clamp or grip, drill a ½-inch (1.3-centimeter) hole through the wooden balls (I found it easiest to use a bench vise and to drill across the grain of the wood).

4. Prep the string lights by removing the ball light covers. Some lights additionally have a rubber ring around each light that serves to hold the ball. This too should be removed so that you have a simple string of LED solar lights.

5. Once the balls have been removed from the lights, cut a hole in the opposite side of each ball, making it like a bead that you can string from one side to the other. This can be done by tearing or cutting away some of the rubbery material.

6. Thread the wooden balls, solar balls, and lights onto the rope. Starting closest to the power source, string lights through a couple of the wooden balls so that you have two wooden balls between the power source and the first light. Then string the rope through these same balls, knotting at the end so that they do not move around. Since you must get the rope and the string of lights through all the beads of string together, I found it easier to do one at a time—first the lights, then the rope, alternating a few at a time.

7. String in a series, so that when you reach a light in the string you can place it within the ball that came with the lights. The electrical cord and the rope will go through the ball, and the light inside will be visible when illuminated. Knot the rope occasionally (stringing the electrical wire through the center of the knot) to keep everything together and add interest to your beaded string.

8. Continue to add the wooden balls, the rubber balls that came with the lights, and knots to the string until you come to the end, where you can knot the rope to secure the fixture.

DIY LIGHT FIXTURES

Materials

- Approximately 24 (2-inch or 5.1-centimeter) wooden balls (more for a longer string of lights)
- String of solar-powered LED lights with balls
- Paint pens
- Spray paint
- Drill with ½-inch (1.3-centimeter) wood bit
- Rope: two times longer than string of lights

Scandinavian Wild

Gardens of the way North are required to deal with the harshest and shortest of seasons, but this style always seems to have a beautiful, lush wildness that is worth emulating no matter where you are. Part cottage, part shelter, and always enhanced with classic grace, the Swedes call this *Mormors trädgård* ("Grandma's garden") because it recalls the casual, homey places that so many Nordic grandmas still tend. They are the summer retreats of northern climates and they tend to be packed tight with plants and flowers. A bit rampant, they are slightly more colorful and controlled versions of the wilderness beyond.

Plants are required to be tough and hardy because they have to put up with less-than-pleasant growing conditions much of the year. There are plenty of opportunistic self-seeders that migrate and put down roots wherever they want. And because the growing season is short, things bloom together that might not line up elsewhere, creating special combinations otherwise only achievable by clever nursery people who specialize in forcing plants to perform when and how they wish.

This romantic tangle is strongly infused with modern Scandinavian design and Gustavian influences, all adding up to a look that is both casual and elegant, rustic but refined, carrying with it a fresh-faced, cheerful appeal.

casual

elegant

rugged

rambling

unpretentious

Wild & a little unkempt

Whether this garden grows in the farthest polar reaches or not, it should still look like Mother Nature is winning the battle—hands down. Wildness is not only acceptable, it is the element that makes this style look so desirable. It is on the brink; it has a survivalist quality, and its rugged, barely tamed beauty adds its own elements of surprise. Don't stress a weed or two—though everything should be planted so tightly that there is barely room for wayward plants—and don't be swayed by a compulsion toward too much trimming and pruning.

Saunas and hot tubs

Even though saunas were invented in ancient Greece, Finland is their true home. The popularity and related culture of these hyperheated rooms is spread widely through Baltic, Scandinavian, and northern European countries. In some places, family saunas are more common than family automobiles and often saunas are placed outside in the garden. Taking advantage of icy temperatures, treatment for many ailments involves heat baths and steam sessions, followed by cold-water dunks. Tubs and saunas can be heated in a variety of ways, but tradition and natural simplicity favors wood-fired options. A stylish cedar hot tub or a shed or outbuilding that is turned into a sauna will provide an inviting garden destination year-round.

Round pole fences

Made of unsplit young trees that are easily found nearby, the round pole fence is common throughout the Scandinavian countryside. Constructing the fence involves driving pairs of posts into the ground and then laying, either horizontally or diagonally, the round poles between the uprights. The round poles are lashed to the uprights with binding cord. The resulting fence is uniquely elegant, but rustic, and capitalizes on locally found materials.

Eco charm

Edge living, as this style implies, means that a harmonious agreement must be made with the landscape and its ways of taking control. Learn to accept wildlife and the desire of various creatures to share your garden, accommodating them in a way that makes everyone safe and happy. Find ways to gather water, manage pests, and fix problems in ways that don't pollute the surrounding area or leave long-lasting chemical traces. As with this pool, incorporate garden features in a way that underlines wildness rather than trying to dominate it.

LOCAL LIGHT, LOCAL MATERIALS

Beautiful, polarized light is characteristic of locations that are close to the geographic poles, and certain colors will look particularly stunning in this glow whereas others will not. Similarly, stone has a way of looking most beautiful near its quarry. The creamy shades of Yorkstone look gorgeous in the English landscape because they complement the other natural stone in the region. Gray granite is prevalent and popular through much of eastern North America, and more colorful sandstones find an appropriate home in the west. Not only is it cost effective and environmentally responsible, but choosing local materials will often help you avoid color schemes that never quite settle into the landscape. To create gardens that feel natural and appropriate, take into account the quality of the light and the colors, forms, and materials that are found naturally in the region. You will have a hard time trying to make a Falu red house not glow in tropical sun, just as you would struggle to tone down the yellow brightness of English Cotswold stone against anything other than the typically gray British sky.

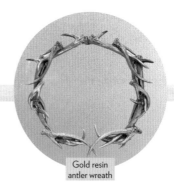

Gold resin
antler wreath

Dovecote

Gingham cloth

Black
picket fence

Black
iron urn

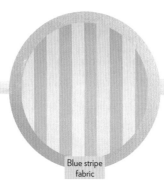

Blue stripe
fabric

Filigree metal
plant stand

Resin deer head
with colored antlers

Blue and white
outdoor fabric

Cast iron
armillary

White
deck chair

Galvanized
drum planter

Gustavian and gold

Grayed pastels and lots of white and cream are the mark of Gustavian design. Named for King Gustav III of Sweden, who himself was heavily predisposed to French classics, there is a preference for painted furniture, light colored wood, and simple lines. A formal version might add shiny or gilded things like this gold resin antler wreath. Informal versions are more rustic and highlight the simple lines of a glass cloche or a modern wooden chair. A garden-ready chaise and classical bust could come straight from Versailles, but an unassuming dovecote is more down to earth. The dramatic juxtaposition between the informal and very formal is what makes the look interesting but unfussy.

Baroque garden chaise

Sculptural garden bust

Crofter's cottage

Gingham checks, Falu red (named for the copper mine at Falun in Sweden, where the red pigment originated), black or white picket fences, and simple furnishings are ubiquitous in the Scandinavian countryside. A Finnish saying that loosely translates to "a red house and a potato field" evokes the same sentiment as the American version of "Mom and apple pie." Poor farmers and crofters embrace the traditional red color and their picturesque homes and gardens make use of simple details such as rustic treillage and plain but elegant plant vessels.

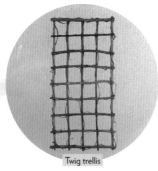

Footed planter bowl

Twig trellis

Black, white, bright color

Long summer days are short compared to the nearly unending winter nights that make it necessary to capture and reflect as much light as possible. A fresher approach to the classic white backdrop with pastel accents is to use brighter, clearer fore colors, such as turquoise. These flashy accents reflect light and brightness. Mix and match styles to pique interest. Pair a lightweight amoeba-shaped chair with an ornate, heavy, black iron urn and an elegant turquoise plant stand, then add irony and humor with offbeat decorations and clean, classic fabric. Keep it uncluttered and only infuse enough color to lend character and surprise.

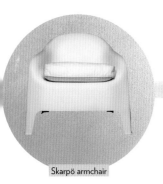

Skarpö armchair

Classic obelisk

Nordic nautical

Take a page from the seafaring life and use deep blue, stark white, soft beige, and stone gray colors; the addition of any other hue will ruin the serenity of the palette. Nautical touches such as deck chairs, armillaries (navigational instruments showing celestial spheres) as garden ornaments, and coastal wall sconces will add detail to the naval theme. Quirky topiary that isn't pruned too strictly and containers with clean modern lines soften the orderliness.

Lavender topiaries

Nautical garden light

Fava beans

Red potatoes

Turnips

Rugged & hyper hardy

Planting zone guides help gardeners to know if a plant will survive in their area. Lower numbered zones (4 and below) are intensely cold in the winter, zones 9 and above are generally considered tropical. Choose plants such as lupine, delphinium, sweet peas, monk's hood, and mallow, that can all survive in zones lower than 5. These plants are also used to performing in shorter planting seasons.

Sweet pea

Mallow

Delphinium

Lupine

Monk's hood

Hearty vegetables

Fava beans, turnips, and potatoes are grown quickly while the season allows, then safely stored in the temperature-moderated underground until they are needed in the kitchen. These vegetables work well in cold climates; their earthy flavors warm us in wintery garden dishes.

Bergenia

Traditional varieties

Plants come into and go out of favor just like everything else. Old favorites such as bergenia will recall the fashions of gardens from a different era. Just like donning a vintage dress can bring soft charm to a modern fashionista, traditional plants will help recall the gardens of grandparents and another generation of gardeners.

Wild beauties

Plants that have an independent mind of their own and a will to live freely can survive outside of the garden and without human care. All our garden plants were at some point cultivated or bred from wild versions of themselves, but those that still maintain that free spirit (perhaps because they are great self-seeders) will pop up where you least expect them and never fail to keep the garden from looking too planned.

Wild rose

Martagon lily

Astrantia

Aruncus

RIGHT PLANT, RIGHT PLACE

Picking up a gardening book, walking through a nursery, or talking to an experienced plant person, you often hear the phrase "right plant, right place." What is meant by this common phrase? Simply, if you grow the right plant in the right place, you will vastly increase your gardening successes. And if you don't, well, you will have to spend a lot more time on maintenance and your plants might not thrive—in fact, oftentimes they will up and die. Even if you are an epically talented gardener, it is sometimes impossible to overcome the problems of a plant that is poorly suited for its location. When measuring the right plant, right place factor, make sure the conditions match the plant's needs and the site's offerings. If they don't, trust that there is always something that will—you just need to find it. Ask the following questions, then choose plants accordingly.

- **How much light** does the planting space receive, for how long during the day? Full sun, part sun, deep shade, or something else?

- **How much water is needed?** What is the quality of the water? You can spend your time constantly watering a heavy drinker, but if you plant it in a bog, it will likely be happier.

- **What is the exposure to wind and variable temperatures?** Sometimes in very cold climates, a warmer microclimate somewhere in the garden can offer better odds for success. Conversely, a harsher microclimate than expected might explain why something didn't work out.

- **What kind of soil do you have**: clay, chalk, acidic, fertile, compacted, sandy, or other? What kind of drainage is called for?

- **Do the hardiness zones match?** If they don't, you might quickly find that more-expensive perennials become annuals.

- **Will the neighbors get along?** Struggles with plants in close proximity can spell trouble. Competition for water, light, and other resources can become a battle to the death. Make sure your plants play well together.

- **Do you have site issues** such as shallow dirt depths, or overhead wires and rooflines? If they obstruct growth, plant choices will be impacted.

Red currant

Gooseberry

Raspberry

Bountiful berries

Currants, gooseberries, and raspberries are staples of northern gardens and provide the basics for lots of sweets and desserts. These prolific producers can be planted in their own berry patch or used as backdrop shrubs at boundaries or in large beds.

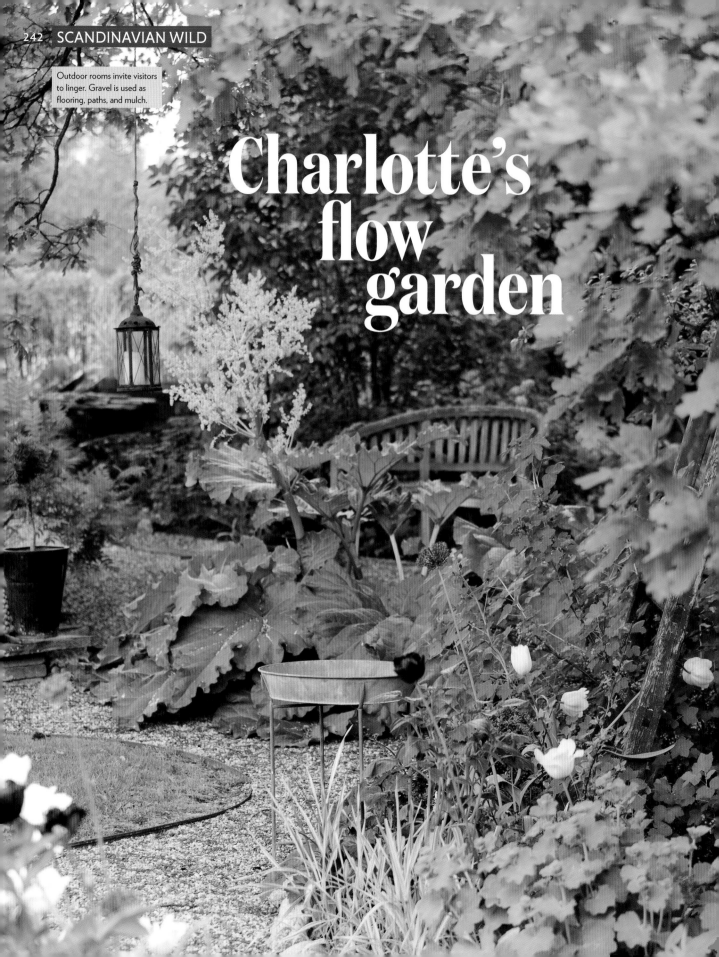

Outdoor rooms invite visitors to linger. Gravel is used as flooring, paths, and mulch.

Charlotte's flow garden

When summer comes, everything moves outside. From breakfast to dinner and as much time in between as possible, the garden is the place to be. Charlotte's garden is a laboratory for her writing and photography, as well as a cherished place for her to spend the relaxed time she considers essential for her well-being. "Gardening for me is health care and a place of desire and creativity, but also rest and recovery," she says. Like most gardens, this is a place in flux; every year the place is expanded (lovingly, by the hands of Charlotte and her family) and new construction projects are undertaken to grow the garden and explore new ideas.

Furniture and accessories add decorative interest and make the garden more livable.

As the garden evolves, Charlotte plans to add a large rose garden.

"With pots, stools, small tables, seating areas, statues, columns, and other things, I furnish the different rooms in the garden. I like the feeling."
—Charlotte Andersson

An old stove, moved outside, warms the garden.

MAKING MICROCLIMATES & STRETCHING THE SEASON

Where the growing season is short, there are many tricks that gardeners can employ to make garden time last a little longer. Highly practical changes can physically alter the conditions of a site, allowing plants to produce or grow longer, but there are also design tricks that make for a garden that retains its beauty through the fall and into the winter.

A microclimate is an area whose growing conditions are different from the surroundings. Warmer or colder, wetter or drier, a microclimate that already exists can be enhanced, or new areas can be created with a little planning. Here are some of the things that impact microclimates.

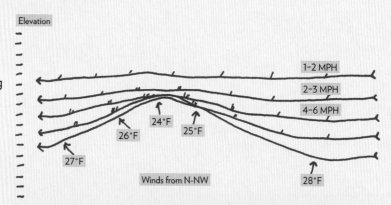

Elevation

1–2 MPH
2–3 MPH
4–6 MPH

24°F
26°F
25°F
27°F
28°F

Winds from N-NW

Elevated decks, balconies, and roof gardens. These will not benefit from the effects of ground warming. Plants in these areas will likely be more prone to damage by cold winds that can freeze roots and aboveground foliage. You may have to consider that this placement is a zone or two colder than the rest of the garden. Moving plants into a garage or shed or at least to ground level will help them withstand the cold season.

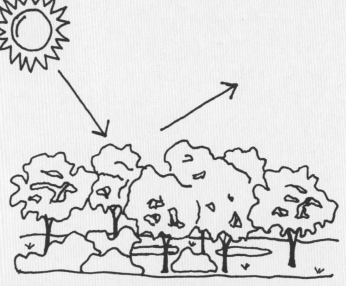

Raised beds (particularly those facing south or toward the equator). Beds that are set above the surrounding ground can help soil thaw and drain earlier in the spring, allowing for a head start on a garden.

Trees and needy plants. These can not only block sun from reaching plants underneath, but can also be competitive, causing less-aggressive plants to not get all the resources they need.

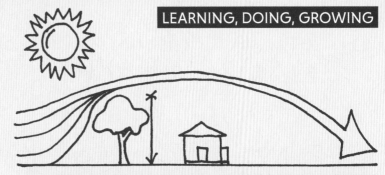

EXTENDING THE SEASON

- **Use protection.** Cold frames, plastic covers, individual plant cloches, and hoophouses will all warm garden temperatures, allowing plants to grow earlier or later in the season.

- **Mulch and insulate.** A nice insulating layer will protect roots and help retain ground heat. Adding leaves, hay, or other mulch late in the season will help plants grow later into the fall and may also help them better survive the winter.

- **Choose long-lasting plants.** Enduring garden all-stars have beautiful flowers or features in the summer and interesting characteristics in the fall and winter. Look for plants that have a pleasing overall shape, notable seed heads, or a distinct appearance in snow and frost. Evergreens often fall into this category.

Adjustments around the house. Your home will absorb and radiate heat and it will change the way that air moves. Depending on the direction of the prevailing winds, you may find that warmer zones exist on the opposite side of the house. Wind patterns change their flow around your home and turbulence forms on the edges. It is possible that turbulent, higher wind speeds will cause extra damage to tender plants located at the corners of buildings, so protect vulnerable plants by planting them on the protected side of the house, away from the building's edges.

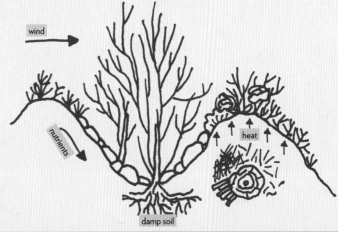

Certain soils. In some cases, soil can alter the effects of ground frost. The air pockets in lighter soils are more insulating to lower soils, but more prone to ground-level frost, whereas heavy clay soils will act like paved surfaces and help to moderate surrounding temperatures.

Topographic effects. Deep valleys, hilltop locations, large bodies of water, and even groups of buildings (as in urban areas) will all have more significant and less controllable effects on microclimates and may give rise to extended areas (such as entire valleys or hillsides) that behave outside the expected hardiness zone.

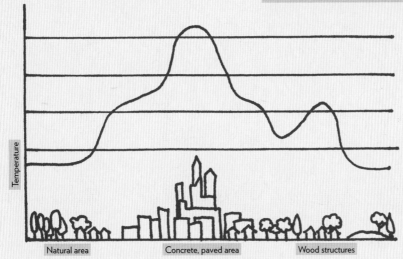

Fences and walls. Edifices can protect plants from wind by creating sheltered areas, but they can also produce areas where cold air gets trapped—making the possibility for damage even worse. Pay attention to how frost melts in these areas; if it is the last place to thaw, it's likely that cold air is being trapped.

Rocks, ponds, and paved surfaces. These gather heat and radiate it slowly at night; the reflected heat can make for a milder adjacent climate. Paved surfaces can also alter water flow if they are impermeable, and may create spots that are wetter than elsewhere.

Sophisticated Taj

romance

Taj means "crown" in Hindi, and there is a definite majesty to this style of garden. Like a good Bollywood movie, it combines a global fusion of cultures and traditions to tell a romantic, captivating, and altogether wonderful (if sometimes over-the-top) story. A kaleidoscope of colors, it is meant to put us on imaginary overload and transport us to a dreamy, unearthly, exotic place. And who doesn't crave a dreamy place to step into after a long day in the real world?

For influences, look no further than the vivid, hand-painted movie posters from the cinema of India, the luxurious saris and textiles that define the region, and the intricate details of adornment worn by beautiful women to enhance pleasure, sensuality, health, and desire. Food, spices, music, and festivals are all decked in bold, saturated color and intense flavor—and so is the garden that springs from a civilization of deep passion.

Romantic staycation

Our gardens are our personal utopias. They should always ease our stress and provide a calming refuge. Making them transformative places can help us escape from the stress of daily life and return us mentally to a favorite vacation, holiday, or time in our lives. The garden is a perfect spot for a space dedicated specifically to relaxing and romance.

Luscious light

Devise the right lighting scheme and every evening the garden will transform into a magical place. Turn off overhead flood lights and opt instead for a more flattering mix of colored lanterns that each cast their own special glow. Add in candles and a warm fire.

Rich layers

This style is about opulence and desire. The rich layers of fabrics, plants, and color are stirring and vivid. Oversaturated sensory excess erases the walls of the garden and transports us to another place.

Scarlet raj

A luxurious Indian traveling tent can take the place of a gazebo, pool house, or a shady pergola during the summer season. Weighty British colonial furniture with its turned-wood detailing provides seating and is kept cozy with the addition of plenty of patterned kantha floor cushions. The umbrella stand has exotic lotus flower details and can also be used as a small sculpture; with the addition of wooden planks, a pair can become a low table.

Jaipur
garden tent

Kantha
floor cushions

Persimmon paradise

Use large-scale architectural elements to screen off poor views or ugly walls and infuse ambiance where there wasn't any before. Import stores and architectural salvage yards frequently carry large teak pieces that can be installed to create instant mood. Keep it fresh and avoid becoming too theme-like by offsetting an expensive-looking, hand-painted umbrella with a budget metal stool that adds some zesty tangerine color. Industrial steel chairs finished with varnish take on a warm brown tone and work well with heavy wood and rich orange.

Carved
teak panel

Painted umbrella

Regal magenta

Keep bright and sometimes overbearing colors in line by pairing them with earthy hues such as olive green. The tufted ottoman is made of stained concrete—a perfectly solid and charming outdoor accent to this drapey design. Bright mosquito net curtains will envelop and protect an outdoor sitting area, and brass details in the lighting and chairs further enhance the rich tones.

Fuchsia mosquito
net curtain

Stained concrete
ottoman

Saffron drama

Cheery yellow becomes dramatic when combined with black. The thin-lined, tailored chair looks like an indoor piece but is constructed of metal and weather-ready materials. Layer in an outdoor rug, ornate lanterns, and black mesh mosquito netting to keep away biting bugs while you're luxuriating.

Gathered
insect screen

Outdoor armchair

British colonial-style chair

Red wall light

Lotus umbrella stand

French steel chair

Round metal accent table

Persimmon pot

Metal rocking chair

Violet hanging light

Large molded pillar candles

Aluminum fire table

Metal lantern

Yellow outdoor rug

Sacred plants

Ancient Indians worshipped plants because they believed them to be the home of divine spirits. Certain plants were believed to have magical powers granted by the spirit that possessed them. Though science has taught us that many plants have powerful properties that aren't at all magical, these revered plants are still regularly used in rituals.

Lotus flower

Fig

Holy basil

Banyan tree

Ayurvedic medicinals

Ayurveda ("knowledge of life") was established thousands of years ago by ancient sages in India. These traditional healers believed a person cannot be of sound body if he or she is not also of sound mind and spirit. Ayurvedic medicine identifies over 1,500 plants that have medicinal qualities commonly used in modern medicine. Ayurveda encourages all people to know and grow these plants for well-being of mind and body.

Castor oil is derived from the exotic castor plant.

Beautiful thorn apple flowers conceal poisonous seeds used in salves and ointments.

Lime

Crocus sativus

Hibiscus

Culinary

Indian and Asian cooking focuses primarily on vegetarian dishes and spices. Though many true Indian spices cannot easily be grown outside the tropics, there are some that can be cultivated in gardens most anywhere.

Coriander (cilantro)

Eggplant

Cosmetic beauties

Indian culture celebrates beauty as an expression of godliness. The Indian goddess Lakshmi, for example, is said to be the embodiment of beauty and her presence is frequently associated with the cherished lotus flower.

Chives

Exotic aromatics

Jasmine

Cabbage rose

Flowers are woven into everyday life in India, and abundant floral garlands are used to celebrate all aspects of the culture. Gardens, and specifically fragrant flowers, are recognized for their tranquilizing effects and are even a regular part of treatment for patients in India with mental disorders.

Faced with a grading issue, Laura created two levels, placing the water-fire feature at the garden's center. Arches, arabesque forms, and elephant accent pillows help guests feel transported.

Laura's exotic jewel box

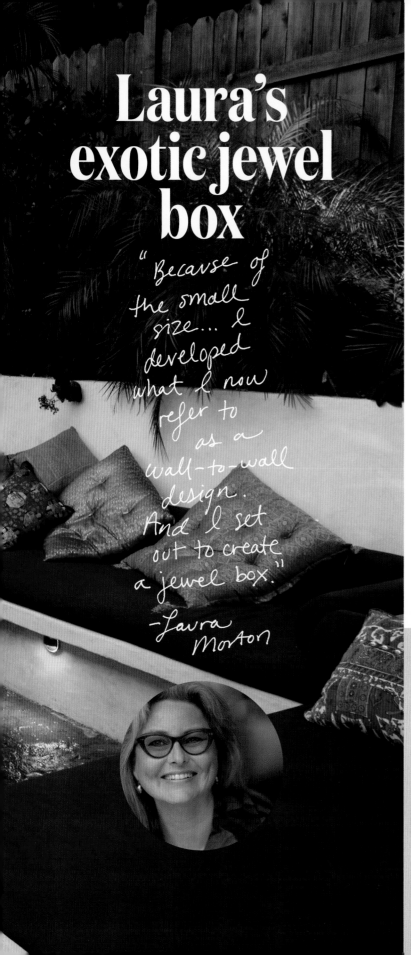

" Because of the small size... I developed what I now refer to as a wall-to-wall design. And I set out to create a jewel box."

—Laura Morton

G arden designer Laura Morton fashioned this sumptuous terrace for a client who needed a place she could enjoy as a lounge, a work space, and an area for entertaining—an outdoor retreat that could be accessed from the bedrooms of the house. Drawing on her previous work as a jewelry artist, Laura transformed the garden into an exotic hideaway. It was an obvious success when, after completion, the owner asked a date to wait in the garden while she finished getting ready. Immediately upon entering the space, he suggested they stay in and order Chinese food instead. Later, after the couple was living together, they hired Laura to design another garden for them.

The color scheme of sky-blue and violet came from a neighbor's visible plumbago and morning glory vines.

Artist Mark Rothko, trips to North Africa, a love of fabrics, the sumptuous mogul gardens of India and the client's own Indian heritage were all part of the design inspiration.

UPHOLSTERY & OUTDOOR FABRIC BASICS

You can haul your silk drapes outside if you want—but they are likely to be quickly ruined. I don't recommend it if you want to be a bit more relaxed about your life (and not fretting over what is happening moment by moment with the weather). I would rather have fabrics that reduce stress and leave me unbothered when someone spills their lemonade or a flash rain shower chases us inside before we can grab the lounge cushions.

There are a variety of outdoor fabric options; each has points worth considering.

Cotton. A natural material, cotton releases stains easily, can be soap washed if needed, and can be treated with UV protectors and stain guards. There are many different weaves, and even if you can wash them, you may not like how they look afterward; some cottons will lose their sheen or nap. Use cottons outdoors where you prefer a casual, lived-in look that might be a little wrinkled and relaxed. Heavyweight canvas is an excellent choice for sturdy outdoor projects such as hammocks. Don't machine-dry them; they can shrink.

Linen. Made from the flax plant, linen has natural rot resistance. This fabric will also wrinkle easily, but maintains a beautiful texture and strength. It can be combined with cotton or rayon for easier care. Many of the best linens for outdoor use are available from European manufacturers.

Solution-dyed acrylic or woven polyester. These are the most popular outdoor fabrics because they are affordable and easy to care for. Sunbrella is one well-known brand whose products are touted for their quick-dry feature (reducing mold) and fade resistance. These fabrics are water repellent and mildew resistant.

Printed acrylic. In printed acrylic you'll find many of the same features as other acrylics or polyesters but unlike solution-dyed fabrics, patterns are printed on the fabric and can be more inclined to fade.

Nylon. A man-made polymer fabric, nylon is extremely durable, mildew and rot resistant, and is also resistant to UV degradation. It can be very handy for flags and screens as it handles wind well, too. Use with care around fire because it melts rather than burns.

Vinyl. These fabrics—which are essentially plastic—are not very breathable (so can be sweaty if used in upholstery), but they are immune to water damage and very handy for tablecloths, placemats, and other applications where comfort is not a concern.

DESIRABLE TRAITS OF OUTDOOR FABRIC

- They won't fade; or if they do fade, they just look better with time.

- They are stain resistant and don't require dry cleaning. (Mild soap and water? Yes, please!)

- They won't hold water in a way that encourages them to get stinky, moldy, dank, or generally disgusting. I like cushions that are made of fast-draining marine foam.

Xeric Hacienda

traditions

painted

Rainwater isn't all it's cracked up to be. It swells, freezes, causes mold and rot, encourages mosquitoes, and washes things away. New England (where I currently live) isn't exactly waterlogged (in fact, it is quite balanced) but the humidity and all that goes with it make me long for the arid western climes of my youth. Cool, comfortable evenings that follow warm days beckon us to move outside to eat and lounge under the stars—to really use outdoor space as we might another part of the home. Desert dwellers often begrudge the lack of water, but I say embrace it. Use xeric (low-water) gardening techniques and design elements from native cultures to create an oasis where you can celebrate family, traditional customs, art, and natural beauty.

Big skies, *really* long views, colorful landscapes, abrupt mountains, and dramatic contradictions all inform the Xeric Hacienda style. Because it's nearer the equator, the light in such gardens can have dramatic effects on the mood of a landscape. It is the main reason certain colors work so much better in some places than in others. I could no sooner get away with a fuchsia wall in New England than my nearly black house would work in Arizona. Bright pinks and purples, electric blues, and vivid yellows, oranges, and reds all reflect the beautiful and abundant light of these regions and give the hues their character. This garden celebrates light and color and works with the realities required by water conservation—while imparting an exotic, south-of-the-border sense of style.

desert

vibrant

sizzle

Mix & match texture

Wrought iron, stone, earth, and rustic wood (usually heavily marked with age) are used in solid and simple ways. This type of garden can get creative with the use of gravel (try various colors and textures to make designs and paths, or to delineate areas of the garden), finishes (stucco, both painted and natural, and concrete are great options), and smooth tiles to add flair and pattern.

Essential water

In the midst of hot and dry, water provides welcome, cooling relief and soothing sound. Tiered fountains are typical focal points in courtyards, but wall fountains are also common. If you have impermeable surfaces, consider channels for the water when it does rain. You can plan for a rain garden at the end of a drainage channel, or make rills to retain water for aesthetic, cooling, or play purposes. Kids of all ages love nothing more than a stream of water running through the garden.

Family altars

Carefully assemble keepsakes and items that recall family and loved ones. Combine them on a table or shelves, along with candles and either fresh or paper flowers, for a beautiful and constantly evolving garden shrine. Freely include the festive spirit of regional celebration decor and even religious, mythological, and superstition-based icons that are important to you. Play with color symbols that are used in the commonly seen *papel picado* (perforated paper) decorations. Some of the meanings include purple (for pain, suffering, grief), white (for hope and purity), pink (for celebration), red (for the Catholic Church and blood), yellow and orange (for marigolds, sun, light), and rainbow for all other fiestas.

Hefty doors

In hacienda style design, doors come in all sizes and are simply everywhere. They are required for making a grand entry into the inner garden but are often repurposed as tables and other furniture. These doors are rugged and romantic and generally have oversized nails and hinges that go along with the thick, rustic wood from which they are made.

Handcrafted elements

Hand-painted stencils adorn walls, and the rusty remnants of generations past are often remade into folk art and used liberally.

Cultured *casa*

Sometimes a garden's style can be easily defined in just a few pieces. Think about ways to keep the formula simple. Here, chair + pattern + planter + other accessory = a unique twist on the look. Use white for a refined, almost preppy, air. Traditional materials such as iron and terra-cotta are used to build modern furniture and container shapes. Tiles in primary colors recall naval flags and pair well with the near-black and navy blue of the mesh chair and relaxed hammock, respectively.

String hammock

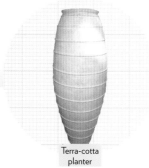

Terra-cotta
planter

Terra-cotta *terraza*

Burnt sienna, ochre, and umber aren't just romantic-sounding paint colors. They are natural pigments and their first use dates back to the cave homes of prehistoric man. Use these colors to connect a garden *terraza* (terrace) to the landscape. Rusty metalwork and furniture that is simple and solid pair well with these basic colors. A succulent kissing ball is a clever and charming alternative to hanging potted plants.

Metal bird
silhouette

Succulent
kissing ball

Traditional *hogar*

Talavera-style painted terra-cotta as well as unpainted containers and chiminea fireplaces are extensions of the *artesanía* culture and the traditional way of *hogar* (home) life. Tile can be used throughout the garden in decorative elements or as flooring over a concrete base. The fireplace, footed planter, and furniture all share curved characteristics.

Mexican chiminea

Terra-cotta
footed planter

Vibrant *fiesta*

An impromptu party might break out at any moment when you use fun colors that reflect the light. It doesn't take much to overdo it, so stick to one or two colors and a few selected pieces. Here the hanging planter and oilcloth (for dressing a table) coordinate, and the chair and papel picado pennants provide a secondary dash of brightness. Keep the backdrop neutral.

Papel picado

Hanging planter

Colorful tile

Biscayne chair

Earthy tile

Reclaimed wood
and iron chair

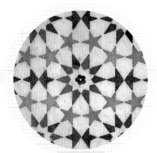

Artisanal tile

Wrought iron
chair

Mexican
oilcloth fabric

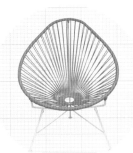

Pink Acapulco
chair

GARDEN TYPOGRAPHY

Just as in graphic design, typography can bring a strong sense of mood and style to a project. If an image is worth a thousand words, typography junkies understand that a simple letter with just the right serif curve—or lack thereof—can speak volumes. These house number styles use typography to express different looks for a variety of garden styles.

Silver leaves

Gray or light-colored foliage reflects light, reducing heat and thus water loss from transpiration, making these plants good choices for the xeric garden.

Smoke tree

Gray agave

Verbascum

Red-hot poker

Red-tipped agave

Mediterranean sea holly

Architectural lines

Make use of what are often called architectural plants—choices whose distinctive characteristics tend to be structural, and whose features tend not to be soft but rather tall, pointy, perfectly spiraled, supremely orderly, or in possession of some other striking shape or feature. Because these qualities catch your eye, it is not as necessary to have the groupings of plants that might be required with other styles. Instead, one fantastically perfect agave (for example) can create a focal point. You don't want to crowd out the view of these plants, so give them the space they need to shine. That said, I often find that where one works, so, too, will three or five, but that is a matter of space restrictions and personal preference.

Roundleaf buffaloberry

Orange iris

Weeping blue atlas cedar

Sempervivum

Succulents

Succulents and their fleshy, water-storing leaves do well in dry environments. In fact, they will quickly turn to mush and die if you let their feet stand too long in water. Use them in containers (I love them planted in interesting bowls and used as centerpieces), as ground covers, or in vertical gardens.

Gaillardia

Showy goldenrod

Blue flax

XERISCAPING ESSENTIALS

Don't assume that a xeric garden has to be sparse or dry in appearance. It can be quite lush if you choose plants wisely and are able to retain a dense cover. You'll need to do more than just buy native plants that are purported to survive naturally in your region, however.

While a well-established specimen will thrive, your brand new baby will need a little TLC. You will have to water even low-water plants in the beginning. Most of these plants are able to survive by having extensive root systems that gather the nutrients they need, but babies and new plants don't have that yet—so you will need to provide water until they establish themselves. This usually takes a year, but sometimes can take longer depending on the plant (ask the nursery where you purchased it for specific advice).

Most xeric plants need good drainage; you may need to amend your soil to make it friendlier to these plants (particularly if your plot was back-filled during the construction of your home). If you live in the most drought-stricken of areas, you may even need to raise the beds and soil level to accomplish this (sometimes the natural soil can be nearly impossible to break up).

Dry gardening is a little counterintuitive in that you can easily overfeed your plants. Many of these specimens will do better if you do not plant them in richly organic soil; a little stress tends to bring out their best.

Horizontal surfaces should retain as much water as possible, so aim for permeable surfacing. Permeability means that water can move through a surface and reach the roots beneath. Gravel, rammed earth, non-mortared pavers, and mulches are all good permeable surfaces for water retention.

Parry's penstemon

Apache plume

Purple poppy mallow

Catmint

Natives

Look around and see what grows wild where you live. This will be the first step toward understanding the characteristics of your environment and using plants that have naturally adapted. It is also helpful to think of other areas in the world that are similar to yours, and research native plants from those places. Xeric gardeners should not only look to desert natives of southwestern North America, but also to the *maquis* plants of the Mediterranean, and the desert and grassland plants of South Africa (just to name a few).

Rubber rabbitbrush

Yarrow

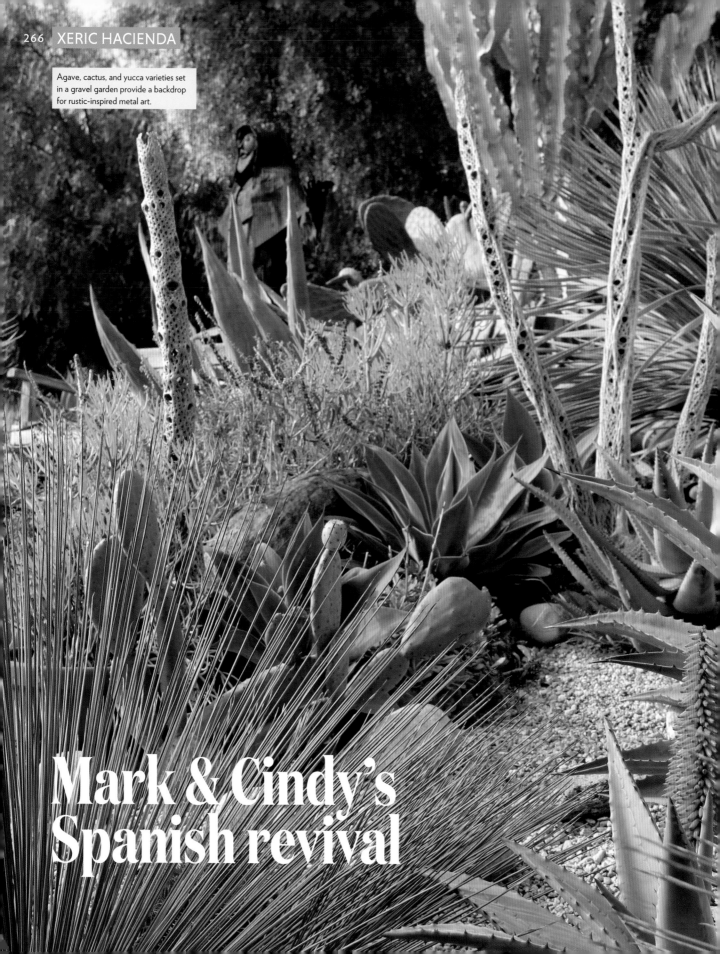

Agave, cactus, and yucca varieties set in a gravel garden provide a backdrop for rustic-inspired metal art.

Mark & Cindy's Spanish revival

"Barrio Viejo in Tucson is a sweet, beautiful place my wife and I love. It has a primitive beauty; the colors and atmosphere are magical."
—Mark Evans

A central fountain is common in courtyards and entries. This three-tiered feature adds lushness to a garden filled with desert plants.

The hardy and drought-tolerant slipper plant is striking against a white wall.

Mark and Cindy's house, dubbed the Bear Flag (after the iconic "sporting house" in John Steinbeck's novel *Cannery Row*), was a wreck when they bought it. They filled twelve large garbage bins with brush and debris from the overgrown garden before they could start leveling, installing irrigation and drainage, and rebuilding the terraces. The garden was planted with drought-tolerant cactus and succulents, partly for fire prevention—a serious concern in California's Laguna Hills.

Inspired by the Barrio Viejo neighborhood in Tucson, Arizona, and the architecture of their home, Mark and Cindy let their penchant for antiquing and flea markets take over. The garden is filled with art and treasures collected throughout the southwestern United States.

FIRESCAPING FUNDAMENTALS

According to the National Center of Ecological Analysis and Synthesis (NCEAS), the frequency of wildfires around the world has increased by over four hundred percent since the 1970s, when records started being kept. In the western United States, the increase is over six hundred percent. While wildfires serve a necessary purpose in forested ecosystems, and are needed to help trees, vegetation, and the soils in which they grow to remain healthy and stable, the cost to private property is spiraling at similar rates.

If you live in an area prone to wildfires, factoring firescaping principles into your garden plan could mean the difference between having a house and not. Practically any plant material will burn, but if you choose plants that are less flammable and follow a few other precautions, you can create a beautiful garden and add a layer of protection to your home.

CREATING DEFENSIBLE ZONES

- Don't plant traditional foundation plants. Junipers, conifers, and any broadleaf evergreen shrub should be no closer than 30 feet (9 meters) from the house. These have oils, resins, and waxes in their foliage that are particularly flammable.
- Use ornamental grasses and berries sparingly; they can easily ignite.
- Choose low-growing plants with high moisture content.
- Deciduous trees are generally more fire resistant because they have higher moisture content when in leaf, and a lower fuel volume when dormant.
- Maintenance is even more important than planting. Keep tree limbs at least 15 feet (4.5 meters) from chimneys, power lines, and structures. Irrigate any specimen trees that you choose to have closer to buildings.
- Use inorganic (fire-resistant) mulches.
- Fences and garden structures should be constructed of nonflammable materials such as rock, brick, or cement.
- Water features, pools, ponds, or streams can be used as fuel breaks. A fuel break is an area where there is nothing to feed the fire—used strategically, they can provide a protection zone.

PLANT HANGER DIY

1. Prepare the dye in a plastic bucket as the bottle prescribes.

2. Drop in beads, making sure they are fully submerged. The longer they are in the water, the darker the beads will become; an overnight soaking will achieve maximum darkness.

3. Drain the beads and let them dry completely. Their color will lighten and soften as the wood dries and shrinks back to its normal shape and size.

4. Cut three equal lengths of string. The length should be about 12 inches (30 centimeters) longer than you wish the height of the hanger to be. Knot them together, about 8 inches (20 centimeters) from one end. Begin stringing beads (I used small beads) on the short end of the group of strings (all three strings go through each bead together). This will be your hanging loop. Once you have enough to make about 7 inches (18 centimeters), loop it over to make the first knot, so that the beads are tight and you have a beaded loop about 3 inches (7.6 centimeters) tall.

5. Separate the three strings on the bottom end, and string an equal number of beads onto each. I used eighteen ¾-inch (2-centimeter) beads on each string. Set this aside.

6. To make the bottom ring that the pot will sit in, cut a string about 3 feet (1 meter) long. Pick three beads that will be your joints and drill a small hole in each bead, perpendicular to the existing bead hole. Do not go all the way through the bead—only deep enough to intersect the existing hole (the finished bead will have three holes: two across from each other and the third on the top of the bead between the first two).

7. String beads onto the loop string, spacing the joint beads evenly. I did a joint bead, then seven regular beads, then a joint, then seven more, until I had used all three joint beads. As you add each joint bead, use a latch hook or crochet hook or some other small tool that will fit into the joint bead and pull a loop of the string through the top hole, so you can tightly attach (with a knot) the top three strings of the hanger to the bottom loop. The knot should be hidden inside the joint bead once you pull the thread back through. After you have attached all three strings through all three joint beads, finish the hanger by tightly tying off the base loop and trimming the strings.

Materials
- A spool of linen thread (preferably waxed) or other strong thread or line that will assume tight knots
- Wooden beads ½ inch to 1 inch (1.3 to 2.5 centimeters) in diameter
- Rit dye in preferred color

Low Country Shaman

It is not surprising to me that Dutch, Belgian, and Danish garden design has developed as it has. Working in a densely populated region that is flat and wet leads to certain necessities. Homes must be organized in much the same way that American suburbs are laid out, often side by side on rectangular pieces of land. Craving vertical relief, gardeners are drawn to hedges that break up sight lines and add interest on a human level.

For all the practicality that lowland gardens bring to the design scene, however, the Dutch Wave roused a renewed interest for environments that were sympathetic to both man and nature. It has become a signature of Dutch and Belgian garden design to embrace the modern while honoring ancient environmental truths. Ancient wisdom, or shamanic knowledge, recognizes that while gardens have become a luxury, we cannot cultivate them purely for our aesthetic purposes. We must find ways to balance our desire for beauty and nurturing with a commitment to ecologically sound living places for other creatures. The Dutch Wave brought a renaissance of wild plants and ways to combine them so that they had significant design impact. Lowland gardens have taught us how to pleasingly combine wildness with formality—and a touch of humor. Though the notion is becoming more commonplace, and it sounds a bit silly when I say it, I credit the Dutch for reminding us that gardening can be inspired by nature.

contrast

resourceful

panoramas

practical

rectilinear

Rectilinear formality

Dutch-style gardens are recognizably rectangular and often surrounded by full hedges, which add vertical interest. Except within the plantings, curving lines are uncommon. Even the furniture is geometrically shaped. These gardens have historically been associated with ordinary citizens (versus the royalty of French and English styles) and are well suited to suburban design worldwide.

Organized utility

Functional spaces provide aesthetic pleasure as well as what people need to enjoy the garden. Generous eating areas with shade cover are roomy, and these gardens are dense with functionality and efficiency. Water butts, compost heaps, play areas, and planting beds are neatly incorporated—often enclosed and separated by low barriers of boxwood or other similarly dense and clipped border plants.

Black, white, & shades of gray

Low Country gardens fearlessly embrace gray scales. Black can be scary in the garden but it lends depth and is often a surprisingly beautiful backdrop for plants. Whites provide a crisp, clean contrast, and hues of silver and gray add a sleek, modern touch or warm patina.

Slide the scale

Oversized everyday items always spark a reaction. The challenge of seeing an item at a new scale challenges our perception of what it should look like and makes us see in a new way—like a rediscovery. Gardens of this style frequently employ extra-large pots. You can play with other large items like lights or architectural details, but containers are a great way to get the effect and add some sophisticated whimsy.

Coleus

Elderberry

Wood-accented planter

Fire with wooden stand

SPREAD SOME BLACK MAGIC

Using black can seem risky, but if done right, its formal decency can be classy and beautiful.

- Paint your front door black.

- A black background will make the colors in front of it look lighter. Play with this if you dare. Paint your home or an outside wall black.

- Large planters are a good way to bring in the power of black. Consider making them even more substantial by placing them on a plinth (a base or foundation that adds height).

- A structure will seem larger when painted black.

- So-called black plants—which are in fact dark purple or another shade, but never true black—are eye-catching and provide a great contrast to surrounding plants.

Wire sculpture by Rupert Till

Modern rectangular fire pit

Soft-sided planters

Red fire pit

Deep purple tulip

Black calla lily

Zinc-lined wood and rope planter

Large steel fire bowl

Outdoor lamps

White and
wicker sofa

Stylish spa

Infuse the garden with spa-like serenity. Natural woven seating with clean white cushions complements the similar wood and white mix of the planter. Garden lighting, such as these tall lamps, can either stand alone or hang, and don't need to always hide in the shrubbery. Let them become a focal point.

Concrete table

Woven chair

Dark and sleek

This type of collection comes together with the consistency of dark-colored elements, but such schemes can become a little ominous. A zinc fire pit and concrete table share a similarity of hue. Mesh chair detailing helps keep things light, but it is a fanciful piece of wire sculpture that makes sure a sense of humor is maintained in a garden that could start to feel a bit heavy.

Galvanized
gooseneck light

Minimalist
wood furniture

Upmarket industrial

Bright red fire pits, galvanized metal lighting, and sack containers are urban and gritty. They could find an edgy home in the back garden of a modern home just as easily as in a rooftop oasis. Simple, sturdy furniture is timeless and pairs with many styles.

Yellow
barn light

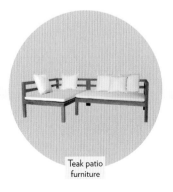

Teak patio
furniture

Pastoral barn

Silvered wood, twig art, and rustic details are kept contemporary with the addition of sleek furniture and colorful accents. Blond wood is a finish that recalls Danish modern design, but is not often found in landscape furniture. To achieve the look, mahogany can be bleached with peroxide, then stained with a mustard-colored pigment. A teak sofa will silver in time unless regularly treated with wood oils.

Pleached hedge

Stately hedge

Helpful hedges

Hedges give this style of garden its structure. Often they are used to mark boundaries, but they can also become playful features. Privet, hornbeam, boxwood, holly, yew, juniper, and many varieties of deciduous shrubs can be clipped in a traditional manner (with chamfered sides and flat tops), or go a little crazy—give them wavy tops or taper them down to the ground and back up again.

Widespread grasses

Add these for an updated and consistent element. Tall and straight grasses can be used as visual barriers and hedges. Flowy, vase-shaped grasses give movement to borders. Short, mounded grasses can be excellent ground covers and edging plants.

Calamagrostis brachytricha

Pennisetum orientale

Miscanthus sinensis

MAKING WATTLE WORK

Wattle is constructed with poles that have twigs or branches intertwined. Produced in the same basic way as woven fabrics, wattle has been used in combination with daub (essentially mud) to build structures for over six thousand years. Without the daub, wattle, which is fairly easy to construct from garden prunings, has a variety of potential uses.

- Make raised beds by creating wattle panels that are lashed together and filled with dirt.

- Wattle panels make excellent screens and walls for dividing the garden into usable spaces.

- Use solid uprights, or keep things flexible (and movable) and construct a fence.

- Decorative bed edging keeps errant hoses and pets from trouncing flowers.

Eupatorium maculatum

Salvia nemorosa 'Caradonna'

Thalictrum

Echinacea purpurea

Rudbeckia fulgida

The Dutch Wave

This planting style is noted for introducing a series of previously lesser known (and used) plants. Dutch designers started using informal and indigenous plants as relief from formal herbaceous borders in the early 1920s. The plants they chose were eventually paired with clipped hedges as experiments progressed. These airy and more ethereal plants have found homes in many other styles, but they are particularly suited to this style.

Verbena hastata f. rosea

Monarda 'Mohawk'

Helenium 'Sahin's Early Flowerer'

Filipendula

Sanguisorba officinalis 'Red Thunder'

Jakob & Yvette's modern Danish garden

The house was built around the century-old copper beech that towers over the front and back gardens. A long, wide, low hedge separates sitting and play areas.

A gas grill became a charcoal grill to hang on the wall. Concrete pavers are wall mounted as minimalistic counters.

" Even though our home faces the ocean, we are always in the back because it is the nicest."
—Jakob Roepstorff

In 1957, during the era of famed Danish architect Arne Jacobsen, another contemporary architect, Vagn Højmark, designed and built this modern seaside home in the fishing village of Klampenborg, on the outskirts of Copenhagen. The garden, which was part of the original design, has changed little since, but remains a vision of the Low Country design aesthetic we still admire. The patio is south facing: a sunny spot away from the notable regional winds. Here, Jakob, Yvette, and their family frequently enjoy a glass of wine, outdoor dining, and the comfort of the fireplace. The simple but elegant rectilinear design includes a trimmed boxwood hedge that is precisely 1 meter high by 4 meters wide by 20 meters long—and very precisely maintained. A winding old wisteria and cobbles used for the uncovered patio provide contrasting sinuous and rugged elements to the otherwise plain garden. Jakob and Yvette love the functional clarity of the design, and in their modifications—creating the grilling area, removing a deceased bamboo hedge, and replacing a small pond with an in-ground trampoline—they have maintained the simple sophistication.

CONTAINER SAVVY

Consider the three S's when planning a container garden. Getting each right will make certain that your plants are happy and your efforts rewarded.

Selection. Choosing plants for a container garden doesn't have to be tricky if you resolve to keep it simple. The idea of putting four, five, or even more varieties in one container is a surefire recipe for needless struggle. Plants are like people; roommates need to be able to live together. Shade lovers and sun lovers don't mix, arid plants with water lovers will not be pals. The logistics of trying to find a love match with plants can be torture—never mind that what you really want is for them to look good with each other. I don't recommend putting more than three different plant types in a container; in fact, I have a preference for just one. You will save yourself a whole lot of grief by keeping it simple. One plant, one pot not only lets you cater to the needs of that particular baby; you can also mix and match, making new arrangements with other singularly potted plants whenever you feel like it. I also like to keep new shrubs in a container while I decide where I will permanently plant them; it allows me to experiment with placement and combinations easily before I commit plants to the ground.

Size. Undersized containers are the reason for most container plant failures. The bigger the container, the easier it is to maintain. Be realistic about your own habits and if hand watering is required, remember that small containers will need much more attention in the form of frequent waterings, so go as big as you can. Besides being easier to maintain, larger containers make a more impactful design statement. Why waste extra effort on something small and unremarkable, when you can have something bigger and more impressive—with less trouble?

WHEN TO CHANGE YOUR SOIL

Soil does wear out over time and it becomes necessary to repot container gardens. It's time to replace the soil if you notice any of the following.

- A crusty ring on the inside of the pot at the soil line

- A yellow or white crust on the surface of the potting mix

- Obvious crowding of the plants

- Roots growing out of the drainage hole

Soil. The stuff in the bottom of the pot is arguably the most important element of a container garden—and the most ignored. Don't just use dirt from your backyard, and do give it all the attention you give everything else in the pot. The roots are the heart of the plant and if they are not healthy and happy, you won't have a pretty plant. Buy or make a soil that is a good mix of peat, perlite, coir, and compost, designed to drain well and withstand regular watering over time. Soil that doesn't drain well (the problem with using regular dirt) won't properly aerate the roots of your plants. There are many good mixes; nursery people usually have their preferred brand or personal recipe. Ask them what they use and why. Mulch your containers as you would the rest of your garden. I prefer to use compost, as it not only helps with water retention, but also provides a slow drip of nutrients to your plants every time you water.

THE RULE OF THIRDS

It isn't a hard and fast directive, but keep in mind the rule of thirds, which is good to apply to visual compositions. Things usually look better in a dynamic arrangement. The idea is to visually break down what you are looking at (in this case, a container planting) and imagine a 3-foot-by-3-foot (1-meter-by-1-meter) grid of boxes over it. The main elements of the visual image will be more arresting if they fall near those one-third lines. So, for example, if you are planting in a container a tall grass that will ultimately grow to 4 feet (1.2 meters), then you might consider a 2-foot-tall (.5-meter) pot, which will give you a composition in which one-third is container, and two-thirds is plant. Or perhaps you have a taller container and you want to plant dangling plants; the length that they hang down might fall at a one-third line. You can tip this on its side and play with the horizontal impression, too.

ANNUALS VS. PERENNIALS

Annual

- A plant or flower you will have to replant each year (because it doesn't survive the winter)

- Easy to grow, long flower life, fast growing, versatile, generally happy in lots of settings

- Dies or doesn't bloom again after the first season; more expensive in the long run

Perennial

- A plant or flower that will grow back every year for several or many years

- Less labor and planting, less expensive, blooms annually, fills more space over time

- Short flower cycle (a few weeks, generally), so ensuring continual blooms in the garden requires extensive planning

Bucolic Zen

Zen-influenced gardens are not something to shy away from; in fact, they are particularly suitable matches for contemporary and low-slung, mid-century architecture (which can look a lot like the traditional Japanese garden teahouse).

The Asian garden most familiar to me lived adjacent to a Gasho steakhouse restaurant in the '70s, where, when I was kid, we would go on special occasions for "hibachi" dinners. The garden always seemed to lose some of its aura when packs of suburban kids were racing around it, finding endless joy in crossing little bridges and spotting koi in such an otherworldly place. I remember the sculptural trees and the overtly composed nature of it all. It seemed like a wonderfully real theme park. I think back on that and marvel at how such a beautiful thing could exist for so long in the middle of a shopping center parking lot. A high fence certainly helped to protect this gem from the nearby sprawl. The garden was transformative; the moment you walked into that secretive place, it was like you had your passport checked to enter a different world—and you would instantly forget that a strip mall lived just behind the evergreen trees. I believe every garden should aim to have this level of mystical appeal.

soulful

contemplative

serene

soothing

harmonious

Miniaturize nature

The first versions of the Japanese garden we know today were found on the island of Honshu, which is known for its rugged volcanic mountains and narrow valleys punctuated with streams, waterfalls, and lakes. These gardens emulated nature's majesty and sought to miniaturize it with the use of boulders as mountains, sand as water, and trees that were kept small and in scale with the little landscape. The idea of capturing nature and manipulating it to heighten its grandeur is also expressed in bonsai pruning. To create a regionalized version of a Zen garden, embrace your surrounding landscape—bonsai a tree that is native to your region and emulate the peaks, oceans, and wildness near you.

Asymmetry

Guided by a basic aesthetic that calls for all things to be natural, Japanese design intentionally seeks to leave things in their most likely state. By this logic, asymmetry is more desirable than symmetry, as completely balanced symmetry is not often found in nature. Use odd numbers of things and employ the trick of placing them in triangles.

Find serenity in the void

Nothing is crowded and bare spaces are just as important as those that are occupied. The lack of visual clutter is what enables these gardens to maintain their serenity. Ground-hugging plants preserve space by staying low and not tumbling over other plants.

KOI

Koi are relatively easy garden pets (they can be very social and personable animals) and can add beauty and enjoyment to your garden. Bred to look like living jewels, they are symbols of love and good luck and are a *feng shui* way to attract prosperity. Keeping koi doesn't have to be difficult, but it does require a few design considerations.

- **These fish are big.** Koi are a type of carp. They eat well, excrete a lot of waste, and will consume most water plants—so don't bother with pond greenery.

- **Koi are colorful, which makes them an easy target.** Herons, raccoons, and other birds and animals can threaten them, and precautions need to be taken to protect koi from becoming prey.

- **Don't make your pond too big.** You should be able to reach to all areas of the pond with a net, so that you can capture fish as needed and easily perform maintenance.

- **Give the pond some shade.** Koi don't like to bake all day and overhanging buildings or trees (preferably those that will not drop debris in the pond) will provide cover from the sun and some level of protection from predators.

- **Make sure the pond is close by.** It will become a destination in the garden and you want it to be easily accessed and viewable.

Urban *karesansui*

Follow the guidance of the most extreme style of minimal Japanese garden, the karesansui, where only gravel, rocks, and sand are used. The white upholstery and the shape of the stool recall the reflective quality and smooth lines that are drawn in the sand, and the moon rock lamps that glow from within and cobblestone-like outdoor rug put a new twist on the symbolic stone island.

Simple white sofa

Rustic tea

Traditional tea gardens are known for their rustic simplicity. A *tsukubai*, which is a small stone water basin, provides for ritual washing, but is also frequently combined with a bamboo pole to create a simple garden fountain. Other rustic elements in the tea garden include stone fountains, pebble paths, simple ceramic birdhouses, and natural wood furniture.

Rustic teak table set

Eclectic Edo

The smooth organic shapes of modern garden chairs are a graphic contrast to the classic zigzag bridge. The zigzag design is also used on paths and is meant to make the follower focus on the moment at hand. Pretty verdigris accents such as Japanese-inspired light fixtures, iron lanterns, and ceramic chimes make for a nice color accent. Chimes are traditionally used to summon spirits and disperse negative energy.

Zen lounge chair

Modern Shinto

Connect with the spirituality of nature by using uncomplicated lines and subtle twists on ancient designs. The rustic bench fits modern proportions, water takes on new shapes and interesting movement, and outdoor fabric displays ancient fretwork patterns in trendy colors. Layer in rustic but sleek-shaped planting vessels and a simple teak table to add to the sophistication.

Traditional block bench

Modern
outdoor rug

Bronze-colored
planter

Moon rock
lights

Wood peanut
stool

Black basalt
stones

Ishidoro
stone lantern

Tsukubai fountain

Teardrop birdhouse

Zigzag bridge

Japanese
wind chime

Taisho-era cast
iron lantern

Rustic pagoda
lantern

Fretwork fabric

Tall jar
planters

Abstract fountain

Teak
side table

The beauty of gravel gardens

Gravel can do so much more than just provide a walkable surface. Gravel of different colors can create patterns within the surface, and when it is placed around plants it also is an effective mulch. Gravel makes it possible for planting borders to disappear; without formalized planting beds, the whole garden becomes softer and more natural. Single specimen plants whose roots are completely surrounded by gravel become elevated versions of themselves as the gravel acts as a picture frame. Just as with interior design, a mediocre piece of art becomes special when properly framed.

Conifers

Conifers are the heart of the year-round Zen garden. They are low maintenance and beautiful regardless of the season. They also come in a variety of shapes, sizes, and colors—so designing with them can be just as exciting as working with flashier perennials. A focus on evergreens will heighten your awareness of variations in color and contrasting textures. Remember that in winter, a conifer will be the star of the garden, while in summer it may be a backdrop to something else.

Spider lily

Scotch moss

Japanese forest grass

Silver bell

Black mondo grass

Japanese maple

Cherry blossoms

Japanese black pine

Amazing specimens

Once you forgo the traditional flower bed, the drama and excitement of a garden must come from something else. Japanese gardens often use single specimen plants for eye-catching seasonal displays. One example is the spectacle of blooming cherry trees: a perfect excuse for celebration. Other seasonal plant displays are similarly feted in Japanese culture. Fill your garden with a few special plants unique enough to stand on their own.

CLOUD PRUNING

You might assume that cloud pruning, or *niwaki*, is the art of training trees and shrubs to look like clouds. In fact, the cloud-like appearance is a side effect of pruning, with the intention to distill the plant down to its essence. It is similar to a caricature portrait you might have done at a local fair. The artist focuses on your most prominent qualities, highlights them, and the final piece is a cartoonish but recognizable version of you. These caricature trees are typically smaller than their free-growing siblings but they have tremendous personality.

Reiner & Gesine's roji

A cultivated contrast exists between the clipped hedges, cloud-pruned pine trees, and raked gravel vs. the natural grasses and ferns, rough-barked trees, and rugged boulders.

The North German climate didn't agree with plants from Japan, so the garden was created with European varieties.

The garden's namesake roji ("dew-covered path").

A variety of plants (not just trees) are grown in the bonsai garden.

"To make a little maintenance in the evening light; listening to the nightingale in the tree above; raking leaves on a quiet, foggy day— these are magical moments."
—Reiner Jochems

An elaborate birdhouse rises from the ferns

In 1992, Reiner and Gesine set out to create a garden for their business; something they could use to experiment with plants and materials, but also something they could learn from. As designers who specialize in Japanese gardens, they wanted to learn how long it would take to start from nothing—a completely blank slate—and build something truly extraordinary. Ten years later, they have a remarkable *roji* ("dew-covered path through the tea garden") in northern Germany that their customers and other garden lovers enjoy visiting. It continues to teach them about the evolution of a garden over time.

STONE MASONRY BASICS

Stonework is one of the biggest investments you can make in an outdoor landscape; it is the backbone of most gardens. Its timeless beauty will ground your garden and make it fit in with its surroundings. Because of its longevity, expense, and importance, and particularly because of its structural implications, I tend to recommend everything but the most basic jobs be left to professional stonemasons. Whether you opt to self-build or hire a professional, it is imperative that you know what you are buying so you can communicate effectively about what you are trying to create.

KNOW YOUR ROCKS

Different types of stone have varying characteristics that will impact the construction and cost of your wall or garden feature. The main characteristics of stone are its weight, its workability, and its overall strength.

A quality like workability can impact cost, in that a more workable stone might initially be more expensive than a less workable alternative, but the labor to shape and dress the less workable stone might be so much that it is ultimately more expensive. Weight may also affect cost, with the expense of delivery and equipment needed to maneuver stones during construction. Strength is an important consideration; weaker stones are not always best for structural masonry. Stones with low strength also should not be used in walls or flooring.

Type of rock	Sub-type of rock	Weight	Workability	Strength
Igneous. Generally good for texture and performance				
	Granite	Heavy	Hard	High
	Basalt	Heavy	Medium to hard	Medium to high
Metamorphic. A widely varied stone with similarly varied applications				
	Slate	Medium	Easy	Low (but stronger than shale)
	Quartzite	Medium	Medium	Medium to high
	Gneiss	Medium to heavy	Medium to hard	Medium
	Marble	Heavy	Medium	Medium to high
Sedimentary. Generally good for consistent shape				
	Clay shale	Medium	Easy	Low
	Sandstone (soft)	Light	Easy	Low
	Sandstone (dense)	Medium	Medium	Medium to high
	Limestone	Heavy	Medium to hard	Medium to high

SOURCING

Since the Stone Age, craftsmen have gathered up rocks to transform them into tools, structures, and art. In the beginning, the stone was whatever was handy, but now we can gather our materials from all corners of the world. Keep in mind the following considerations when sourcing stone for your project.

- **Quarried or harvested.** Stone from a quarry will have been cut relatively recently, displaying clean, fresh edges and shapes. Quarried stone will not have any of the character that comes with a stone that has been lying in a field for decades or more, gathering lichen, the signs of age, and the general patina of weathering.

- **The *terroir* of your stone.** As with wine and agricultural products, the specific set of characteristics that comes with the climate, the history of the land, and origination point of your stone (its terroir) will help guide your decision making about which stone to use. This sense of place will be imbued upon your landscape, so make sure it fits.

- **Ethical concerns.** Know where your stone was quarried or harvested, as well as how and by whom. Foreign stones—particularly those coming from countries where labor laws are less strict—are often cheap because children are employed in the quarry. Or perhaps irresponsible harvesting practices are wreaking severe environmental damage upon the landscape.

- **Know the rules.** There are often local regulations around gathering stones; many locales restrict the dismantling of old stone walls. Wherever you wish to harvest stones, first make sure removing rocks from the area is legal.

STONE WALLS: THINGS TO CONSIDER

- **How much variation in size and color?** Mixing types of stone can make for a more natural look, by adding a blend of textures and hues.

- **How many rocks are chipped?** It's preferable to keep chips to a minimum, and to space them as far apart in the wall as possible.

- **How old is the stone?** Freshly quarried stone will differ starkly from aged stone in appearance, and seamlessly mixing the two can be very difficult. Natural aging generally looks best. Lichen and moss can help.

- **Where is the stone from?** Look local. Native stone is not only cheaper and easier to source, but it will look like it belongs in your landscape.

- **How are the rocks shaped?** Are they overly smooth? Are there multiple cuts? Try to find rocks that fit well together, to keep the mortar joints as small as possible.

KEY VOCABULARY

Ashlar masonry Masonry in which stones are cut into uniform shapes (rectilinear or sometimes trapezoidal) and stacked so that only very small and tight mortar joints are needed.

Capstone The stone that goes across the top of a wall or structure.

Drystone wall A stone wall that is constructed with no mortar. The wall is flexible and relies on friction and gravity for its strength.

Dry-stack wall A stone wall that looks like a drystone wall but is not. The wall is mortared but the mortar is recessed in the wall so it cannot be seen.

Mortared wall A stone wall that uses visible mortar to hold the wall in place.

Re-pointing The process of raking out old, weakened mortar joints in a stone or masonry wall and replacing them with new, stronger mortar.

Rubble masonry Rough, unhewn stones laid in mortar without organization. This type of masonry looks very haphazard and coarse.

Slipform stonemasonry Usually used for short walls (under 2 feet, or .5 meters). A temporary form is used to stack and contain facing rocks and stones. Concrete is poured behind the rocks and rebar is used for additional strength, making for half-stone, half-concrete construction.

Veneer Thin (non-structural) stones that are glued or mortared to a solid surface to look like a structural stone wall.

ACKNOWLEDGMENTS

Thank you for your patience with the long hours and your generosity with the kitchen table (Rob, Meredith, and Isaac). Thank you for the time and peace of mind and a willingness to jump into my crazy organization system (Kendra and Mom). Thank you for the help with all my other "little" projects and things that drive me nuts; their repair gave me tremendous peace and the energy to keep going (Dad). Roanne, Leslie, Jen, Shannon, Shelley, Jen, Cori, and Meredith, your amazing talents and constant friendship inspire me in more ways than you can ever know. Kelly, thank you for your contagious patience, constant support, and beautiful photography.

Julie Talbot, this is a lovely read because of you and I am so grateful. Anna and Bree, I am immensely thankful for your skills; you have been so helpful in refining and sculpting my ideas into more beautiful and interesting things.

I am so privileged to have had the opportunity to work with the homeowners who shared their private utopias, and the designers and artists who inspired this collection. I think I must expand my constant refrain: Gardeners are the nicest people– but so, too, are the artists, makers, designers, and photographers I got to work with in writing this book.

XO

Rochelle Greayer

THE LITTLE GREEN BOOK

A GUIDE TO *CULTIVATING GARDEN STYLE* RESOURCES

(Artists, designers, and homeowners by chapter)

RETRO ROCKERY

Annie Rocchio, Sun and Glory
sunandglory.com

Lauren Block
lavendergreyevents.com

Pam Penick
penick.net

Dig It Gardens
digitgardens.com

Jeff Andrews
jeffandrews-design.com

Leslie and Patrick Bunnell

CULTIVATED COLLECTOR

Daniel Nolan for Flora Grubb Gardens
floragrubb.com

Dotty Dewitt

Ken Marten, Hermetica London
hermeticalondon.co.uk

Reuben Munoz
ranchoreubidoux.com

ENCHANTED BOHEMIAN

Clara Baillie

ABSTRACT VOGUE

Topher Delaney
Seam Studios
tdelaney.com

Tony Heywood and Alison Condie
heywoodandcondie.com

Sim Flemons and John Warland
flemonswarlanddesign.com

Laureline Salisch, Seung-Young Song, Patrick Nadeau, Konrad Loder

ESAD Reims
esad-reims.fr

Tom Sulcer

Jette Mellgren
jettemellgren.dk

Willow Pool Designs
willowpooldesigns.co.uk

HOLLYWOOD FROUFROU

Art Luna
artlunagarden.com

Daniella Witte
daniellawitte.blogspot.se

Jim Douthit, A Blade of Grass
abladeofgrass.com

Eric Aust
austarchitect.com

Ruthie Sommers
ruthiesommers.com

Peter Fudge
peterfudgegardens.com.au

WHERE TO SHOP

DESTINATIONS & INSPIRATION

We travel every day. Bloggers welcome us into their online realms and graciously give away inspiration and information, just as tangible destinations leave an imprint on our perspective and help us understand our world. I am grateful for the hard work that goes into sustaining these places so that you and I can enjoy our visits—both virtual and in person.

GARDENS

Babylonstorenen, South Aftrica
babylonstoren.com

Barnsley House
barnsleyhouse.com

Bernheim Gardens
bernheim.org

Bloedel Reserve
bloedelreserve.org

Cambo Estate
camboestate.com

Chaumont Festival of Gardens
domaine-chaumont.fr

Chelsea Flower Show
rhs.org.uk

Cornerstone Gardens
cornerstonegardens.com

Filoli Gardens
filoli.org

Fondazione Andre Heller
hellergarden.com

Hampton Court Palace Flower Show
rhs.org.uk

Jacobstuin
jacobstuin.nl

Jardin Majorelle
jardinmajorelle.com

Malvern Spring Flower Show
rhs.org.uk

Mankas Boat House
mankas.com

Mendocino Coast Botanic Garden
gardenbythesea.org

New York Botanic Garden
nybg.org

Pensthorpe
pensthorpe.com

Portland Japanese Garden
japanesegarden.com

Raleigh Hotel
raleighhotel.com

ROJI Gardens
roji.de

Tower Hill Botanic Garden
towerhillbg.org

Trentham Estate
trentham.co.uk

BLOGS

Lindsey Boardman, Filthwizardy
filthwizardy.com

Natalija Brunovs
natalija.com.au

Trinidad Castro and Johan de Meulenaere, Atelier de Champagne
atelierdecampagneantiques.blogspot.com

Suzanna Clarke, The View from Fez
riadzany.blogspot.com

Laura Distin, The Ironstone Nest
theironstonenest.com

Linda Dresselhaus, Itsy Bits and Pieces
itsy-bits-and-pieces.blogspot.com

Chelsea Fuss, Frolic
frolicblog.com

Emily Green, Chance of Rain
chanceofrain.com

Pella Hedeby, Stil Inspiration
stilinspiration.se

Jon at Mississippi Garden
mississippigarden.blogspot.com

Audrey Kitching
audrey.buzznet.com

Irene Knightly, La Ferme de Sourrou
lafermedesourrou.blogspot.com

Grace Light, Poetic Home
poetichome.com

John and Marci Middlebrook, Big Sky Artisans
bigskyartisans.wordpress.com

Pia Myrberg, Torvans
torvans.blogspot.com

Fifi O'Neill, Fabulous Fifi
fabulousfifi.typepad.com

Matti and Megan Salomaki, Far Out Flora
faroutflora.com

Mariana Sjöberg, MS Design
ms-design.se

Joshua Stenzel, Green Haven Designs
greenhavendesigns.blogspot.com

Loi Thai, Tone on Tone Antiques
toneontoneantiques.blogspot.com

TROPICAL NOIR

Thomas Schoos
schoodesign.com

Eric Brandon Gomez
ericbrandongomez.com

Cezign
cezign.com

Raymond Jungles
raymondjungles.com

Kevin Beer
hollywoodforeverkevin.com

HANDSOME PRAIRIE

Adam Woodruff
adamwoodruff.com

Amy Hamilton
amyhamilton.ca

ARTY ISLAM

Jeffery Bale
jefferygardens.com

Creative Outdoor Solutions
creativeoutdoorsolutions.com.au

Cleve West
clevewest.com

Lucy Sommers
lucysommers.com

SCANDINAVIAN WILD

Jinny Bloom
jinnyblom.com

Charlotte Andersson
tradgardsflow.blogspot.com

SOPHISTICATED TAJ

Heather Lenkin
lenkindesign.com

Laura Morton
lauramortondesign.com

XERIC HACIENDA

David LeRoy
bernardtrainor.com

Mark and Cindy Evans

LOW COUNTRY SHAMAN

Studio Toop
studiotoop.nl

Amir Schlezinger
mylandscapes.co.uk

Nelleke Langius
langiusdesign.nl

Jaap De Vries
jakobstuin.nl

Rupert Till
ruperttill.com

Jakob and Yvette Roepstorff

BUCOLIC ZEN

Ben Young, Ben Young Landscape Architecture
byla.us

Bluegreen
bluegreenaspen.com

Nikki Coulomb
nikkiartwork.com

ROJI
roji.de

Scrap Hound Studio
scraphoundstudio.com

Earth City Landscapes
earthcitylandscapes.com

Micheal Tavano
michaeltavano.com

WABI SABI INDUSTRIAL

Peter Fudge Gardens
peterfudgegardens.com.au

Dan Kowalski
flippsf.com

HOMEGROWN ROCK 'N' ROLL

Jamie Newton
concretewheels.com

Ryan Marshall
ryanulyssesmarshall.com

Jon Wheatley and Mary Payne

PLAYFUL POP

Ben Lalisan
benlalisan.com

Barbara Butler
barbarabutler.com

B. Jane Gardens
bjanegardens.com

LilyPond
lilypond.nl

Gallagher Designs
gallagherdesigns.com

Blasen Landscape Architecture
blasengardens.com

Stephanie Green, Green Green Design
greengreendesign.com

Charlotte Rice
rice.dk

COURANT COTTAGE

Leah Steen
revivalhomeandgarden.com

Jim Charlier
artofgardening.org

Marquette Clay

PRETTY POTAGER

John Fluitt

Meg Turner
mturnerlandscapes.com

Brooke Giannetti
brookegiannetti.typepad.com

ORGANIC MODERN

Elizabeth Montgomery, BoxHill Design
boxhilldesign.com

Margaret Grace, Grace Design Associates
gracedesignassociates.com

Jakkelyn Iris
jakkelyniris.com

XTEN Architecture
xtenarchitecture.com

JL Designs
jldesignsandevents.com

Flora Grubb
floragrubb.com

B. Jane Gardens
bjanegardens.com

Marnie Lewis
marnielewisdesign.com

Susie Gibbons
flowerpowerpictures.com

Todd Boland, Memorial University of Newfoundland Botanical Garden
mun.ca/botgarden

Urban Hedgerow
urbanhedgerow.com

Molly Wood
mollywoodgardendesign.com

PLUSH YOGA

Suzanne Biaggi and Patrick Picard

Marianne Kaplan
pebbleandcomosaics.com

Jeffery Bale

Hugh Main and Marc Wittenberg
spiritlevel.com.au

FOREST TEMPLE

Clive Rundle
cliverundle.com

Matthew Cunningham
matthew-cunningham.com

John Cullen, Celtic Gardens
celticgardenimports.com

Tamara Codor
codordesign.com

Robert Cannon
opiary.com

Green over Grey
greenovergrey.com

SACRED MEADOW

Roy Diblik, Northwind Perennial Farm
northwindperennialfarm.com

Michelle Derviss
dervissdesign.com

Miriam Goldberger
eco-lawn.com

Oheme Van Sweden
ovsla.com

John Little, The Grass Roof Company
grassroofcompany.co.uk

EARTHY CONTEMPORARY

Ketti Kupper, Ketti Kupper Conscious Living Landscapes
kettikupper.com

Deborah Carl
deboracarl.com

Mo Mullan
myarthabit.com

Arterra Landscape Architects
arterrallp.com

Exteriorscapes
exteriorscapes.com

Reynolds Sebastiani
reynolds-sebastiani.com

Deb Silver
deborahsilver.com

Kirby Roper, Kirby Design
wireballs.com.au

Doyle McCullar
doylemccullar.com

Fernando and Karin Ballarena

GARDEN ACCESSORIES

Balcony Gardener, The (UK)
thebalconygardener.com
Ready-made container gardens, outdoor furniture, and accessories.

Buddha Groove
buddhagroove.com
Buddha garden statues.

Bungalow 5
bungalow5.com

Casablanca Market
casablancamarket.com
Moroccan imports and artifacts.

Chaka
chakamarketbridge.com
Fair trade market for unique home decor.

Connected Goods
connectedgoods.com

Cox and Cox (UK)
coxandcox.co.uk
Accessories, light fixtures, outdoor play gear, and containers.

Cyan Design
cyandesign.biz

Dan 300 Group, The
(Australia)
dan300.com.au
Colorful retro-inspired textiles and rugs.

Elizabeth's Embellishments
elizabethsembellishments.com
Cottage and rustic French-style accessories, benches, and trellises.

Eva Solo
evasolo.com
Danish-designed everyday home products.

Gardecor
gardecor.com

Idyll Home (UK)
idyllhome.co.uk
Vintage, modern, and unique home accessories and industrial lighting.

J Schatz
jschatz.com
Handmade ceramic birdhouses and bird feeders.

Japanese Connection, The
thejapaneseconnection.com
Importers of handmade, traditional Japanese arts and crafts.

Haiti Metal Art
haitimetalart.com
Metal art from Haiti.

India Rose
indiarose.com
Online bed, bath, and candle shop.

Inside Avenue
insideavenue.com
Hollywood Regency–style planters and accessories.

Kirklands
kirklands.com

Karma Kiss
karmakiss.net

Kouboo
kouboo.com

La Fuente Imports
lafuente.com
Talavera decor.

Lekker Home
lekkerhome.com
European-inspired modern and contemporary garden furniture.

Loyal Loot (Canada)
loyalloot.com
Collective of Canadian artists offering handcrafted items.

Merci
merci-merci.com
French design store selling furniture and planters worldwide.

Mquan
mquan.bigcartel.com
Handmade wabi sabi bells and birdhouses.

Our Boat House
ourboathouse.com
Nautical furnishings.

Present and Correct
presentandcorrect.com

Rice (Denmark)
rice.dk
Family-friendly colorful homegoods.

Shop Wright
shopwright.org
Frank Lloyd Wright–inspired homegoods.

Society6
society6.com

Tazi Designs
tazidesigns.com
Moroccan lanterns and imports.

Uncommon Goods
uncommongoods.com
Online shop for unique and unusual gifts.

Unurth Home
unurthhome.com
Modern ceramic planters and garden wares.

Wabi Sabi Atelie (Brazil)
wabisabiatelie.com
Wabi sabi–style objects.

Yard Envy
yardenvy.com

ANTIQUES

1st Dibs
1stdibs.com
High-end garden and architectural antiques.

Amighini
salvageantiques.com
Architectural artifacts and doors.

Eleanor Brown Boutique
eleanorbrownboutique.com

Mecox Gardens
mecox.com
Outdoor furniture and antiques.

R.T. Facts
rtfacts.com
Garden and architectural antiques.

Rare Finds Warehouse
rare-finds.com

Ruby Lane
rubylane.com
Antiques and art.

Watson and Co.
watsonandco.com
Antiques and salvage.

BARBEQUES

Barbecook
barbecook.com
Colorful and compact barbeque grills.

BEADED SCREENS

Hippie Shop
hippieshop.com
Source for bead screens.

BEES

Bee Thinking
beethinking.com

Crown Bees
crownbees.com
Source for mason bee gear.

Evans Cedar Beehives
evanscedarbeehives.com
Cedar bee hives.

BONSAI

Miami Tropical Bonsai
miamitropicalbonsai.com

CABLE RAILINGS

Arcat Cable Railings
arcat.com

CARAVANS

Pod Caravans
podcaravans.co.uk
Stylish camper caravans.

CHICKEN ARCHITECTURE

High Country Doc Woody Chicken Coop
amazon.com
Chicken houses and nesting boxes.

Holland Hen Houses
hollandhenhouses.com
Charming handcrafted chicken houses.

CONTAINERS

Aidan Gray Home
aidangrayhome.com
Wide variety of metal and mesh planters.

Architectural Pottery
architecturalpottery.com
Architectural, modern, and large planters.

Asian Ceramics
asian-ceramics.com

Bacsac
bacsac.fr/en
French-made, soft-sided industrial growing containers.

Bauer LA
bauerpottery.com
Vintage American-styled pottery.

Campania
campaniainternational.com
A wide selection of containers and sculpture.

Gainey
gaineyceramics.com
Plant containers of all shapes and sizes.

Iota Garden
iotagarden.com
Modern planters.

Jamali Garden
jamaligarden.com

Kelly Lamb Studios
kellylamb.net
Faceted and artistic vessels.

NDI Natural Decorations Inc.
ndi.com
Floral and botanical reproductions.

Ore Containers
orecontainers.com
Corten steel planters, fireplaces, and garden elements.

PAD Outdoor
padoutdoor.com

Petersen Pottery
petersenpotterycompany.com
California-based maker of stoneware planters.

Room and Bloom (Australia)
roomandbloom.com.au
Affordable Australian homewares.

Seibert and Rice- Italian Terracotta Pottery
seibert-rice.com

Steel Life
shopsteellife.com

Thrifted and Made
thriftedandmade.com

Terrapot
terrapot.co.uk
Terra-cotta containers.

Vandersar (Netherlands)
vandersar.nl
Vases, pots, and dishware.

Wallter
foldbedding.com

Yield Design
shop.yielddesign.co
Modern wooden containers.

ETSY SHOPS

Apartment 528
etsy.com/shop/Apartment528
Vintage housewares and furniture.

Ay Mujer
etsy.com/shop/AyMujer
Papel picado.

Baloolah Bunting
etsy.com/shop/BaloolahBunting
Buntings.

Bent Tree Gallery, The
etsy.com/shop/TheBentTreeGallery
Rustic wood accents, baskets, and fiber art.

Bird and Feather Co.
etsy.com/shop/BirdAndFeatherCo
Handmade containers and air plants.

Bon Jour Frenchie
etsy.com/shop/bonjourfrenchie
Driftwood art.

Bragging Bags
etsy.com/shop/braggingbags
Shabby chic decor.

Busy Bee Quilting Shop
etsy.com/shop/thebusybeequilting
Fabric.

By Camille Designs
etsy.com/shop/byCamilleDesigns
Outdoor doily rugs.

Cotton Light
etsy.com/shop/cottonlight
Handmade lanterns.

Dog Biscuit Designs
etsy.com/shop/DogBiscuitDesigns
Dodecahedron Corten fire pit.

Dohler Design
etsy.com/shop/DohlerDesigns
Reclaimed furniture.

Earth Sea Warrior
etsy.com/shop/EarthSeaWarrior
Air plants artistically mixed with objects.

Hodi Home decor
etsy.com/shop/
hodihomedecor
Faux taxidermy.

JoJo Shaiken Photos
etsy.com/shop/
JoJoShaikenPhotos
Fine art photography.

Kari Herer Photography
etsy.com/shop/kariherer
Photography
Photography.

Mossology
etsy.com/shop/Mossology
Moss and stone gardens.

Past Perfect Patterns
etsy.com/shop/
PastPerfectPatterns
*Downloadable vintage knitting
and crochet patterns.*

Philly Fabrics
etsy.com/shop/phillyfabrics
Fabric.

Remakerie, The
theRemakerie.etsy.com
Repurposed homegoods.

Selvedge
etsy.com/shop/SelvedgeShop
*Vintage fabric and sewing
patterns.*

Serenity in Chains
etsy.com/shop/
SerenityInChains
*Chainmail decor and
accessories; lotus candles.*

Succulent Babies
etsy.com/shop/
SucculentBabies
Online source for succulents.

Topiary Classics
etsy.com/shop/TopiaryClassics
Live topiary.

White Faux Taxidermy
etsy.com/shop/
WhiteFauxTaxidermy
Colorful faux taxidermy.

Zen Ceramics
etsy.com/shop/ZenCeramics
Ceramics inspired by nature.

FABRIC

Beverly's
beverlys.com

Bon Marche
bonmarcheonline.com
*French outdoor fabric and patio
furniture.*

Classic Modern (UK)
classic-modern.co.uk
Vintage fabric and accessories.

**Delany and Long (to the
trade only)**
delanyandlong.com

Dwell Studio
dwellstudio.com

Fabric.com
fabric.com

Hable Construction
hableconstruction.com

Link Outdoor
linkoutdoor.com

**Madder and Rouge (New
Zealand)**
madderandrouge.co.nz

Marimekko
marimekko.com

Maxwell Fabrics
maxwellfabrics.com

Mexican Sugar Skull
mexicansugarskull.com
Oilcloth.

Spoonflower
spoonflower.com
*Design-your-own custom fabric
prints.*

Tommy Bahama Fabric
tommybahama.com

Trina Turk /Schumacher
trinaturk.com

FARM AND
GROWER SUPPLY

Growers Edge
growers-edge.com

**Nasco Farm and Ranch
Supply**
enasco.com/farmandranch/

Veseys
veseys.com

FENCING

The Bamboo Fencer
bamboofencer.com
Bamboo panels.

FIRE

Camping World
campingworld.com

Elena Columbo
firefeatures.com

Hearth Product Fire Pit
hpcfire.com

John T Unger
johntunger.com

Mod Fire
modfire.com

Paloform (Canada)
paloform.com/
*Modern fire pits; fireplace
surrounds; wall claddings in
concrete, Corten, and stainless
steel.*

FOUNTAINS

Backyard X-Scapes
backyardxscapes.com

Garden Fountains
garden-fountains.com

**NVA Creative Garden
Granite**
nvaus.com

FURNITURE

American Design Club
americandesignclub.com
*Collective of young American
designers.*

Anthropologie
anthropologie.com

Archiexpo
Archiexpo.com
*Online resources for
architectural products.*

Artwood (Sweden)
artwood.se

Asian Art Import
asianartimports.com

Ballard Design
ballarddesigns.com

Bobby Berk Home
bobbyberkhome.com

Boxhill
shopboxhill.com

Brown Jordan
brownjordan.com
Luxury outdoor furniture.

Capital Gardens (UK)
capitalgardens.co.uk

Casa Mexicana Imports
mcssl.com
Mexican decor.

Cezign
cezign.com

Circa50
circa50.com

Compo Clay
compoclay.com
Furniture, containers, accessories.

Connox
connox.com
Inflatable furniture.

Cozy Days
cozydays.com

Crib Candy
cribcandy.com

Deesawat
deesawat.com

Design Within Reach
dwr.com

Direct From Mexico
directfrommexico.com

Domani
domani.be
Belgian-style containers, fountains, and furniture.

Edmond (France)
edmond.tm.fr

EMU
emuamericas.com

Equator Homewares (Australia)
equatorhomewares.com

Fab
fab.com
Flash sale site offering a wide variety of homegoods.

Fermob
fermob.com
French outdoor furniture.

Flipp
flippsf.com

Fousse
fousse.nl
Playful Dutch-designed furniture.

Freedom (Australia)
freedom.com.au

Freeline (Netherlands)
free-line.nl

Frontgate
frontgate.com

FURNITURE AND ACCESSORIES

Amazon
amazon.com

Galanter and Jones
galanterandjones.com
Heated furniture.

Garden Items (UK)
gardenitems.co.uk

Graham and Green (UK)
grahamandgreen.co.uk

Halo via GJ Styles
gjstyles.com

Hayneedle
hayneedle.com

HomArt
homart.com

Home Decorators
homedecorators.com

Home Garden and Patio
homegardenandpatio.com

Hudson Furniture
hudsonfurnitureinc.com
Furniture that celebrates the form and texture of the trees it is made from.

Iconic Dutch
iconicdutch.com

Ikea
ikea.com

Il Giardino Di Legno (Italy)
ilgiardinodilegno.it

Innit Designs
innitdesigns.com
Acapulco chairs and modern Mexican furniture.

Ipe Furniture
ipefurniture.com

Iron Accents
ironaccents.com
Iron furniture and decor.

Janus et Cie
janusetcie.com

Jason Phillips Design
jasonphillipsdesign.prosite.com
Industrial and graphic furniture.

Jayson Home
jaysonhome.com

John Kelly Furniture
johnkellyfurniture.com

Joss and Main
jossandmain.com

Kathy Kuo Home
kathykuohome.com

Kenneth Cobonpue
kennethcobonpue.com

Layla Grayce
laylagrayce.com

Linens and Things
lnt.com

Loll Design
lolldesigns.com
Modern outdoor furniture from recycled plastics.

Massant (Belgium)
massant.com
Reproduction outdoor chairs from the 17th, 18th and 19th centuries.

Milan Direct
milandirect.com.au

Micheal Trapp
michaeltrapp.com

Mod Livin
modlivin.com

Modernica
modernica.net

My Own Bali
myownbali.com

Nectar Imports
shopnectar.com

Nest Vintage Modern
nestvintagemodern.com

Niche
nichebeverly.com
Los Angeles–based, high-end contemporary furniture.

Nova 68
nova68.com

One Kings Lane
onekingslane.com

Organic Modernism
organicmodernism.com

Padma's Plantation
padmasplantation.com

Paola Lenti (Italy)
paolalenti.it
Modern outdoor furniture, lighting, and pavilions.

Pfeifer Studio
pfeiferstudio.com

Phillips Collection, The
phillipscollection.com

Pier 1 Imports
pier1.com

Plodes
plodes.com
Furniture and fire.

POLaRt
polartdesigns.com

Potted Store
pottedstore.com

Pottery Barn
potterybarn.com

Pure Modern
puremodern.com

Red Modern Furniture
redmodernfurniture.com

Reed Bros Furniture
reedbrosfurniture.com

Relax Tribe (Europe)
relaxtribe.com

Revival Home and Garden
revivalhomeandgarden.com

Room and Board
roomandboard.com

Rosenberry Rooms
rosenberryrooms.com
Modern and green kids' gear.

Royal Botania
royalbotania.com

Serena and Lily
serenaandlily.com

Shop Horne
shophorne.com

Skargaarden (Europe)
skargaarden.com

Slide Design (Italy)
slidedesign.it

Soane (UK)
soane.co.uk

Strathwood Patio Furniture
strathwoodpatiofurniture.com

Studio Liscious
liscious.com

Target
target.com

Terrain
shopterrain.com

Foundary, The
thefoundary.com
Modern, rustic, industrial, and mid-century furnishings.

Tine K
tinekhome.com

Tolix
tolix.fr/en

Un Jenesaisquoi deco (France)
unjenesaisquoi-deco.fr

Unica Home
unicahome.com

Urban Barn (Canada)
urbanbarn.com

Urban Outfitters
ubanoutfitters.com

Vivaterra
vivaterra.com

Wayfair
wayfair.com

West Elm
westelm.com

World Market
worldmarket.com

Worlds Away
worlds-away.com

Y Living
yliving.com

Yorkwood Furniture Co.
yorkwoodco.com

Z Gallerie
zgallerie.com

Zachary A Design
zacharyadesign.com
Lightweight concrete furniture.

GABIONS

Midwest Construction Products
gabionbaskets.net

GREENHOUSES

Keder Greenhouses (UK)
kedergreenhouse.co.uk

The Greenhouse People (UK)
greenhousepeople.co.uk

HAMMOCKS

KW Hammocks
kwhammocks.com

INDUSTRIAL / POTTING SINKS

Alape
alape.com

LATTICE

Lattice Stix
latticestix.com

LIGHTING

Arroyo Craftsman
arroyo-craftsman.com

Barn Light Electric
barnlightelectric.com

Bellacor
bellacor.com

Coe Studios
coestudios.com

HANDMADE LIGHTS

Coleen and Company
coleenandcompany.com

Destination Lighting
destinationlighting.com

Manufactum
manufactum.com
Lighting and other accessories.

Moda Flame
modaflame.com
Tabletop lighting and fire features.

My Light Source
mylightsource.com

Paloform
paloform.com
Lighting and fire features.

Serralunga
serralunga.com

Shades of Light
shadesoflight.com

Vintage Marquee Lights
vintagemarqueelights.com

Y Lighting
ylighting.com

NATURAL POOLS

Bionova Natural Pools
bionovanaturalpools.com

Lily Pond Natural Pools (Netherlands)
lilypond.nl

NURSERIES AND PLANTS

A Plant Affair (Southern California)
plantaffair.com

Annie's Annuals (Southern California)
anniesannuals.com

Bailey Nursery
baileynurseries.com

Blue Stone Perennials
bluestoneperennials.com

Classic Nursery (Washington)
classicnursery.com

Dancing Oaks Nursery
dancingoaks.com

Detroit Garden Works (Michigan)
detroitgardenworks.com

Flora Grubb Nursery (San Francisco, California)
floragrubb.com

High Country Gardens (Sante Fe, New Mexico)
highcountrygardens.com

Lambley Nursery (Australia)
lambley.com.au

Moss and Stone Gardens
mossandstonegardens.com

Proven Winners
provenwinners.com

Rolling Green Nursery (Southern California)
rollinggreensnursery.com

Snug Harbor Farm (Southern Maine)
snugharborfarm.com

Terrain (Pennsylvania and New York)
shopterrain.com

Wildflower Farm (Canada)
wildflowerfarm.com

Winston Flowers (Boston)
winstonsflowers.com

Briellaerd Nursery (Netherlands)
briellaerd.nl

Crocus (UK)
crocus.co.uk

Moss Acres (Pennsylvania)
mossacres.com

My Plantopia
myplantopia.com
Tropical and indoor plants.

Northwind Perennials
northwindperennialfarm.com

Preston Bisset Nurseries and Country Shop (UK)
thenurseries.com

OUTDOOR RUGS

Angela Adams
angeladams.com

Dash and Albert
dashandalbert.com

Momeni
momeni.com

OUTDOOR SPAS

Hikki Natural Spas (Sweden)
hikki.se/hikki-naturspa

PLAY STRUCTURES

Barbara Butler
barbarabutler.com
Imaginative, colorful, custom play structures and tree houses.

RAISED GARDEN BEDS

The Farmstead
gardenraisedbeds.com
Cedar mortise-and-tenon raised garden beds.

Scout Regalia
scoutregalia.com
Modern raised beds and furniture.

SCULPTURE

Orchard Pottery (UK)
orchardpottery.com
Sculpture in stoneware, bronze, or cold-cast resin.

Opiary
opiary.com
Planted sculpture.

TerraSculpture
terrasculpture.com

SEEDS

Outside Pride
outsidepride.com

Terroir Seeds
underwoodgardens.com

SHEDS AND OUTBUILDINGS

Tumbleweed Tiny House Company
tumbleweedhouses.com
Imaginative small buildings.

STAINED GLASS

Pompei Glass
pompeiglass.com

SWINGING GARDEN SOFAS

Wilverley
wilverley.com.

TENTS

Indian Garden Company
indiangardencompany.com
Indian garden tents and accessories.

TERRARIUMS

Hermetica
hermeticalondon.co.uk

TILE

Mexican Tiles
mexicantiles.com

Saint Tropez Boutique
sainttropezboutique.us
Moorish tiles.

TOOLS AND ACCESSORIES

Fog Linen
foglinenwork.com
Linen clothing and aprons.

Garden Trading (UK)
gardentrading.co.uk

Kaufmann Mercantile
kaufmann-mercantile.com
Quality and durable tools, outdoor wear, and accessories.

Kinsman Garden
kinsmangarden.com

Plow and Hearth
plowhearth.com

Lowes
lowes.com

TUTEURS, ARBORS, TRELLISES

Arboria
arboria.com

Hen and Hammock
henandhammock.co.uk

M. Turner Landscapes
mturnerlandscapes.com

Terra Trellis
terratrellis.com

Wooden Garden Obelisk (UK)
woodengardenobelisk.co.uk

Yard Arbors
yardarbors.com

UMBRELLAS

Hedgerow Studio
hedgerowstudio.com
Hand-painted garden umbrellas.

WATER FEATURES

Stone and Water (UK)
stoneandwater.co.uk

PHOTOGRAPHY CREDITS

Credits for photography, except where noted for design.
Photography by author, except where noted.
Thanks are offered to those who granted permission for use of materials. While every reasonable effort has been made to contact copyright holders and secure permission for all materials reproduced in this work, we offer apologies for any instances in which this was not possible and for any inadvertent omissions.

Table of Contents, pages 2–3, left to right, row 1: courtesy of Galanter and Jones, 123rf/Natalia Bratslavsky, courtesy of Milan Direct Homewares, courtesy of Seam Studios, courtesy of Streamline Inc., Dan Kowalski; row 2: 123rf/ Eric Isselee, Therese Hagstedt (design: Charlotte Rice), Michael Garland, Sally Nex (design: Malvern Spring Gardening Show), Trina Roberts (design: Molly Wood Gardens), 123rf/ Irina Belousa; row 3: courtesy of Matthew Cunningham, Wikipedia/Derek Ramsey, courtesy of J Schatz, Flickr/Jack Holloway, courtesy of Backyard X-scapes, courtesy of Pensthorpe; row 4: courtesy of Kathy Kuo Home, courtesy of Kathy Kuo Home, Ashley Camper, Marcus Ryan/ courtesy of Lambley Nursery, Robert Vonnoh, Rochelle Greayer.

Page 6, bottom: Flickr/Ryan Somma.

Page 7, top: 123rf/tang90246; center: 123rf/fashionweek; bottom: Vincent Van Gogh.

Table of Contents, pages 10–11, left to right: Kate Sluman, Jeffery Bale, Laura Kicey for Terrain, courtesy of Jayson Home.

Pages 12–13, clockwise from top left: courtesy of Vintage Marquee Lights, Flickr/ Lori Desormeaux, Kate Sluman, Brandi Welles, 123rf/Anna Bogush, 123rf/Sandra Cunningham, 123rf/pauljune, 123rf/JosÃ© Barcelo.

Pages 14–15, clockwise from top left: Pam Penick (design: Dig It Gardens Austin TX), 123rf/Barbara Helgason, 123rf/pauljune, Grey Crawford (design: Jeff Andrews).

Pages 16–17, left to right, row 1: courtesy of Etsy Selvedge Shop, courtesy of Kmart, courtesy of Classic Modern, courtesy of Yliving, courtesy of Potted; row 2: courtesy of Classic Modern, courtesy of Plodes, Malm Fireplace (design: Design Within Reach), Shannon Lester, courtesy of Potted; row 3: Dwell Studio, courtesy of Galanter and Jones, courtesy of Modfire, courtesy of Pad Outdoor; row 4: courtesy of Etsy Busy Bee Quilting, courtesy of 1stdibs, courtesy of Vivaterra, courtesy of Potted.

Page 18, upper left: Wikimedia/Wouter Hagens; plant row 1: Wikimedia/Manfred Werner, Wikimedia/Manfred Werner; plant row 2: Public Domain; plant row 3: Wikimedia/Stan Shebs, Wikimedia/Ghislain118; plant row 4: Wikimedia/Jerzy Opioła; plant row 5: Shutterstock/Supertrooper; bottom left: Wikimedia/ Wouter Hagens.

Page 19, top: 123rf/labrynthe; bottom right: 123rf/Tamara Kulikova; bottom left: 123rf/ Yuriy Brykaylo.

Page 21, center: Kelly Fitzsimmons.

Pages 24, top: RHS Lindley Library; lower right: Caitlin Atkinson (design Flora Grubb); bottom left: Etsy Earth Sea Warrior Ursula Manaf-Pitt.

Page 25, clockwise from upper right: 123rf/Anna Chelnokova, courtesy of Grace at

Poetic Home, Ken Marten, Audrey Kitching, courtesy of The Southern Home, Flickr/Umbrella Shot.

Page 26, top: 123rf/Thomas Black; bottom: iStock/AtWaG.

Page 27: Jessica Turnbow.

Pages 28–29 left to right, row1: 123rf/photographieundmehr, courtesy of Wayfair.com, 123rf/Jolanta Dabrowska, courtesy of Lattice Stix; row 2: 123rf/Thaweeporn Traiwittayayont, courtesy of Wayfair.com, Flickr/Rae Lowenberg, Laura Kicey for Terrain; row 3: 123rf/DeGraaf Erik, Flickr/Don Burkett, courtesy of Buddha Groove, 123rf/aelita2, courtesy of Micheal Trapp; row 4: courtesy of Ipe Furniture, 123rf/Feng Yu, courtesy of Campania International, 123rf/Ganna Poltoratska, Wikipedia.

Page 31, top: Marianne Majerus (design: Susan Bennett and Earl Hyde, GB); bottom: 123rf/Brenda Kean.

Page 32: Reuben Munoz.

Page 33: all images by Reuben Munoz.

Page 34: Reuben Munoz.

Page 36–37, clockwise spiral from top right: Jeffery Bale, Rochelle Greayer, Gary Rogers, Roger fry, Flickr/Loz Pycock, Flickr/ernop, Flickr/antidigital_da.

Page 38, bottom: Heather Edwards.

Page 39: Wikimedia/Garry Knight.

Pages 40–41 left to right, row 1: courtesy of Angela Adams, courtesy of Red Modern Furniture, courtesy of West Elm, courtesy of Fermob; row 2: courtesy of Momeni, courtesy of Milan Direct Homewares, courtesy of 1stdibs, courtesy of phillyfabrics; row 3: Etsy Camille Designs, courtesy of Serenaandlily, courtesy of Destination Lighting, courtesy of Hippieshop; row 4: courtesy of Dash and Albert, courtesy of Soane, courtesy of Blazing Needles, courtesy of World Away.

Page 42, clockwise spiral from top center: Rochelle Greayer, Flickr/Amanda Slater, Rochelle Greayer, Rochelle Greayer, Flickr/Caitriana Nicholson, Rochelle Greayer, Flickr/Frank Mayfield.

Page 43, top left: Flickr/Louise Docker; Plant row 1: Flickr/Cuong Nguyen, Flickr/Maja Dumat; bottom left: need to check credit; Plant row 2: Flickr/Hiroyuki Takeda, Flickr/Carsten aus Bonn; bottom: Shutterstock/Vilor.

Page 44: Sophie Hitchens/Light Locations.

Page 45, top left: Sophie Hitchens/Light Locations; top right: courtesy of Clara Baillie; center left: courtesy of Clara Baillie; center right: Sophie Hitchens/Light Locations, bottom right: courtesy of Clara Baillie.

Page 49, clockwise spiral from top left: Chales Hawes, Tom Sulcer, Flickr/Yohann Legrand, Flickr/Kelly Kilpatrick, courtesy Of Seam Studios, 123rf/miroart, 123rf/subbotina.

Page 50: Flickr/Kelly Kilpatrick.

Page 51: all images by Flickr/Kelly Kilpatrick.

Pages 76–77, left to right, row 1: courtesy of Kathy Kuo Home, Deb Silver, Laura Kicey for Terrain, courtesy of Tumbleweed Tiny Houses; row 2: courtesy of Garden Trading Co., courtesy of R.T.Facts, courtesy of Home Decorators Collection, courtesy of Watson & Co., 123rf/palych; row 3: Laura Kicey for Terrain, courtesy of Bacsac, courtesy of Wayfair.com, courtesy of Compo Clay, courtesy of Black Widow Vintiques; row 4: courtesy of Design Within Reach, courtesy of Jayson Home, Laura Kicey for Terrain, courtesy of Apartment 528, courtesy of MQuan Studio.

Page 78, top to bottom: Littleyard.com/sa11chan21taichan, Wikimedia/Amanda Slater, Wikimedia/Bryan.calloway, Wikimedia/Derek Ramsey.

Page 79: top: Wikimedia/Steve Snodgrass, Wikimedia/Tracy Ducasse, Wikimedia/Till Westermayer.

Page 80–81: all images by Dan Kowalski.

Page 82: Kelly Fitzsimmons.

Page 83: Kelly Fitzsimmons (design: Rochelle Greayer).

Table of Contents, pages 84–85, left to right: 123rf/martateron , Laura Kicey for Terrain, 123rf/Eric Isselee, 123rf/Ilka Erika Szasz-Fabian, 123rf/Irina Belousa.

Pages 86–87, clockwise from top left: Rochelle Greayer, 123rf/kazoka30, 123rf/Tom Gowanlock, 123rf/Stanislav Moroz, Rochelle Greayer, Levi Fussell, Flickr/woodleywonderworks, 123rf/Ans Houben.

Page 88: 123rf/arinahabich.

Page 89, top: Mark Matson; bottom, left to right: GAP/Michael Howes, ryan marshall.

Page 90, left to right, row 1: courtesy of Hayneedle, courtesy of Holland Hen Houses, 123rf/Louella Folsom, 123rf/John McAllister; row 2: Matt Reed/ courtesy of Bee Thinking, 123rf/Harald Biebel, Flickr/Katrina Wiese, jamie newton; row 3: courtesy of Alape, courtesy of Keder Greenhouse, Laura Kicey for Terrain, courtesy of Manufactum; row4: courtesy of Terrapot, courtesy of Growers Edge, courtesy of the Farmstead, courtesy of Terra Trellis.

Page 91: 123rf/Eric Isselee.

Pages 92–93, clockwise from top left: Flickr/Amy Ashcraft, Flickr/Yoshizumi Endo, Flickr/Dwight Sipler, Flickr/Emma Forsberg, Flickr/Toshiyuki IMAI, Flickr/Tara AuBuchon, 123rf/julietphotography, 123rf/martateron, Flickr/Jim Capaldi, Flickr/Quinn Dombrowski, Flickr/Anthony Cramp.

Pages 94–95: Marcus Harpur (design: Jon Wheatley and Mary Pyne).

Pages 98–99, clockwise from top left: 123rf/Giuseppe Ramos, 123rf/Anan Kaewkhammul, 123rf/vitalinka, design & photos by Barbara Butler Artist-Builder Inc., Lindsey Boardman, Ryann Ford (design: b jane gardens), 123rf/Wasan Gredpree, 123rf/YuanHung Liao, 123rf/Elena Anferova.

Page 100, top: Ryann Ford (design: b jane gardens); bottom: courtesy of LilyPond Natural Pools (design: LilyPond).

Page 101, clockwise from top left: 123rf/Pan Xunbin, JoJo Shaiken, 123rf/Thawat Tanhai, 123rf/Pan Xunbin.

Pages 102–103, left to right, row 1: courtesy of Wayfair, Laura Kicey for Terrain, courtesy of Green Green Design, courtesy of Room and Board, courtesy of Yield Design; row 2: courtesy of Gallagher Designs, courtesy of SLIDE srl, courtesy of Doug & Gene Meyer / LINK Outdoor (design: Fabric and trim by Doug & Gene Meyer for LINK Outdoor), courtesy of Vessel USA Inc., courtesy of Orchard Pottery; row 3: courtesy of Sears, courtesy of Loll design, courtesy of Vessel USA Inc., courtesy of the Fulham Group, courtesy of The Balcony Gardnener; row 4: courtesy of Rosenberry Rooms, Laura Kicey for Terrain, courtesy of Barbecook, DYLAN + JENI, courtesy of J Schatz.

Page 104, clockwise from top left: 123rf/boyenigma, 123rf/Maksim Shebeko, 123rf/godrick.

Page 105, clockwise from left: 123rf/Liu Fuyu, Peter Griffin, Petr Kratochvil, 123rf/Iuliia Malivanchuk, 123rf/Marc Parsons, 123rf/designpics, 123rf/Rob Huntley, 123rf/jiravan.

Pages 106–108: Therese Hagstedt (design: Charlotte Rice).

Pages 110–111, top left to right: 123rf/iofoto, courtesy of RHS/Neil Hepworth; center: Flickr/Elaine Eppler, Rochelle Greayer, Flickr/ Leah Steen (design: Leah Steen Revival Home and Garden); bottom: Flickr/Darwin Bell, Jim Charlier, Rochelle Greayer, Flickr/Marie Coleman, Karen Arnold.

Page 112, top: Marianne Majerus; bottom: Trudi Harrison.

Page 113, top: Michael Garland; bottom: 123rf/Matt Caldwell.

Pages 114–115, left to right, row 1: courtesy of Studio Liscious, courtesy of Homart, Jim Charlier, courtesy of Ballard Design; row 2: courtesy of Fermob, courtesy of Wayfair.com, courtesy of Eleanor Brown Boutique, courtesy of Bon Marche; row 3: Laura Kicey for Terrain, Laura Kicey for Terrain, courtesy of J Schatz, courtesy of Schumacher Fabrics, courtesy of Michael Devine/ One Kings Lane; row 4: 123rf/Sally Williams, courtesy of Wilverley, Laura Kicey for Terrain, courtesy of Wayfair, courtesy of Connected Goods.

Page 116, clockwise from top left: Flickr/Ryan Somma, Flickr/Yoko Nekonomania, Flickr/Pamla J. Eisenberg, Flickr/Acid Pix, Kealan O'Neil, 123rf/Le Do, 123rf/Marilyn Barbone, 123rf/Dmytro Sukharevskyy, 123rf/Nataliya Litova, Flickr/By possumgirl2 – Jude.

Page 117, clockwise from top right: Marianne Majerus (design: Dove Cottage, Yorkshire, GB), Flickr/Olivier Bacquet, Flickr/Ryan Somma, Flickr/Emmanuel Keller, 123rf/Eric Isselee, 123rf/Sergejs Bespalovs.

Page 118: all images courtesy Marquette Clay.

Page 119: all images courtesy Marquette Clay.

Page 121: all images by Kelly Fitzsimmons.

Pages 122–123, clockwise from top center: Kim Kruse/University of Florida, Flickr/Jan Käseberg, Middleton Jameson, Malvern Spring Gardening Show by Sally Nex, Flickr/Diana Sorela, Rochelle Greayer.

Page 124: all images by Andrea Jones.

Page 125, top: Flickr/Sandra Mora; bottom: Steven Royce Wright.

Pages 126–127, left to right, row 1: courtesy of Bacsac, 123rf/Tami Freed, courtesy of The Greenhouse People, courtesy of Cox and Cox; row 2: courtesy of Cox and Cox, courtesy of Wayfair, courtesy of M Turner Landscapes (design: M Turner Landscapes), courtesy of Topiary Classics; row 3: courtesy of Wooden Garden Obelisk, courtesy of 1stdibs, courtesy of Terrasculpture, courtesy of Zachary A Design; row 4: 123rf/Ilka Erika Szasz-Fabian, courtesy of Kinsman Garden, 123rf/Rosamund Parkinson, courtesy of Kaufmann Merchantile, courtesy of crocus.

Page 128, clockwise from top left: Flicker/Dwight Sipler, Flickr/@joefoodie, 123rf/zigzagmtart, Flickr/Toru Watanabe, Flickr/Nick Saltmarsh, Flickr/Christia Guthier, Flickr/Joi Ito, Flickr/Nick Saltmarsh, Flickr/Various Brennemans, Flickr/Michael Bentley.

Page 129, top: Andrea Jones; bottom left: Flickr/Ben Hosking, Flickr/derek visser; bottom right: Rochelle Greayer, Flickr/Allan Harris.

Pages 130–131: all images by Brooke Gianetti (design: Brooke Gianetti).

Pages 132–133, clockwise from top left: courtesy of The Phillips Collection, courtesy of The Phillips Collection, Joshua Stenzel (design: Joshua Stenzel), Holly Lepere Photography (design: Grace Design Associates), Taylor Pollack, courtesy of The Phillips Collection, Art Gray (XTEN Achitecture), Dagmara Mach (design: Mickey Muennig) Katie Slater (design: Jakkelyn Iris).

Page 136, top left: Trina Roberts (design: Molly Wood Gardens); top right: Shannon Lester; bottom: Ryann Ford (design: b jane gardens).

Page 137, top: GAP/Susie Gibbons; bottom: courtesy of Marnie Lewis.

Pages 138–139, left to right, row 1: courtesy of Preston Bisset Nurseries, courtesy of Preston Bisset Nurseries, 123rf/Ramzi Hachicho, Rick Dohler, courtesy of Vivaterra; row 2: courtesy of Cottonlight, courtesy of Kaufmann Merchantile, courtesy of John Kelly Furniture, courtesy of Vivaterra, courtesy of John Kelly Furniture; row 3: courtesy of Plow and Hearth, courtesy of Jason Phillips Design, 123rf/Bert Folsom, courtesy of Wayfair.com, courtesy of Jamali Garden; row 4: 123rf/Eetu Mustonen, courtesy of Artwood, courtesy of Zü Galerie, courtesy of Paloform, courtesy of Vandersar.

Page 140, clockwise from top left: Wikimedia/Barbara Studer, 123rf/Anthony Baggett, Wikimedia/cliff, Wikimedia/Saintrain, 123rf/Roman Hraška, Wikimedia/Donovan Govan, Wikimedia/El Grafo, 123rf/Harald Biebel, Todd Boland (design: Todd Boland), Wikimedia/Winfried Bruenken, Wikimedia/Tigerente.

Page 141, top: Far Out Flora; bottom left: courtesy of Miami Tropical Bonsai; bottom right: Rochelle Greayer.

Page 142: Trina Roberts (design: Molly Wood Gardens).

Pages 146–147, clockwise from top left: moss and stone gardens, 123rf/Gina Allen, Rochelle Greayer, Flickr/xhaju, Flickr/Cassandra Kinaviaq Rae, Marianne Kaplan, Flickr/Elliot Brown (design: Giardino Botanico - Fondazione Andre Heller - Gardone Riviera), Flickr/Kelly Kilpatrick (design: Suzanne Biaggi and Patrick Picard), 123rf/Gina Smith, Flickr/Tomas Sobek.

Page 148, top: Jeffery Bale; bottom: Wikimedia/Daniel Schwen.

Page 149: Flickr/Wonderlane.

Pages 150–151, left to right, row 1: 123rf/Kobchai Matasurawit, 123rf/piccaya, courtesy of Crown Bees, courtesy of American Design Club; row 2: Flickr/Mark Pilbeam, courtesy of Eva Solo, 123rf/Evgeny Alekseev, courtesy of Stone and Water; row 3: courtesy of Wayfair, Flickr/Acid Pix, Kendall Mills for the American Design Club, John T Unger; row 4: courtesy of Bent Tree Gallery, courtesy of Loyal Loot, Laura Kicey for Terrain, courtesy of Hen and Hammock.

Page 152, left to right, row 1: Flickr/Alexandre Dulaunoy, Flickr/john Norton; row 2: Flickr/Paul W. Locke, Flickr/Harrison Turner, Flickr/Cathi Baber, Flickr/Pam Gore; row 3: 123rf/serezniy, Flickr/Carolyn; row 4: 123rf/Chris Hill, 123rf/loflo, Flickr/Wendy Cutler, Flickr/I M Swaminathan; row 5: Flickr/Tony Hisgett, Flickr/Chris Darling; row 6: 123rf/Valery Voennyy, Flickr/Tambako The Jaguar, Flickr/Satheeshkumar K, Flickr/Karen Roe.

Page 153, left to right, row 1: 123rf/madllen, 123rf/Andrey Nekrasov, 123rf/Richard Griffin; row 2: 123rf/Irina Belousa, 123rf/Vladimira Tausova, 123rf/photographieundmehr; row 3: 123rf/Maksim Shebeko, 123rf/Anastasy Yarmolovich, 123rf/Alfio Scisetti; row 4: 123rf/Wu Ruiyun, 123rf/serezniy.

Pages 154–155: Hugh Main (design: Hugh Main and Marc Wittenberg).

Pages 156–157: all images by Kelly Fitzsimmons.

Table of Contents, pages 158–159, left to right: courtesy of Mecox Gardens, Nigel Burkitt (design: FlemonsWarlandDesign), courtesy of Niche Your Home, courtesy of Lowes.

Pages 160–161, clockwise from top left: Flickr/Molly Mazilu, 123rf/George Mayer, Flickr/Janne Hellsten, Flickr/Carissa Rogers, courtesy of Barnsely House, Flickr/Garry Knight, John Cullen (design: Celtic Design Celtic Gardens), Matthew Cunningham, Flickr/Thomas Lieser, Flickr/John Christopher, Flickr/Alexis Lê-Quôc.

Page 162: Matthew Cunningham.

Page 163, top: Wikimedia/Daderot, Greg Lehmkuhl/courtesy of Terrain.

Pages 164–165, left to right, row 1: courtesy of Wayfair.com, courtesy of Mecox Gardens, courtesy of Frontgate, Laura Kicey for Terrain, courtesy of Pfeifer Studio; row 2: courtesy of And Made, courtesy of Morgann Hill Designs Etsy Shop, courtesy of Frontier Stove, 123rf/Mark Payne; row 3: courtesy of Direct from Mexico, courtesy of Moss and Stone Gardens, 123rf/Zhang Xiangyang , courtesy of Campania International; row 4: courtesy of 1stdibs, courtesy of Wayfair.com, courtesy of Belacor, courtesy of Barraveld International, courtesy of Codor Design.

Page 166, clockwise from top: Flickr/brewbooks - J Brew, Flickr/Brighton Plants, Green Over Grey (design: Green Over Grey), Flickr/John Donges, Flickr/Nico Nelson.

Page 167, clockwise from top left: Flickr/Barbara Eckstein, Flickr/Elizabeth Escher, Flickr/Dendroica cerulea - John B., Flickr/Jeff Hart, courtesy of String Gardens (design: String Gardens), Flickr/Takashi Hososhima.

Pages 168–170: Emma Jane Harbour (design: Clive Rundel).

Page 172–173, clockwise from top left: 123rf/Napat Kumphol, Flickr/Kelly Kilpatrick, Sound of Music, 123rf/Irina Burakova, 123rf/Warren Goldswain, Wikimedia/Derek Ramsey, Adam Woodruff (design: Northwind Perrenials).

Page 174: 123rf/Maksim Shebeko.

Page 175, top: 123rf/Vladimir Salman; bottom: courtesy of Matthew Cunningham Design.

Pages 176–177, left to right, row 1: courtesy of Iconic Dutch, courtesy of Unica Home, 123rf/Thawat Tanhai, 123rf/Pan Xunbin, 123rf/Thawat Tanhai; row 2: courtesy of Deesawat, courtesy of Iconic Dutch, courtesy of Zanotta (design: Zanotta), Deposit Photos/paulmhill, courtesy of Rare Finds; row 3: courtesy of Idyll Home, courtesy of Pure Modern, courtesy of Graham and Green, 123rf/happyalex, Miriam Goldberger (www.eco-lawn.com); row 4: courtesy of Massant, courtesy of Pod Caravans, courtesy The Dan 300 Group Australia, courtesy of Uncommon Goods, courtesy of Unurth Home.

Page 178, left to right, row 1: Wikimedia/Christian Fischer, courtesy of Mississippi Garden, courtesy of David Salman/High Country Gardens; row 2: Rochelle Greayer; row 3: Wikimedia/Forest & Kim Starr; row 4: Wikimedia/Bj.schoenmakers, Wikimedia/TeunSpaans, Wikimedia/Pauk; row 5: Robert & Mihaela Vicol.

Page 179, left to right: Michelle Derviss (design: Van Sweden for Cornerstone Festival of Gardens in Sonoma), Rochelle Greayer, 123rf/menuha.

Pages 180–181: Jane Seibre (design: John Little).

Pages 184–185, clockwise from top left: Flickr/Chris Parfitt, courtesy of Exteriorscapes LLC (design: Exteriorscapes LLC), courtesy of Kirby Design and Great Balls of Wire (design: Kirby Design), courtesy of Debora Carl Landscape Design (design: Deb Carl), courtesy of Arterra LLP, Landscape Architects/ Michelle Lee Wilson Photography (design: Arterra LLP, Landscape Architects), Marianne Majerus (design: Modular, GB), courtesy of Ketti Kupper Conscious Living Landscapes (design: Ketti Kupper Conscious Living Landscapes), Flickr/Nigel Burkitt (design: FlemonsWarlandDesign), Michael Mullan (design: Mo Mullan).

Pages 186–187, left to right, top: Caitlin Atkinson (design: Reynods Sebastiani), texturezine, 123rf/Wu Ruiyun, texturezine, psdgraphics, mayang; bottom: courtesy of Deb Silver (design: Deb Silver), Rochelle Greayer (design: Medocino Coast Botanical Garden), Marion Brenner (design: Zeterre).

Pages 188–189, left to right, row 1: Ore Containers, courtesy of Wayfair.com, Flickr/Billy Bob Bain, courtesy of Wayfair.com, courtesy of Zachary A Design; row 2: courtesy of Wayfair.com, 123rf/Mike Peel, 123rf/Stepan Ermakov, courtesy of Wayfair; row 3: courtesy of Ore Containers, Circa50, Rochelle Greayer, courtesy of Ore Containers, courtesy of Wayfair; row 4: courtesy of Shop BoxHill.com, courtesy of Arcat Cable Railings, Flickr/Brian Pursel, courtesy of Hable Construction, Skargaarden (design: Carl Jägnefelt och Joacim Wahlström).

Page 190, top left to right: Marianne Majerus, 123rf/Alison Bowden, Flickr/Allan Harris; bottom, clockwise from left: Marianne Majerus (design: Sue Moss USA), Flickr/Jack Holloway, Flickr/bobrpics.

Page 191, left: Marianne Majerus (design: Charlotte Rowe, GB); right, top to bottom: 123rf/Maria Sbytova, Petr Kratochvil, Photaki/Miguel Ángel López Moreira.

Pages 192-193: all images by Eric Rorer (design: Doyle McCullar).

Pages 196–197, clockwise from top left: Flickr/Dan Meineck, 123rf/Jennifer Grush, courtesy of KOUBOO LLC, courtesy of Eldreds (design: Paul Jacoulet), 123rf/Nataliia Peredniankina, Rochelle Greayer, 123rf/yuri2011, 123rf/Lijuan Guo, courtesy of Cezign (design: Cezign), courtesy of Proven Winners.

Page 198: Richard Felber Photography (design: Raymond Jungles).

Page 199, top: Steven Brooke Photography (design: Raymond Jungles); bottom: Marion Brenner (design: Raymond Jungles).

Pages 200–201, left to right, row 1: courtesy of Niche Your Home, courtesy of Barnlight Electric, courtesy of NVA Creative Garden Granite, courtesy of Tommy Bahama, courtesy of Backyard X-scapes; row 2: courtesy of Shop Boxhill, courtesy of Z Gallerie, courtesy of Cost Plus World Market, courtesy of Sophitatiki, courtesy of Wayfair. com; row 3: courtesy of Wayfair.com, courtesy of Schumacher/Trina Turk (design: Trina Turk), courtesy of Hayneedle; row 4: courtesy of Niche Your Home, courtesy of Gainey Ceramics, courtesy of Cost Plus World Market, courtesy of Fabric.com, courtesy of Vessel Architectural Pottery.

Page 202, counter-clockwise from top left: 123rf/Arthit Buarapa, 123rf/Alexander Morozov, 123rf/canoness, 123rf/Kanda Euatham, 123rf/Nathaporn Tunthong.

Page 203, clockwise from top left: Flickr/Amanda Slater, 123rf/happystock, Flickr/Frank Schulenburg, Flickr/Chris Stott, Flickr/hickoryrose, 123rf/ekays,

Pages 204–205: Rochelle Greayer (design: Kevin Beer).

Pages 208–209, clockwise from top left: Emily Green (www.chanceofrain.com), courtesy of Beverlys, 123rf/Vladimir Nikulin, 123rf/Jeanne Hatch, Adam Woodruff, Flickr/Amanda Slater, Photo by Loi Thai (ToneOnToneAntiques.blogspot.com), courtesy of Pompei Glass, 123rf/Dan Kosmayer.

Page 210, top: Flickr/Aleks Peterson; Bottom, left to right: 123rf/Christopher Nuzzaco, Flickr/Michael J. Andersen.

Page 211: courtesy of Pensthorpe (design: Pensthorpe).

Pages 212–213, left to right, row 1: courtesy of the Ironstone Nest, courtesy of Bauer LA, courtesy of Halo Styles, courtesy of Wayfair.com, courtesy of Dash and Albert; row 2: courtesy of Aiden Gray Home, courtesy of Bauer LA, Amy Hamilton, courtesy of Wayfair.com, George Ong; row 3: courtesy of Bauer LA, courtesy of Arroyo Craftsman, courtesy of Reed Bros Furniture, courtesy of Lowes; row 4: courtesy of Bauer LA, courtesy of Coe Studios (design: Coe Studios), courtesy of Archies Island (design: Archies Island Furniture), courtesy of Shop Wright.

Page 214: Andrea Kennard.

Page 215, clockwise from top left: Adam Woodruff, Flickr/Harsh Patel, Kealan O'Neil, Flickr/Ted Bobosh, Flickr/John Hurd.

Pages 216–217: all images by Adam Woodruff.

Table of Contents, pages 220–221, left to right: 123rf/Pauliene Wessel, courtesy of Indian Garden Company, courtesy of Gardecor, 123rf/daicokuebisu.

Pages 222–223, clockwise from top left: 123rf/Christian Jung, Jeffery Bale (design: Jeffery Bale), Flickr/A. Davey, Flickr/Heather Price (design: Majorelle), Flickr/Woody Anthony, Flickr/Dave Patrick, Suzanna Clarke, 123rf/Santhosh Kumar, Canstock/marzolino, Tim Turner Photography (design: Creative Outdoor Solutions), Bridgeman Art Library.

Page 224, top: Rochelle Greayer (design: Cleve West for Chelsea Flower Show 2012); bottom: Flickr/elfon.

Page 225, top: Public Domain Barbur's Garden; bottom: Flickr/Cara Stewart.

Pages 226–227, left to right, row 1: courtesy of Paola Lenti, courtesy of Wayfair, courtesy of Kenneth Cobonpue, courtesy of Linens and Things; row 2: Tina Suddell, courtesy of Salvage Antiques, Sarah Hepworth /courtesy of the Remakerie Etsy Shop, 123rf/Valentyn Volkov Volkov; row 3: courtesy of Royal Botania, courtesy of Wayfair, Shutterstock/evaschmidt, 123rf/Graça Victoria, courtesy of Tine K; row 4: courtesy of Vivaterra, courtesy of Kathy Kuo Home, 123rf/Hans Bijzet, courtesy of Proven Winners, courtesy of Vivaterra.

Page 228, clockwise from top left: Flickr/THOR (geishaboy500), 123rf/balet, 123rf/Natalia Lukiyanova , courtesy of Bailey Nursery, 123rf/Natallia Yeumenenka.

Page 229, clockwise from top right: Flickr/Lauren Mitchell, 123rf/fotogal, Wikimedia/KENPEI, Wikimedia/Calvin Theo, 123rf/videowokart.

Page 230: Marianne Majerus (design: Lucy Sommers).

Page 231 top: Marianne Majerus (design: Lucy Sommers), center: courtesy Lucy Sommers; bottom: Marianne Majerus (design: Lucy Sommers).

Page 233: Kelly Fitzsimmons (design: Rochelle Greayer).

Page 234, top left: 123rf/Thomas Dutour; bottom left: Allan Pollock Morris (design: Jinny Bloom); top right: 123rf/subbotina; bottom right: Chelsea Fuss.

Page 235, clockwise from top right: 123rf/Ann Louise Hagevi, 123rf/Piotr Wawrzyniuk, Mariana Sjöberg, Flickr/Anna Ådén, Wikimedia/michael clarke stuff, 123rf/virtuelle.

Page 236, top: Allan Pollock Morris (design: Jinny Bloom); bottom: courtesy of Hikki Natural Spas.

Page 237, top: Stefan Holm; bottom: Ryan Scott.

Pages 238–239, left to right, row 1: courtesy of Hodi Home Décor, 123rf/Goce Risteski, courtesy of Polart, courtesy of Wayfair; row 2: courtesy of Delany and Long, Public Domain, Laura Kicey for Terrain, courtesy of Elizabeth's Embellishements; row 3: courtesy of 1stdibs, courtesy of Delany and Long, courtesy of Kirklands, courtesy of Faux White Taxidermy, courtesy of Ikea, courtesy of 1stdibs; row 4: courtesy of Delany and Long, courtesy of Wayfair, courtesy of cozy days, courtesy of Aidan Grey Home, courtesy of Snug Harbor Farm, courtesy of Wayfair.com.

Page 261, top left: Flickr/Lisa Chamberlain; top right: Janine Robinson; bottom left: courtesy of Haiti Metal Art.

Pages 262–263 left to right row 1: courtesy of KW Hammocks, courtesy of 1stdibs, courtesy of St. Tropez Boutique, courtesy of Iron Accents; row 2: courtesy of Iron Accents, courtesy of Rolling Green Nursery, courtesy of Mexican Tiles, courtesy of Uncommons Goods, courtesy of La Fuente Imports; row 3: courtesy of Capitol Gardens, courtesy of Seibert and Rice, Flickr/Alex Jacque, courtesy of Home Garden and Patio, courtesy of Haiti Metal Art; 123rf/sazler, courtesy of Wallter, courtesy of Mexican Sugar Skull, courtesy of Innit, courtesy of La Fuente Imports.

Page 264, plant row left top to bottom: Flickr/Brian Fuller, Flickr/Zion National Park, Flickr/Fred Clark, Flickr/Scott Robinson; plant row center top to bottom: Flickr/Louise Docker, Flickr/Ken Bosma; plant row top left to right: Flickr/Minette Layne, Flickr/Amante Darmanin, Flickr/Lillian Bennett; bottom right: Flickr/Kelly Fitzsimmons.

Page 265, top left: missing credit info; plant row one left to right: Flickr/Phil Hauck, Flickr/megan k hines; pant row 2 left to right: Flickr/Kimberly Kling, Flickr/Mike Tungate, Flickr/R. Philip Bouchard, Flickr/Allan Harris; plant row 3 left to right: Flickr/Matt Lavin, Flickr/Sarah (Rosenau) Korf.

Page 266: Janine Robinson.

Page 267, bottom left: Janine Robinson; center: courtesy of Mark and Cindy Evans; top right: Janine Robinson.

Page 269: all images by Kelly Fitzsimmons.

Page 270, bottom left: missing credit info, 123rf/drobm, 123rf/Anton Gvozdikov.

Page 271, top left: Robert Vonnoh; top right: courtesy of Studio Toop; center: courtesy of Grainedit; bottom left: Koen de Waal; bottom right: Koen de Waal / courtesy of Domani.

Page 272, top: Marcus Harpur; bottom left: Jeltje Janmaat.

Page 273, top: Dario Fusaro (design: Giardino Segreto); bottom: Amir Schlezinger.

Pages 274–275, left to right, row 1: 123rf/Serhii Lohvyniuk, 123rf/Vladimir Nenov, courtesy of Modernica, courtesy of Moda Flame, courtesy of Y Lighting, courtesy of Artwood; row 2: courtesy of Rupert Till, courtesy of Paloform, courtesy of Iota Garden, courtesy of Wayfair, courtesy of Bacsac, courtesy of Modfire, courtesy of Barn Light Electric, courtesy of Freeline; row 4: 123rf/Solatges Irina, 123rf/Tamara Kulikova, courtesy of Artwood, courtesy Elena Columbo, courtesy of Barn Light, courtesy of Free Line.

Page 276, clockwise from top left: Flickr/La Cita Vitta, Flickr/Christian Guthier, 123rf/Ольга Юсупова, Flickr/Mebs Rehemtulla (QUOI Media Group), Wikimedia/Dominicus Johannes Bergsma, Flickr/M. Marcus Vicente.

Page 277, clockwise from top left: 123rf/Marina Kuchenbecker, Rochelle Greayer, 123rf/Nataliya Hora, Flickr/Carl E Lewis, Flickr/AnnaKika, Jaap de Vries (design: Jaap de Vries), Flickr/John Shortland, Flickr/ Jacob W. Frank (National Park Service), Flickr/Col Ford and Natasha de Vere, Flickr/Col Ford and Natasha de Vere, Flickr/Frank Mayfield.

INDEX

ABOUT THE AUTHOR

Rochelle Greayer was co-founder and editor of *Leaf Magazine*, a digital magazine "for garden makers"; creator of the popular garden blog *Studio 'g'*, named one of the ten best garden blogs by *Better Homes and Gardens*; and a weekly columnist (The Gardenist) for *Apartment Therapy*, "one of the most influential interior design sites on the Web," according to *Forbes* magazine. A graduate of the English Gardening School in London, she has designed gardens for private residences and hotels around the world, including a garden at the Hampton Court Palace Flower Show, earning a coveted medal from the Royal Horticultural Society. Prior to her garden design success, Rochelle was a physicist rocket scientist (yes, really), riding in the cockpits of F-14s and helping launch Russia's first commercial satellite.

Finding pleasure today in more earthbound endeavors, Rochelle's garden style reflects her Colorado roots—as close to Handsome Prairie as you can get in the middle of New England, with healthy dashes of Sacred Meadow, Forest Temple, and Homegrown Rock 'n' Roll thrown in. Her garden supplies flowers and vegetables for her two children to sell at the local farmers' market she started with friends.

133 S.W. Second Avenue, Suite 450   6A Lonsdale Road
Portland, Oregon 97204-3527   London NW6 6RD
timberpress.com   timberpress.co.uk

Printed in China
Book design and illustrations by Breanna Goodrow

Library of Congress Cataloging-in-Publication Data
Greayer, Rochelle.
  Cultivating garden style: inspired ideas and practical advice to unleash
your garden personality/Rochelle Greayer. —First edition.
      pages cm
  Includes index.
  ISBN 978-1-60469-477-2
  1. Gardens—Styles. 2. Gardening. I. Title.
  SB457.5.G74 2014
  636.8—dc23
                        2014009479
A catalog record for this book is also available from the British Library.